The *Lazy*

Intellectual

Maximum Knowledge,
Minimum Effort

Richard J. Wallace and James V. Wallace

Adamsmedia
Avon, Massachusetts

Published by
Adams Media, a division of F+W Media, Inc.
57 Littlefield Street, Avon, MA 02322. U.S.A.
www.adamsmedia.com

ISBN 10: 1-4405-0456-3
ISBN 13: 978-1-4405-0456-3
eISBN 10: 1-4405-0888-7
eISBN 13: 978-1-4405-0888-2

Printed in the United States of America.

10   9   8   7   6   5   4   3

Library of Congress Cataloging-in-Publication Data
Wallace, Richard J.
The lazy intellectual / Richard J. Wallace and James V. Wallace.
p. cm.
ISBN-13: 978-1-4405-0456-3
ISBN-10: 1-4405-0456-3
ISBN-13: 978-1-4405-0888-2 (ebook)
ISBN-10: 1-4405-0888-7 (ebook)
1. Education, Humanistic. 2. Self-culture. I. Wallace, James V. II. Title.
LC1011.W26 2010
370.11'2—dc22
2010027244

This publication is designed to provide accurate and authoritative information with regard to the subject matter covered. It is sold with the understanding that the publisher is not engaged in rendering legal, accounting,
or other professional advice. If legal advice or other expert assistance is
required, the services of a competent professional person should be sought.
—From a *Declaration of Principles* jointly adopted by a Committee of the
American Bar Association and a Committee of Publishers and Associations

Many of the designations used by manufacturers and sellers to distinguish
their product are claimed as trademarks. Where those designations appear
in this book and Adams Media was aware of a trademark claim, the designations have been printed with initial capital letters.

This book is available at quantity discounts for bulk purchases.
For information, please call 1-800-289-0963.

Contents

Introduction

If we were to look up the term *lazy* in a dictionary, we might expect to find some unflattering connotations. Let's skip over such definitions as "adverse or resistant to work," "slothful," and "sluggish," and adopt a more positive, charitable perspective. If instead we consider lazy as "economical" or "avoiding waste," we get a much better picture of the idea behind *The Lazy Intellectual*.

This book, then, is an economical reference full of fundamental knowledge that represents the core of a well-rounded education. Whether you want to refresh your memory of a long-since forgotten course, missed the subject entirely and desire to get a small dose of the essentials, or merely wish to be able to say something intelligent on a topic without having to put in a great deal of study, this book will help.

In the following ten chapters, *The Lazy Intellectual* lays out the indispensable facts, crucial high points, and fascinating elements of a basic, comprehensive knowledge foundation. From the teachings of Aristotle to those of Zeno, from mythological deities Athena to Zeus, from the Arabic language to Dr. Zamenhof's Esperanto, and from the literary efforts of M. H. Abrams to those of Emile Zola, this book offers an intensive miscellany of information.

In almost all cases, the biggest problem in assembling this book was determining what to leave out. The exclusionary process was highly subjective but, by offering a brief and entertaining glimpse into an immense universe of knowledge, this book will hopefully encourage the reader to pierce the veil of learning further. In the meantime, enjoy the low-effort scholarship of *The Lazy Intellectual*.

Chapter One

Philosophy

Philosophy is the study of our most fundamental beliefs and the rational grounds underlying the concepts of being and thinking. The word "philosophy" comes from the Greek *philosophos* meaning "love of wisdom." This chapter considers some of the main tenets of Western philosophical thought in a roughly chronological sequence.

Early Greek Philosophy

The Pre-Socratics

Philosophy in the Western world began in ancient Greece with Thales, Anaximander, and Anaximenes.

THALES (ca. 625–c. 545 B.C.) was a man of broad interests in science and mathematics and likely traveled to Egypt to learn practical skills. He eschewed supernatural or mystical explanations for the world around him and tried to give rational explanations for natural phenomena. Thales believed that water was the source of all things and also subscribed to the doctrine of hylozoism, the theory that all matter possesses life or can feel sensations.

ANAXIMANDER (610–545 B.C.) was a student of Thales and is known for inventing the sundial and providing the first map of the Greek world. Anaximander disagreed with his teacher and contended that the original substance of the universe was not matter like water, but rather must have been something more immaterial. He thought the fundamental, ultimate stuff of the universe must be the infinite.

ANAXIMENES (580–475 B.C.) said that cosmic air, or mist, extended everywhere, pervading all things in the universe, and was the primordial element.

These three philosophers differed from earlier approaches by explaining the world with natural rather than divine causes.

Pythagoreans

Members of the Pythagorean School, a secret religious society founded by Pythagoras, believed in following strict moral, ascetic, and dietary rules to enable their souls to reach a higher level and be liberated from the "wheel of birth." They also believed that numbers were the essence of all things. These early Greeks tried to understand the world in a rational manner and did not think that natural events were determined by the wills of gods. They laid the groundwork for later philosophers by questioning where things came from.

HERACLITUS (540–480 B.C.) changed the focus of early Greek philosophy from emphasis on the ultimate constituents of the world to the problem of change. His main contribution to philosophy is his thought that unity exists in diversity, that reality is one and many at the same time. Contrary to Heraclitus, **PARMENIDES** (ca. 515–450 B.C.) thought that all change is an illusion of the senses. The same is true of diversity and motion: they are unreal appearances. Like Parmenides, **ZENO** (490–430 B.C.) took the view that common sense led to absurd conclusions.

- - - - - - - -- --- -- - - - - -- - - - - - - - - - -- - - - - - - -- - - - - - - - - - - -- - - -- --- ----

Person of Importance
Pythagoras

Pythagoras (ca. 580–500 B.C.), one of the most celebrated and controversial of the ancient Greek philosophers and mathematicians, founded a brotherhood of disciples known for its belief in the purification of the soul. He believed in reincarnation, that all living things must be interrelated, and that mathematical principles could explain all of reality. Pythagoras is traditionally credited with the first use of the term "philosophy."

Socrates: The First Moralist

Without writing a single word, **SOCRATES** (ca. 470–399 B.C.) is arguably the most important philosopher in the history of Western thought. What we know of him comes from the dialogues of his student Plato, as well as from the accounts of Xenophon, Aristophanes, and Aristotle. His philosophical mission began with an oracle, or divinely appointed authority, who had declared him the wisest living person. He set out to disprove the oracle and went about Athens questioning others, concluding that: "Real wisdom is the property of God."

Socrates thought that philosophy ought to be concerned with practical questions about how to live and the nature of the good life. Because of these concerns about values, he essentially invented the field of philosophy known as "ethics." Socrates deserves a distinctive title in the history of thought as the first moralist. According to Socrates, if a person fully understands what the good is in any given situation, then he will do that good; goodness and knowledge is the same thing. Vice or evil is therefore the absence of knowledge. Socrates's second ethical doctrine is that wrongdoing harms the doer more than it harms the recipient of the action.

Repeatable Quotable

I know you won't believe me, but the highest form of Human Excellence is to question oneself and others.—*Socrates*

Socrates sought definitions of terms like *justice* and *virtue*, *love* and *piety*. He thought that one couldn't know what love and virtue were unless one could define these terms. He used inductive reasoning, starting with particular statements like "This generous action is virtuous," hoping to establish more important generalizations like "All generous actions are virtuous."

Plato

Born in Athens, **PLATO** (ca. 428–348 B.C.) was twenty-nine years old when his teacher Socrates died. In the course of his lengthy life, Plato used dialogues, an inherently dramatic form, to pour forth a complete system of philosophy, and made contributions to every branch of philosophy, leaving behind a system of thought that is breathtaking in its breadth and depth.

In 387 B.C., Plato founded the Academy in Athens for the study of philosophy, mathematics, logic, the sciences, and legislative, political and ethical ideas. The Academy lasted for several centuries after his death and is regarded by many to have been the first university.

Plato believed that engaging with ideas he called forms, chief among these being justice, beauty, and equality, would lead to the understanding necessary for a good life. These forms were the most important components of reality, underlying what we know of the world and insuring order. Plato attempted to show the rational relationship between the soul, the state, and the universe, and built a systematic, rational treatment of the forms and their interrelations, starting with the supreme idea of Good. He believed that people could, through constant questioning, achieve understanding.

Plato's Dialogues

The first group of Plato's dialogues includes those early writings where the subject matter under consideration is moral excellence. These ideas were also held by Socrates, and included pursuing definitions of courage, piety, friendship, and self-control. The middle group of dialogues includes Plato's theory of forms and accompanying theory of knowledge, his account of the human soul, his political ideas, and his ideas about art. Most notable among the middle dialogues is the incomparable *Republic*, his treatise on the nature of justice. The third and final group of writings is what now might be called *meta-philosophical*. These dialogues are highly technical, showing a concern for logical and linguistic issues.

Aristotle

ARISTOTLE (384–322 B.C.) was a student of Plato's and a member of his Academy. In 335 he founded the Lyceum, a school in Athens that he also directed for twelve years, which was also known as the Peripatetic School for its scholars' habit of walking about. Aristotle delved into many subjects, including metaphysics, logic, aesthetics, ethics, and political thought, and is regarded as one of the most influential figures in the history of Western philosophy. Aristotle was the first person to systematize the rules of logic, the specifics of which can be found in his *Organon*. Aristotle was chiefly concerned with the form of proof and was most interested in syllogism, which he assumed provided certain knowledge concerning reality gained by logical deduction. Besides syllogistic deductive reasoning, there are three laws of thought according to Aristotle.

> *The Principle of Contradiction:* Asserts that a statement cannot be true and false at the same time.
> *The Principle of the Excluded Middle:* Declared that a statement must be true or false; there is no "middle" possibility.
> *The Principle of Identity:* States that everything is equal to itself.

In the *Analytics,* Aristotle considered not only deductive scientific proof or demonstration, but also induction, which enables one to reason from a particular instance to a general conclusion.

Aristotle also was empiricist who claimed that all knowledge comes from experience, beginning with sensory experiences. Physical objects, including organisms, were composed of a potential, their *matter,* and of a reality, their *form.* In living creatures, the soul was the form; plants had the lowest type of souls, animals had higher souls with some feeling, and humans exclusively had rational, reasoning souls. Aristotle also differed sharply from medieval and modern thinkers in his belief that the universe was eternal. To Aristotle, change was cyclical. For example, water might evaporate from

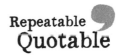

Repeatable
Quotable

All men by nature desire to know.—*Aristotle*

the oceans and rain down again, and rivers might appear and then perish, but overall conditions would never change.

The Stoics

The philosophies of Epicureanism and Stoicism arose after the deaths of Alexander the Great in 323 B.C. and Aristotle in 322, and the wars between the Greek city-states. No longer was knowledge and its pursuit believed to be ends in themselves.

Stoicism was a school of philosophy founded around 300 B.C. in Athens by Zeno of Citium. The essence of their belief was that one should resign oneself to fate, perform one's appointed duties faithfully, and thereby acquire tranquility of mind. According to Zeno, nature has implanted in all people an instinct for self-preservation. One must live a life "in accordance with nature," Zeno said, and for humans that meant living with reason. Reason, which animals lack, leads to virtue. The ethical lesson for us is to do nothing that nature would forbid. The Stoics sought happiness through not only accepting, but embracing whatever happens in life. They believed that, by controlling one's attitude and emotions and remaining free from jealousy or apathy, it was possible to achieve the serenity and happiness that was the mark of a wise person. While everything in the universe behaves according to divine law, happiness comes from existence and is not a by-product of choice. Freedom, therefore, is not the power to alter your destiny but rather the absence of emotional disturbance.

The Stoics believed there were four general types of passion (what they defined as an irrational impulse contrary to nature): distress, fear, appetite, and pleasure. They were further categorized as shown in the following table.

FOUR PASSIONS

	Present Objects	Future Objects
Irrationally judged to be good	Pleasure	Appetite
Irrationally judged to be bad	Distress	Fear

Stoicism coincided with the Christian tradition, even as it was waning as a philosophical movement. Stoicism provided comfort for the Christians, since they knew that the pains of this world are ultimately insignificant in the course of eternity.

Epicurus

EPICURUS (341–270 B.C.) was an atomist who believed that all things were composed of both regularly moving atoms and the void, and that some atoms "swerved in the void," which accounted for free will. To Epicurus, the chief aim of human life is pleasure and true pleasure-filled life required an attitude of imperturbable emotional calm. This calm called for only the simpler things of life. The ultimate pleasure humans seek is the absence of bodily pain and the gentle relaxation of the mind.

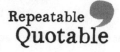

Repeatable Quotable

Don't seek for things to happen as you wish, but wish for things to happen as they do, and you will get on well.—*Epictetus*

St. Augustine

ST. AURELIUS AUGUSTINE (A.D. 354–430) was born in Tagaste, a provincial Roman city in Algeria. When he was thirty-two, Augustine rejected his libertine ways and entered the Christian church. He is considered perhaps the most significant Christian theorist after St. Paul.

As a thinker, Augustine had a great affinity for Plato and his doctrines. While Plato thought of the philosopher's vision of the forms, Augustine referred to religious vision, a theory of *illumination*. "There is present in us the light of eternal reason, in which light the immutable truths are seen," he said. For Augustine, this illumination comes from God.

In his early work *Against the Academics* he addressed himself to the Skeptics of the New Platonic Academy who doubted that human beings could know anything at all with certainty. He reasoned that *you must exist* in order to doubt. In other words, you can prove the absolute reality of your own soul. Augustine said *Si Fallor sum*: if one can doubt then one surely is.

Reason and Faith

According to Augustine, philosophy must include both reason and faith. He believed that reason can never be religiously neutral, that reason and faith are not each independent approaches to the truth. The faith and reason issue also applies to moral knowledge. Contrary to the Socratic dictum that "Virtue is knowledge," and that knowing leads you to pursue the truth, Augustine maintained that knowledge does not produce goodness. According to Augustine, "Faith goes before; understanding follows after."

Fast Fact

Augustine's book *The Confessions* is a landmark in spiritual literature. It is considered the first western autobiography and is a brutally honest record of Augustine's own spiritual journey. His City of God helped to lay the foundation for much of Christian thought during medieval times.

Augustine accepted the notion of Creation as told in Genesis: that God created the world from nothing. Augustine also provided an argument for the existence of God and gave an explanation of how God's goodness could be accounted for in light of the evils in the world. Augustine contends that evil is not a positive reality but a privation—that is, the absence of good. The world is imperfect, but this does not imply that God is imperfect or responsible for the imperfections of the world.

The Platonic element in Augustine's thinking came from his belief that progress in wisdom is made when the mind turns upward toward God, away from the things of this world. Though for Augustine, this movement away from the sensible world toward the spiritual one can only be accomplished if the mind has been purified by faith.

Medieval Thought

The predominant system of theological and philosophical teaching in medieval times was known as *scholasticism*. Two fundamental problems persisted during this period, which lasted from 529 to 1453. The first was the problem of universals, or whether ideas could exist apart from things themselves. The second problem was devising logical proofs for the existence of God.

Person of Importance
St. Anselm

St. Anselm (1033–1109) was an Italian who became the abbot of a monastery in Normandy and was made archbishop of Canterbury in 1093. Like Augustine before him, Anselm tried to provide rational support for the doctrines of Christianity, assuming no boundaries between reason and faith. He thought that natural theology—that is, basing conclusions about God's existence on logical arguments—could provide a rational version of what he already believed. His significant writings include *Monologium* and *Proslogium*.

Other Medieval Thinkers

AVICENNA (980–1037) was a Muslim philosopher who also thought that God's essence necessarily implied his existence. He coupled Anselm with Aristotle to arrive at his own doctrine of Creation: God is at the apex of being, has no beginning, is always active (i.e., in the Aristotelian sense of never being merely potential but always expressing his full being), and therefore has always created. According to Avicenna, then, creation is both necessary and eternal.

AVERROES (1126–1198) was the most distinguished Arabian philosopher of the period and tried to integrate Islamic traditions with ancient Greek thought. Averroes held that there is no conflict between religion and philosophy. Rather, they are just different ways of reaching the same truth. He said there are two kinds of Knowledge of Truth. The first is the knowledge that religion is based in faith and therefore not subject to tests. The second knowledge is philosophy, which was reserved for an elite few who had the intellectual capacity to undertake its study.

MOSES MAIMONIDES (1135–1204) was the greatest medieval Jewish philosopher. A century before St. Thomas Aquinas, Maimonides anticipated three of Aquinas's proofs for the existence of God. Using portions of Aristotle's metaphysics and physics, and relying on concepts like possible and necessary beings, Maimonides proved the existence of a Prime Mover, the existence of a necessary Being (relying here also on Avicenna), and the existence of a primary cause.

PETER ABELARD (1079–1142) was a French theologian and philosopher whose most famous work, *Sic et Non* (Yes and No),

---

exhibited a style of dialectical discussion by setting out more than 150 theological questions to challenge students.

WILLIAM OF OCKHAM (ca. 1280–1349), an English Franciscan, is known for "Ockham's razor," or the principle of parsimony. The principle of Ockham's razor reflects the idea that if you possess two different theories explaining some scientific data, you should choose the one that puts forward the minimum number of entities. In other words, Ockham (commonly spelled "Occam") thought that the simplest solution was often the correct one. Ockham, like Abelard, is also known for his nonrealist theory of universals.

St. Thomas Aquinas

ST. THOMAS AQUINAS (1225–1274) was a prolific writer whose reputation is based largely on his ability to take Aristotle's philosophy— by the thirteenth century translated into Latin across Europe—and join it to Christian thought.

By Aquinas's time, there were two major paths in philosophy, Platonism and Aristotelianism. Aquinas's philosophy is grounded in Aristotle. His terminology of form and matter, substance and accident, and actuality and potentiality, is the very framework Aristotle employed to express his ideas about objects in nature.

Fast Fact

Aquinas was the founder of the system declared by Pope Leo XIII (in the encyclical *Aeterni Patris,* 1879) to be the official Catholic philosophy.

It can be said that Thomas Aquinas synthesized faith and reason to a greater extent than any other philosopher. Aquinas made no sharp distinction between the natural and divine worlds, unlike Augustine, who did so in his *City of God*. He thought that all of creation, both natural and supernatural, and all truth, revealed or rational, emanated from God. Reason and revelation, the two sources of knowledge, do not conflict. Aquinas is regarded by many as the thinker who overcame the discrepancy between faith and reason.

Aquinas's Thought

Like Aristotle, Aquinas was an empiricist and claimed that knowledge came from experience. For Aquinas, sense experience indicated that the universe was a system of causes and effects and lawful behavior. This religious view of the physical world, teleology, says that nature acts as if it were following a purpose or aiming at some mark, and this world system requires a *transcendent* cause, or an intelligent designer.

Aquinas thought that reflection on familiar features of the physical world afforded evidence of God's existence. Because of this, he attempted five proofs to demonstrate the existence of God. Aquinas ends each of the arguments with the conclusion that God is the cause of some reality, since without God the reality would not be explainable.

At various times St. Thomas Aquinas has been ridiculed for being "Aristotle baptized." To his detractors, Aquinas forced Aristotle to fit into his own Christian assumptions about nature and morality. After all, the ideas of Aristotle's naturalism and Aquinas's Christianity are not the same. Nonetheless, the two philosophers agreed more than they disagreed. Aquinas sought to combine reason and revolution, and the resulting fit was a good one save for those instances where reason did not bear fruit and only Scripture could be trusted.

Renaissance Period

During the medieval period, philosophy was often viewed as "the handmaiden of faith." Philosophy could be used to help establish beliefs by making use of reason and argument. When conflict arose between the claims of faith and the claims of reason, that conflict got "resolved" in favor of faith. But the credo of the two phases of the Renaissance is different. The arts and philosophy in the humanistic phase of the Renaissance (from 1453 to 1600) were human-centered, emphasizing the place of humans in the universe. Philosophy during the natural science phase (from 1600 to 1690) was cosmos-centered. The key thinkers of the humanistic period were Desiderius Erasmus and Martin Luther. By the end of the Renaissance, however, the significant figures were scientific thinkers, Nicolaus Copernicus, a mathematician and astronomer, and Galileo Galilei, a central figure in the scientific revolution, in particular.

Erasmus and Machiavelli

DESIDERIUS ERASMUS (1466–1536) celebrated the human spirit in his writings and saw no tension between the classics and religious faith. While his work inspired the Protestant reformers to follow his lead, especially Martin Luther with whom Erasmus feuded, he wished to heal, not break, the church.

NICCOLÒ DI BERNARDO DEI MACHIAVELLI (1469–1527) is undoubtedly the most important political philosopher of the era and is best known for *The Prince*, a work he viewed as an objective view of political reality.

- - - - - - - - --- - - - - - - -- - - - - - -- - - -- - - - -- - - - - - - - - - - - - - - - - --- - - - -

Person(s) of Importance
Copernicus and Galileo

On his deathbed, the Polish astronomer Nicolaus Copernicus (1473–1543) published his work that placed the sun at the center of our solar system. This work famously ran counter to the Ptolemaic system favored by the church. In his time, Galileo (1564–1642), the Italian astronomer, philosopher, and mathematician, took up the cause, based on his own observations of the heavens. He was subsequently condemned by Rome and placed under house arrest. His thinking and experimental methods, however, became the basis for the scientific revolution in seventeenth-century Europe.

Protestant Reformation

MARTIN LUTHER (1483–1546) was outraged by the church's policy of charging a monetary fee for the sacrament of confession—what he thought of as the selling of indulgences—and nailed his famous "Ninety-five Theses" to the door of the Wittenberg Castle church in 1517. In time his bold action would incite a major protest against the church—the Protestant Reformation—that would be felt across Europe. In undercutting the religious authority of the Catholic Church, downplaying subservience to tradition, and placing new importance on the individual, the Reformation caused a ground-swell against all intellectual authorities and traditions.

Fast Fact

Technology was essential to the Renaissance. The invention of the printing press in the mid-1400s made the works of great authors widely available. Under Cosimo de' Medici, forty-five copyists working feverishly for two years had produced just 200 volumes; by the year 1500 some thousand printers had produced over 9 million books.

Early Empiricism

Following the Renaissance, two forerunners of a scientific, experienced-based philosophy were Francis Bacon and Thomas Hobbes. Empiricism (which comes from a Greek word *emperia*, meaning "experience") was a philosophy that stated all philosophy begins with experience.

Francis Bacon

SIR FRANCIS BACON (1561–1626) was an English philosopher, essayist, and statesman. After a failed career as public servant, Bacon spent his last years working on his lifelong project: the reform of learning and the establishment of an intellectual community dedicated to the discovery of scientific knowledge for the "use and benefit of men." He called his project to reform the sciences "The Great Instauration," which meant "restoration" or "renewal." In fact, he completed only the first of three parts, called the *New Organon*.

In the *New Organon*, Bacon introduces his doctrine of the idols that impede knowledge.

> *The idols of the tribe* are innate human weaknesses, such as the tendency to trust one's senses or to discern more order in events than actually exists.
>
> *The idols of the cave* vary between individuals and include prejudices or distortions due to unique backgrounds.
>
> *The idols of the market place* hinder clear thinking and are due to imprecise language.
>
> *The idols of the theater* derive from grand systems of philosophy.

Bacon was opposed to the rationalist tendency inherent in Plato's teachings that dealt with examining the content and meaning of words to attain knowledge. He also made attacks on Aristotle, the other giant of the classical period, for amassing data but making no scientific hypotheses.

Thomas Hobbes

THOMAS HOBBES (1588–1679) became one of the great seventeenth-century philosophers. In *Leviathan* (1651), Hobbes claimed that the physical motions of objects in the external world produce human sensations, and all events in nature and all behavior is determined. The determinism found in nature and human activity also applies to human motivation. Hobbes said that people are egoistic hedonists, always guided by their own pursuit of pleasure. Hence, people are unfailingly self-interested and therefore psychologically determined to seek their own pleasure. Because people live

---

in a state characterized by fear and violence, self-interest compels them to create a government with a strong ruler.

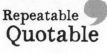

Repeatable Quotable

Hobbes is the father of us all.—*Karl Marx*

While Bacon was a major player in the early empiricist movement in philosophy, he made no important scientific discoveries. Hobbes's reputation as an important thinker in many areas remains and he has been referred to as the founder of modern political science.

Descartes

RENÉ DESCARTES (1596–1650), French mathematician and philosopher, received a Jesuit education, traveled widely for ten years, and finally settled in Holland. Descartes is recognized as "the Father of Modern Philosophy" for his break with medieval thinking and using the methodology of the sciences to establish a rational foundation for truth. Descartes rejected the Scholastic concepts of forms and their causes, and their belief that knowledge began with sense perceptions.

His Philosophy

Descartes's philosophy centered around three goals, the first of which was to eliminate doubt and find certainty. A second goal was his quest for a set of principles, or starting points, from which he could deduce all answers to scientific questions. His third goal was metaphysical for Descartes sought to reconcile his mechanistic view of the universe with his own religious perspective. If the world was a deterministic machine, as Hobbes and other materialists had argued, then how would there be room for human freedom? What need was there for God in such a universe? Descartes wanted to be loyal to two important masters: science and spirituality.

In *Meditations on First Philosophy* (1641), Descartes methodically questions all knowledge, whatever its basis. He then goes on to construct something about which he can be certain: because Descartes doubts, he exists. He states: *Cogito ergo sum* (I think, therefore I am). From this foundation Descartes builds new justifications for the existence of God. One, a causal argument, suggests that his idea of God as a perfect being means that there is some cause of the idea, and that cause must be God. The second argument states that God's essence as a perfect being contains his existence.

Descartes believed that the mind and the body were distinct, and he called this idea "mind-body dualism." Consciousness is the essential property of the mind. By contrast, motion is the essential property of bodily, or material, substance. In *Passions of the Soul*, one of his last works, Descartes attempts to explain the cause-effect relationship between mind and body.

DEFINING MOMENT

On November 10, 1619, while serving in the military, Descartes had a series of dreams or daydreams during which he considered the nature of the world and the meaning of life. This experience led to his work in philosophy as well as analytical geometry.

Spinoza and Leibniz

BARUCH SPINOZA (1632–1677) was a rationalist and, like other seventeenth-century philosophers such as Descartes and Hobbes, systematically laid out his beliefs as if it were a mathematically deduced proof. Though widely criticized—he was even excommunicated for his thinking—Spinoza remains one of philosophy's true original thinkers.

In 1661, he began writing a *Treatise on the Correction of the Understanding,* a work that criticizes Descartes while still illustrating how Spinoza was influenced by his predecessor. He began to write his major philosophical work, the *Ethics,* in 1663, but it was not completed until 1675 and not published until after his death.

In Spinoza's *Ethics,* written in the form of a geometrical treatise, he takes up the subject of the divine nature. He states that only substance is self-caused, free, and infinite, and therefore God must be the only substance. Because everything that exists exists in God, nothing can either be or be conceived without God. The universe contains nothing that is contingent or that could be other than it is. God is free in the sense of being self-determining—and uncaused—and He determines to produce things in a logically necessary manner. Besides calling the universe a "necessary" creation, Spinoza disagrees that God alone is perfect and that the natural order less than perfect.

> **Repeatable Quotable**
>
> [M]en believe themselves to be free because they are conscious of their own actions and are ignorant of the causes by which they are determined.
> —*Baruch Spinoza*

Spinoza asserts that material things are a part of God's nature, which contrasts loudly with Christian views that made God responsible for the creation of the physical world, but had not made God himself material, even in part. People find happiness only through a rational understanding of this system and their place within it.

WILHELM LEIBNIZ (1646–1716) was a German philosopher and mathematician (he developed calculus independently of Isaac Newton). Leibniz held that the world is composed of an infinite number of simple substances, which he called *monads*. Monads are the simplest units of existence and each monad is different. According to Leibniz, everything in the universe unfolds according to a pre-established pattern, and God is an infinitely perfect being who creates the best possible world from an infinite number of possible worlds.

Newton and Locke

SIR ISAAC NEWTON (1642–1727) and **JOHN LOCKE** (1632–1704) were Enlightenment philosophers. Thinkers during the European Enlightenment were confident that man could solve his problems—problems of government, morals, and society included—by the use of reason. Even the universe could be mathematically understood.

Newton

Newton's genius had manifested by his early twenties. He made significant discoveries in mathematics and physics from 1664 to 1667, but his masterpiece, commonly known as the *Principia*, appeared in 1687. This important work set forth the mathematical laws of physics and "the system of the world." Newton had always insisted on adherence to experimental observation and induction for advancing scientific knowledge, and he rejected speculative metaphysics. He believed nature would be revealed through mathematical treatment.

Locke

John Locke was also born in England and was the first great British empiricist. His legacy is vast: he was a notable political, economic, and religious thinker. He was a "latitudinarian," one who conformed to the Church of England but placed little importance on the church's doctrine or practices. He was a broad churchman in theology and a liberal in politics. He argued against the authority of the Bible and the church. Locke maintained that political sovereignty depended upon the consent of the governed and ecclesiastical authority upon the consent of reason. He was also an ardent defender of freedom of thought and speech.

DEFINING MOMENT

Locke's political theory (set forth in 1690 in his *Two Treatises of Government*) defended the doctrine of human liberty and human rights against absolutism. These principles were incorporated into the Constitution of the United States.

Locke's greatest philosophical contribution is his Essay *on Human Understanding* (1690). Locke rejected the traditional belief of innate ideas, but believed that the mind was born blank and acquired knowledge through experience, which is perfected by reflection.

Locke distinguishes between simple and complex ideas, and between ideas and objective reality, or the external world. He also differentiates between the primary qualities of things—solidity, extension, number—and secondary qualities such as color, sound, smell, and taste. Locke's philosophical empiricism was close to Newton and other founders of modern science. His political thought, expressed in his *Two Treatises of Government*, rejected the divine right of the monarch and established the idea of a social contract between citizens.

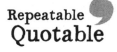

Repeatable
Quotable

In the absence of any other proof, the thumb alone would convince me of God's existence.
—*Isaac Newton*

David Hume

DAVID HUME (1711–1776) was a Scottish philosopher and historian who took empirical philosophy further than did Locke. He applied it relentlessly to issues of how people attain knowledge, to beliefs about God and miracles, and to moral philosophy. When he was twenty-eight, he published his first—and his greatest—philosophical work, the *Treatise of Human Nature* (1739). His reputation for attacking orthodoxies grew with the publication of his *Natural History of Religion* in 1757. His *Dialogues Concerning Natural Religion*, a classic in the philosophy of religion, was published after his death.

Hume tried to describe how the mind acquires knowledge, which he divided into "matters of fact" and "relations of ideas." Relations of ideas include science and mathematics for propositions either intuitive or demonstratively certain. Matters of fact can never be known for certain; their contraries are possible. Hume rejected the existence of metaphysical entities, such as God, soul, or self, as being outside human knowledge. Self, he believed, was a collection of perceptions.

Hume's Beliefs

Hume was a skeptic about God's existence. The existence of the universe is surely an empirical fact, but he thought the existence of God could not be inferred from it since people have neither an impression of God nor of the alleged act of creation. Hume provides a description of the way in which his belief about cause and effect arises. He states that cause and effect is not in the world but in us: we see pairs of events and believe that one is the cause and the other the effect. A "habit of association" is created in the mind through repetition. Hume also discusses morality in the *Treatise*. He believes that moral distinctions are not judgments of reason but emotional responses. Specifically, moral approval is a type of pleasure that people experience, and this pleasure produces additional feelings of love or pride.

David Hume laid the groundwork for the skepticism and strict empiricism of the twentieth century. Hume gave philosophy the impetus to question any and all statements that could not be substantiated with reason or by exacting tests of experience.

Immanuel Kant

IMMANUEL KANT (1724–1804) was born in Konigsberg (now Kaliningrad), East Prussia. In his greatest work, *The Critique of Pure*

Reason (1781), Kant achieved a synthesis of empiricism and rationalist thought. He claimed that knowledge was impossible without accepting truths from both rationalist and empiricist schools. He based his ethics on reason and said that moral duties could be deduced by all rational beings.

He noticed a problem with the empiricist manner of obtaining knowledge. If, as the empiricists said, only particular sensations or particular impressions are known, how is it possible to arrive at necessary and universal knowledge? How can the possibility of scientific knowledge be explained or, more precisely, the relationship between cause and effect, which enables the mind to grasp scientific truths?

Kant believed that humans are active in knowing the world. Although all our knowledge begins with experience, it does not follow that all of it arises out of that experience. Instead of the outside-in approach to knowledge of the empiricists, in which objects cause passive perceivers to have "sensations" (Locke) or "impressions" (Hume), Kant said that the categories of space and time—which he called "forms of intuition"—were imposed on experiences by the human mind in order to make sense of it. Kant termed this basic insight into the nature of knowledge "the Copernican revolution in philosophy."

Understanding

Kant proposed that the mind has "categories of understanding," which catalogue, codify, and make sense of the world. The mind cannot experience anything that is not filtered through the mind's eye and, therefore, can never know the true nature of reality. In this sense, Kant claimed that "perception is reality."

Kant said that, in order to have any knowledge, the mind needs a set of organizing principles. These principles are found in our faculty of the understanding. Knowledge is the product of content (what is sensed) and understanding (space and time as forms of intuition) working together. In other words, both *a priori* and *a posteriori* elements are essential. Without sensation, no object would be perceptible. Without understanding, no object could be conceived. As Kant wrote in *The Critique of Pure Reason*, "Thoughts without contents are empty, perceptions without conceptions are blind . . . Understanding can perceive nothing, the senses can think nothing. Knowledge arises only from their united action."

Kant's *The Critique of Pure Reason* marked the end of the Enlightenment and began a new period of philosophy for German idealism.

Person of Importance
Karl Marx

Karl Marx (1818–1883) was a German social philosopher and the chief theorist of modern socialism and communism.

For Marx, the history of humankind is a tale of the increasing development of man, and one of increasing alienation at the same time. Alienation is the consequence of historical materialism (defined as the idea that a society's economic structure—be it feudalism, capitalism, or communism—determines the nature of its cultural and social structure) determining man's will. In certain kinds of industrial labor, man is alienated from his humanity, his essence, which involves creativity.

Marx wrote the *Communist Manifesto* (1848) with Friedrich Engels (1820–1895), another German socialist whom Marx met in Paris. This work expounds historical materialism ("The history of all hitherto existing society is the history of class struggles") and predicts that communism would overthrow the existing power structure of society. The new banner of communism would read: "From each according to his ability, to each according to his needs." Workers in the new society would no longer be separated from the products of their labor and so alienation would cease.

The first volume of *Das Kapital* was published in 1867 and the second and third volumes, edited by Engels, were not published until after Marx had died. This major work revealed the tenets of Marxism and became the handbook for international socialism. Here, the economic drivers of society and history are explained in terms of labor and wages, and the exploitation of workers is identified as the basis for capitalism. Marx's purpose in *Das Kapital* was to lay bare "the economic law of motion of modern society." He believed these laws were inevitable and would lead to the eventual triumph of the working class

Repeatable Quotable

The philosophers have only interpreted the world, in various ways. The point, however, is to change it.—*Karl Marx*

History has shown that capitalism has the potential to devalue workers and produce alienation on the job. However, capitalism has outlasted and in some cases replaced communism as a successful economic system.

Kierkegaard: The Father of Existentialism

SØREN KIERKEGAARD (1813–1855) was born in Copenhagen, Denmark, and lived the life of a dilettante until age twenty-five when he experienced a reawakening and recommitted to the Christian faith. Kierkegaard's philosophy, by contrast to the grand systems built by Plato and Aristotle, stressed the existing individual and how he lived in the world day to day.

Kierkegaard was influenced greatly by the work of **BLAISE PASCAL** (1623–1662) who believed that, though God's existence could not be proved, men could and *ought to believe* in God's existence. The possibility of infinite gain—including a life of eternal blessedness in the afterlife—far supersedes any sacrifice of material gain in our present finite existence. Kierkegaard agreed that choice, rather than reason and experience, was the starting point for a sound philosophy.

Kierkegaard said that truth is subjectivity; there is no prefabricated truth for people who make choices. Kierkegaard had a higher regard for *subjective* truth than *objective* truth. It is the factor that makes Kierkegaard the "Father of Existentialism." The individual acts on truth, he maintained, and this truth was a manner of existence. Man exists in his truth and lives in it. The highest expression of subjectivity is passionate belief. This is what it means to think "existentially."

> **Repeatable Quotable**
>
> The thing is to find a truth which is true for me, to find the idea for which I can live and die.
> —*Søren Kierkegaard*

Three Stages

The essence of Kierkegaard's philosophy can be seen in his three stages of life experience: aesthetic, ethical, and religious. The aesthetic is a stage of living for the moment, the continual search for diversion, and ultimate futility. This leads to the ethical stage of decision and resolute commitment in which the individual accepts responsibility and follows rules of conduct. Because this lacks personal meaning, the ethical stage leads to the religious stage, one of obedience and commitment to God. This is a personal, subjective experience and relationship, and is, in Kierkegaard's view, a "leap of faith."

Kierkegaard's life and philosophy were centered on existential questions: "How shall I live my life?" "What kind of life is worth living—the aesthetic, ethical, or religious?" "What does it mean to have faith?" "What does it mean to love?" "What does it mean to accept one's suffering and how can one do this?" His discussions of these questions reveal his unfailing and uncanny philosophical acumen.

William James and Pragmatism

Pragmatism is an anti-systematic, anti-empirical, and anti-rationalist philosophy that grew up in America in the nineteenth century. Charles Peirce, John Dewey, and William James were American pragmatists. The practical consequences and meanings of ideas in the real world were more important to them than the theoretical coherence of some of the systematic philosophies of the past.

Although **CHARLES PEIRCE** (1839–1914) was "the Father of Pragmatism," **WILLIAM JAMES** (1842–1910) gave the term its clearest expression. "Pragmatism asks its usual question," said James. "'Grant an idea or belief to be true,' it says, 'what concrete difference will its being true make in one's actual life? . . . What experiences will be different from those which would obtain if the belief were false?'" James insisted that all knowledge is pragmatic because it is difficult if not impossible to settle some philosophical questions—like whether there is a God or an afterlife. James thought that it was best to believe the theory that brings about the best consequences in one's life.

Fast Fact

Charles Peirce founded an organization known as "the Metaphysical Club" that met in the 1870s in Cambridge, Massachusetts, to read and debate philosophical papers. The better-known members of this group included Pierce, William James, and future Supreme Court Justice Oliver Wendell Holmes.

Though the philosophical movement known as *pragmatism* originated about 150 years ago, it is as different and refreshing in the twenty-first century as it was in the mid-nineteenth century. It offered an altogether relaxed attitude about what is true, meaningful, and significant in people's lives. Pragmatism opposed doctrines that believed truth could be reached through deductive reasoning from a priori grounds. In contrast, it held that truth changes as discoveries are made and is relative to the time, place, and purpose of inquiry. What "difference" beliefs make is more obvious—and in some ways more important—than whether those beliefs are true.

Analytic Philosophy

Analytic philosophy, also known as linguistic philosophy, was a twentieth century philosophical movement especially strong in England and the United States. Analytic philosophy concentrated on language—making it unambiguous and concise—and the attempt to analyze statements in order to clarify philosophical problems.

There are at least two reasons for this "linguistic turn" in philosophy. First, philosophers thought science had taken over much of the territory formerly occupied by philosophy. As Moritz Schlick, an early member of the analytic movement, put it, "Science should be defined as the pursuit of truth" and philosophy as "the pursuit of meaning." A second reason for the linguistic turn in philosophy stems from the new and more powerful methods of logic that had been developed in the twentieth century. These methods promised to shed new light on some of the old, philosophical stalemates by eliminating propositions that were vague, equivocal, misleading, or nonsensical.

One striking example of how language and issues of meaning can be applied to philosophical problems is logical positivism, also called *logical empiricism*. In his influential book *Language, Truth, and Logic*, **A. J. AYER** (1910–89) employed a theory called "the verification principle" to statements to see if they are meaningful. The positivists were not trying to decide if a statement was true. They thought that was the job of science. Philosophy's task was to decide what it means to say that a statement has meaning, or that it provides information about the world.

Person of Importance
Bertrand Russell

Bertrand Russell (1872–1970) touched almost every area of philosophy and made major contributions to mathematics and logical analysis. His theory of definite descriptions maintained that sentences were descriptions consisting of a conjunction of separate entities. Each of the entities can be tested to determine if it's true. Logically, any statement that is a conjunction of entities is false if any one of the entities is false. Russell's theory of definite descriptions shows that it is possible to speak sensibly of things that do not exist. Since Russell, it has become a standard tool of logical analysis. There is little question that analytic philosophy changed the manner in which philosophers worked. Using newer methods of logical and linguistic analysis illuminated old philosophical queries in ethics, metaphysics, and epistemology.

Repeatable Quotable

Man is a credulous animal, and must believe something; in the absence of good grounds for belief, he will be satisfied with bad ones.
—*Bertrand Russell*

Sartre and Existentialism

JEAN-PAUL SARTRE (1905–1980) eventually became the leading voice of atheistic existentialism. In his essay "Existentialism and Human Emotions" (1947), he set forth a novel idea of human freedom. He used the phrase "existence precedes essence," which says that there is no such thing as a given human nature. On the contrary, personal choices and acts make up one's identity. Man first exists, and his choices then define his essence: individuals give meaning to facts by deciding how to act. Sartre also rejected the existence of God by pointing out that people are "free agents," and this would not be the case if God existed.

Metaphysics and Ethics

Philosophers like Gilbert Ryle, A. J. Ayer, and Antony Flew brought new life to old metaphysical issues like mind-body interaction, God's existence, and the problem of evil. Their revelations were more about the analysis of concepts and the language used than in introducing new content. But good analytic philosophy brought new understanding to old problems.

Repeatable
Quotable

We are condemned to be free.
—*Jean-Paul Sartre*

Contemporary ethics have added a great deal to the history of ethical thinking in at least two ways. First, there has been increased attention to the meaning of ethical terms such as *fairness, justice,* and *goodness.* In addition, applied ethics including legal ethics, medical ethics, the ethics of sports, the philosophy of warfare, and medical ethics have responded to social concerns.

Cheat Sheet for Philosophy

Aesthetics is the branch of philosophy concerned with the nature of art and the criteria of artistic judgment.

Atomism holds that the universe is composed of invisible, indestructible material particles.

Cultural relativism is a descriptive thesis stating that moral beliefs vary across cultures.

Deists were thinkers in the seventeenth and eighteenth centuries who held that the course of nature demonstrates the existence of God.

Determinism states that all events and actions are caused by an outside force.

Dialectical materialism states that everything is material and that change takes place through "the struggle of opposites."

Dualism is the view that there are two types of substances, or realities, in conscious beings, mind and matter. According to many philosophers, these two substances interact with each other with the body producing mental events and the mind leading to physical action.

Empiricism states that all knowledge derives from experience.

Ethical relativism is the belief that moral judgments depend upon cultural acceptance.

Existentialism is a belief system centered on the individual and her relationship to the universe or God.

Logical positivism is a school of philosophy that attempted to introduce the methodology and precision of mathematics and the natural sciences.

Materialism states that only matter and its properties exist. Even consciousness and various mental states are physical according to this doctrine.

Metaphysics is the study of ultimate reality beyond empirical experience. This branch of philosophy includes free will, causality, the nature of matter, immortality, and the existence of God.

Nihilism is the view that there are no valid moral principles or valucs.

Philosophy is the study of the truths, causes, and principles underlying being, thinking, and conduct.

Rationalism is the theory that reason alone, unaided by experience, can arrive at basic truth regarding the world.

Scholasticism was the philosophy and theology of Western Christendom during the Middle Ages.

Stoicism was a Greek school of philosophy that advocated resigning oneself to fate, performing one's appointed duties faithfully, and thereby acquiring tranquility of mind.

Subjective truth is truth according to some perceiver.

Syllogism is a form of deductive reasoning consisting of a major premise, a minor premise, and a conclusion.

Chapter Two

Music

Music is a form of art whose medium is sound. The basics of music are pitch, rhythm, dynamics, and timbre or texture. Following an introduction to these elements, this chapter will discuss the primary periods of music and the main forms of Western music.

Pitch

Pitch is basically how high or low a sound or note is. Pitch is determined by the speed of a sound's vibrations: the faster a note vibrates, the higher the pitch, and vice versa. In general, smaller objects vibrate faster and produce a higher pitch. A sound that has a definite pitch is called a tone. The distance (measured in what are called steps) between any two tones is called an interval. When tones are eight steps or an octave apart, they sound very much alike. The lower tone in an octave vibrates half as fast as the higher tone. In early music, pitch was the only thing at the composer's disposal.

Dynamics

Dynamics, the second tool discovered by composers, is the difference between loudness and softness in music. Loudness is related to how hard something is vibrating. Utilizing changes in dynamics offers composers different moods for their compositions. These changes can be made abruptly, gradually, or with a sense of rising or falling.

MUSICAL DYNAMICS

Name	Marking	Volume
pianissimo	pp	very soft
piano	p	soft
mezzo piano	mp	moderately soft
mezzo forte	mf	moderately loud
forte	f	loud
fortissimo	ff	very loud

Rhythm

Rhythm, the third tool to be discovered, can be understood as how music flows over time. It's defined as "the particular arrangement of note lengths in a piece of music." Rhythm is measured with a meter and based on a beat, or a regular occurring pulse to music. It divides the music into identical parts of time. Sometimes the beat is heavily emphasized, like in a powerful marching song, and sometimes it's not very important to the song, so it has an airy, floating feeling. A meter is an organization of beats, containing a certain number of notes into a measure. Another part of rhythm is tempo, which is how fast the song is played. Tempo is marked as follows:

Marking	Tempo
largo	very slow, broad
grave	very slow, solemn
adagio	slow
andante	moderately slow
moderato	moderate
allegretto	moderately fast
allegro	fast
vivace	lively
presto	very fast
prestissimo	as fast as possible

Timbre/Texture

Timbre, the fourth and final tool discovered, is the property of a musical sound that describes how the tone resonates. It can be dark, light, airy, hard, mellow, or anywhere in between. Different instruments have different tone colors; thus, a composer can use the same melody but play it on different instruments and keep the piece of music interesting.

Music of the Middle Ages

Gregorian Chants

Gregorian chants started in the Middle Ages as a mix of various chants that had been absorbed by Charlemagne's empire. They were a culmination of Old Testament hymns and Greek and Roman songs. The Gregorian chant period of music lasted from about A.D. 400 to 800. This type of music was still popular for centuries after 800, but new pieces weren't being written or commissioned due to new types of music coming about, including the new invention of polyphonic writing.

Fast Fact

The name Gregorian chant comes from Pope Gregory I, who collected various chants and published them in two books, *Antiphonarium* and *Graduale Romanum*, in approximately A.D. 600.

Secular Music

Although Gregorian chants were the dominant music in the Middle Ages, there were many other types of music outside the church. These were usually love songs written by knights, preserved by clerics, and performed by court minstrels. By the fourteenth century Europe had started to disintegrate as a result of the Hundred Years' War, the weakening of the Catholic Church, and the Black Death plague. Because of this, secular music became more important than religious music. This secular music wasn't based at all on Gregorian chants, and had it evolved to a polyphonic style that included drinking songs and songs where bird calls, dog barks, and hunters' shouts were imitated by instruments or voice.

Form

The Gregorian chant is a voice only, monophonic style of music, meaning that there is only one melody line and no harmony. It wasn't written in what we know as standard music notation and had no written rhythm. By A.D. 700, monks started adding organ lines to Gregorian chants; this marked the beginning of polyphonic music. The secular music that was written after this time was all polyphonic and had a new system of notation in which a composer could write any rhythmic pattern.

Person of Importance
Guillaume de Machaut

Guillaume de Machaut (ca. 1300–1377) was a famous French musician and poet. Born in Champagne, he had many beautifully decorated copies of his music that he distributed to noble patrons. Because of this, most of Machaut's music has survived. He also wrote the Notre Dame Mass, possibly the best known composition of the fourteenth century.

Fast Fact

The Notre Dame Mass is made up of five movements: the Kyrie, Gloria, Credo, Sanctus, and Agnus Dei.

Person of Importance
Francesco Landini

Francesco Landini (ca. 1325–1397) was one of the most celebrated Italian composers of the fourteenth century. He was
born near Florence, and worked there for most of his life.
Blind since childhood, Landini became a famous organist and
scholar. He wrote many songs that had two or three voices, a
new invention at the time.

Music in the Renaissance

During the Renaissance (1450–1600), people held the idea called
"the universal man," that every educated person was supposed to
be musically educated. In other words, educated people should be
able to dance, sing, play an instrument, and read music. As it was in
the Middle Ages, musicians were employed in churches, courts, and
towns and, although the church remained an important figure in
the world of music, the focus gradually began to shift toward royal
courts. The kings and princes competed over who had the best court
musicians. These nobles often took their court musicians with them
when traveling to show them off.

Sacred Renaissance Music

A motet, a polyphonic choral composition set to sacred Latin text, is
a form of sacred Renaissance music. The Renaissance Mass is set to
ordinary Masses and is a longer composition than the motet. Aided

by the development of the printing press, secular music had become more and more popular as the Renaissance age progressed. The printing press helped increase the amount of written music; indeed, thousands of collections were produced. Because of this newfound wealth of musical material for the masses, every educated person was expected to be able to sing and read music.

Secular Renaissance Music

One type of secular music was the madrigal, which is set to a poem concerning love. Like a motet, the madrigal uses both homophonic and polyphonic textures. It originated in Italy around 1520 and was usually sung by aristocrats. A simpler form of vocal music was the ballett, a dancing song made for several solo voices. It was mostly homophonic in texture. In this form, the same music is used for each stanza and the words "fa-la" are used during the refrain.

DEFINING MOMENT

In 1588 there was a large volume of Italian madrigals published in London, which encouraged English composers to start writing madrigals. This English model was lighter and more humorous than its Italian counterpart.

Renaissance Instrumental Music

Although it was still on the backburner to vocal music, instrumental music became more important during the Renaissance. Usually instruments accompanied singers and played music that was written for voices, a tradition that carried on even into the fourteenth century. By the sixteenth century though, instrumental music was not tied to vocal music. That is, songs were written explicitly for instruments. Most of this music was made for dancing, most often in royal courts. There were several types of dance music written in the duple meter, such as the pavane or passamezzo, the faster triple meter, like the galliard. Even with all these instrumentalists, there was no such thing as a standardized orchestra.

Form

As in the Middle Ages, vocal music was more prominent than instrumental music. This, in conjunction with the boom in literature during the Renaissance, created a close connection between words and music. Composers from this era often used a technique called word painting, where poetic images are represented musically. An example of this would be to pair the word "ascending" with rising musical lines. In spite of this emphasis on emotion, Renaissance music was generally expressed in a balanced way, with no extreme contrasts of any kind.

Renaissance music was mostly polyphonic, usually containing four to six parts of the same melodic interest. However, homophonic texture was used in lighter music, such as dances. Another innovation of the Renaissance was the use of the bass register, thus expanding the pitch range to more than four octaves.

- - - - - - - - - -- -

Person of Importance
Josquin des Prez

Josquin des Prez (ca. 1440–1521) was a master of Renaissance music. He wrote many Masses, motets, and even a large amount of secular music. He was a big influence on many later composers, and earned the praise of many of his contemporaries.

Baroque Music

The Baroque period in music lasted from 1600 to 1750. Of all the composers during this time, two stood out: George Frideric Handel and Johann Sebastian Bach. In fact, Bach was so important that his death in 1750 is used as a marker for the end of the period. The Baroque can be split up into three parts: early Baroque (1600–1640), middle Baroque (1640–1680), and late Baroque (1680–1750), the last of which is the best known period.

The early period saw the creation of opera, a dramatic play sung to an orchestral accompaniment. By the middle phase, all of Europe was consumed by this new musical style. Baroque also showed the new importance of instrumental music, with violins being the most popular medium. By the late period, instrumental music was as popular as vocal music, a first in music history.

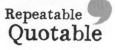
Fast Fact

The fugue, a polyphonic song that has one theme, was one of the most important types of music in the Baroque period. There are different melodies that arise throughout the song and imitate the subject, or main theme.

A Baroque orchestra consisted of ten to forty players. The most common instruments were found in the bass section (harpsichord, cello, double bass, and bassoon) and the strings section (violins and violas). Woodwinds, brass, and percussion were variable and not always used.

Person of Importance
Johann Sebastian Bach

Johann Sebastian Bach's (1685–1750) career is usually used to mark the high point of the Baroque period. By the time Bach was eighteen, he was a church organist in Arnstadt. But his stay was short-lived because church authorities thought his music was too complicated. When he turned twenty-three, Bach found a position at Mühlhausen, where his fame grew through reports of his virtuoso piano playing. His exploits included improvising fugues and playing with his feet better than other performers could with their hands. By 1708 Bach had secured a post in the court of Weimar. By 1717 Bach took a lucrative post as court conductor for the prince of Cothen. Bach was a master in every area save opera, where he never ventured.

- - - - - - - - - --- -- - - - -- - - - - - - - - - - - - - --- - ------------------- ----

Person of Importance
George Frideric Handel

George Frideric Handel (1685–1759) was a master of opera and oratoria (a smaller scale religious opera). Handel was hired as a violinist and a composer in the opera house in Hamburg, and by 1710 was the music director to Elector Georg Ludwig of Hanover. However, while Handel was employed, he asked to go on leave to London where one of his operas was being produced. It was granted on the condition that Handel only stay for a reasonable length of time. This reasonable length of time turned out to be fifty years. He soon became England's, and the queen's, favorite composer. He brought the then exotic Italian opera to England, and during his lifetime he wrote thirty-nine such pieces.

Baroque Music Forms

A Baroque piece typically started out with a homophonic texture, and evolved into a complex polyphonic flavor. By 1680 minor and major scales were the basis of most compositions. The beat of the song is emphasized in a Baroque composition, giving the piece a driving energy rather than the loose feeling of Renaissance music. While the volume levels stay mostly constant throughout a piece, the changes that do occur are sudden and abrupt.

An important part of Baroque music is *bass continuo*, which is an improvised bass part played in conjunction with the chords being played by the harmony instruments. For example, a harpsichord player's left hand would be playing chords, and his right hand would be improvising a bass line to go along with it.

Classical Style

The Classical Era (1750–1820) went from the complicated, polyphonic, and hard to play and sing music of Baroque, to a simpler, easier to sing and remember style that we all know as classical. By the mid-eighteenth century, composers were experimenting with contrasting moods in a single piece. By 1770 the classical style was fully developed with the works of Joseph Haydn, Wolfgang Amadeus Mozart, and Ludwig van Beethoven. By the time classical music really caught on, music had become a commodity for the masses. Thus composers started writing simpler music that amateur musicians could play. They also started writing comic operas rather than the serious, mythological plots of the baroque period.

Classical compositions usually have several movements. They are usually arranged in a certain order: fast movement; slow, lyrical movement; dance-related movement; and fast, heroic movement.

Classical Music Forms

Sonata

The sonata is a form for a single movement of a symphony or other composition usually used for the first part of a piece. It has three sections: the exposition that introduces a theme, the development where the themes are played by different instruments or in other various ways, and the recapitulation where the themes return.

Minuet

The minuet, usually used as a third movement, was originally a stately dance song with curtsies and bows. However, the minuet form that is used in symphonies are for listening, not dancing, and is written in triple (3/4) meter.

Symphony

The biggest contribution to music made in the classical era was the development of the symphony, a long piece that usually lasts between twenty and forty-five minutes. A symphony usually contains four movements, each of which has a different emotion. A theme that is introduced earlier in a piece will rarely appear in later movements.

Concerto

A concerto is a three-movement composition made for an instrumental soloist and an orchestra. The soloist is the star of this composition and needs to be very talented in order to play this type of music. The concerto's tempo changes from fast to slow and back to

---

fast. Prior to the nineteenth century, there was usually a complete, unaccompanied, improvised showcase by the soloist during the first movement and sometimes again in the third. But improvisation went into decline after the eighteenth century, and composers started writing down the solos.

Chamber Music

Chamber music is supposed to be played in an enclosed room in a home or palace. It was fashionable for aristocrats to entertain their guests with chamber music, a type usually played by a smaller group, numbering between two and nine musicians. Chamber music usually contains four movements, like a symphony, and didn't need a composer; instead the musicians relied on each other to coordinate dynamics. The most typical type of chamber music is the string quartet consisting of two violins, a viola, and a cello.

Person of Importance
Joseph Haydn

Joseph Haydn (1731–1809) was the first of the classical masters. He came from a folk music background; his father used to play and sing peasant and folk songs. Haydn went into service of the Esterhazys when he turned twenty-nine. From 1761 to 1790 he composed more than 150 pieces for performances in palaces and houses at the request of his patron. Haydn had met Mozart in the 1780s, and they became quite close friends. Haydn once said, ". . . Mozart is the greatest composer the world possesses now."

Haydn stayed in London from 1791–1795, writing twelve symphonies while there, and then returned to Vienna where he wrote masses for the new prince. Haydn's music was folksier than his contemporaries; his dances were less formal, without bows and curtsies.

Fast Fact

Haydn's popularity grew so much that, when he died in 1809, French generals and an honor guard of French soldiers were in attendance at his memorial service even though Napoleon's army was occupying Vienna.

Person of Importance
Wolfgang Amadeus Mozart

Wolfgang Amadeus Mozart (1756–1791) was probably one of the all-time greatest child prodigies. By the time he was six, he could play various instruments, improvise fugues, write minuets, and read music perfectly. By eight, he wrote his first symphony; at age eleven he wrote an oratorio; and by twelve he wrote his first opera. At fourteen, Mozart visited the Vatican and heard the choir of the Sistine Chapel perform. Mozart heard the work once and then wrote down a near-perfect version of it purely from memory, all the while making additions. His transcription was discovered but, instead of being punished according to the Vatican's rules, he was knighted by the pope because he remembered it so accurately. By the time Mozart was twenty-five, he traveled to Vienna and there met with critical acclaim. His operas were the talk of the town and one, *Le Nozze di Figaro* was the most popular song of the time. However, his popularity began to decline as the tastes of the Viennese started to change. While he was writing a commissioned German opera, he was visited by a stranger who requested a requiem, or a mass for the dead. Unfortunately, Mozart died from rheumatic fever before the requiem could be finished.

- - - - - - - - --- -- - - - - -- - ---

Person of Importance
Ludwig van Beethoven

Many consider the works of Ludwig van Beethoven (1770–1827) to be the highest form of musical genius. When just sixteen he was sent to improvise for Mozart, who said of the young composer, "Keep your eyes on him; someday he will give the world something to talk about." By the time Beethoven was twenty-two, he left to study with Haydn in Vienna. Beethoven was considered a rebel; he thought an artist deserved as much respect as nobility. Beethoven was never a servant as Haydn was; he always made money from lessons, concerts, and publishing.

When Beethoven was twenty-nine, he felt the first symptoms of deafness and suffered an emotional crisis afterwards. His works following this crisis show new power and heroism. By 1818 Beethoven was completely deaf, and he stopped playing piano and conducting. Luckily, he didn't stop composing, and he wrote many piano sonatas, string quartets, and the renowned Ninth Symphony, all while totally deaf.

Classical Form

Classical compositions often show variety and contrasting moods within a single piece. This varies from Baroque in which a single emotion is used throughout the piece. Classical music is mostly homophonic, which again differs from Baroque's complicated polyphony. Classical music also uses gradual dynamic changes, crescendo and decrescendo, that were not used prior to this time period. Because of these gradual changes, the harpsichord and organ were phased out in favor of the piano. During this time, *basso continuo* was also phased out, because more music was written for amateur musicians who couldn't improvise a bass line. The orchestra also expanded to contain:

Strings: 1st violins, 2nd violin, violas, cellos, double basses
Woodwinds: two flutes, two oboes, two clarinets, and two bassoons
Brass: two French horns, two trumpets
Percussion: two timpani

This arrangement could be expanded to as many as sixty players.

Blues

The blues is an important type of music as it provides the backbone for jazz, rock and roll, and many other genres. The blues originated at the end of the 1800s as an amalgam of gospel, work songs, and field hollers. At first there was no set style or form, but by the early 1900s the first real form of blues—country blues—was realized and came to be performed by one person singing with a guitar accompaniment. This clarification was made possible by the 1912 publication of *Memphis Blues* and the release of *St. Louis Blues* in 1914 by W.C. Handy. By the 1920s, the blues had become the music of African Americans. Blues records flew off the shelves by the millions and many artists, like Bessie Smith, became nationally known. Robert Johnson, one of the blues most influential artists, set up in the 1930s the structure that virtually all following blues would conform to after him. Chicago became the center of blues music in the 1920s through the 1950s. Blues has continued to be a popular form of music that is still played by a small group of three to seven musicians.

- - - - - - - - --- ----

Person of Importance
Bessie Smith

Bessie Smith (1894–1937), sometimes called "the Empress of Blues," is considered one of the best blues singers of all time. Smith started her singing career at a young age by singing on the street to earn extra money for her family. Later Smith joined a traveling vaudeville company, but as a dancer because the troupe contained the famed singer Ma Rainey. By 1913 Smith had her own act in Atlanta, and by 1920 Smith's reputation had grown throughout the South and she was signed by Columbia Records. Three years later Smith's records were smash hits for Columbia, and she became one of the highest paid recording artists of her day. Smith made 106 recordings during her Columbia days, but the Great Depression all but killed her recording career and most of the recording industry along with it. Bessie Smith died of injuries received in an auto accident in 1937. She was buried without a marker until 1970 when Janis Joplin and Juanita Green bought one for her.

Types of Blues

Country Blues

Country blues is an acoustic guitar-driven type of blues usually played by one person who sings and plays the guitar, although harmonica players are also occasionally present. It was created through a fusion of gospel, ragtime, and Dixieland jazz, and its early stars included Charley Patton and "Blind" Lemon Jefferson.

Chicago Blues

When African Americans traveled north to work in factories of northern cities during the Great Migration, they brought country blues with them. Once in Chicago, the blues became amplified with the newly invented electric guitar. This new style was much more energized than its country counterpart. Chess Records was founded in Chicago in 1952 and became the biggest seller of blues records. This style of music was one of the foundations of rock and roll.

- - - - - - - - --- ----

Person of Importance
Muddy Waters

Muddy Waters (1913–1983) was one of the first players in the Chicago blues scene. He got his thick, dark guitar sound from

Son House and his technique from Robert Johnson. By 1940, Waters had opened his own juke joint in Chicago where he provided the live music. There he was discovered by bluesman "Big" Bill Broonzy, who took him to record for Columbia. Waters later recorded with Chess Records, where his early hits reached national levels. Waters went to England in 1958 and greatly influenced British blues, including Eric Clapton and Keith Richards. In 1977 Waters made a comeback on Johnny Winter's label. There he continued his reign as the blues king until 1982. Muddy Waters died in his sleep in 1983.

Texas Blues

Texas blues was created in the 1920s by oilfield workers, and it varied from the other types of blues because it was usually played with more swing. Early stars included Blind Lemon Jefferson, who used his jazz background to improvise solos and play single string guitar accompaniment. Many new artists came to work in the bourgeoning urban centers of Dallas and Houston in the 1930s. Guitarists such as T-Bone Walker were electrifying audiences with new sounds that would migrate to Chicago and be perfected there. By the 1970s, the Texas scene was revitalized due to the blues/rock and roll mix of Edgar and Johnny Winter and Jimmy and Stevie Ray Vaughn.

Blues Form

The blues are usually played with what is termed "call and response." The lyrics are sung in three-line stanzas, each with the same melody

---

and rhythm. The first and second line are exactly the same, musically speaking, and the third is similar but is played with more finality. The blues are typically set to a framework that is twelve bars in length, a style known, coincidentally enough, as twelve-bar blues. These songs frequently only have three chords. The rhythm is usually in 4/4 meter with a swing, but this is very flexible and the song's structure allows players to play around the beat.

--- ----- --- ------ ------------- ---- ------------------- ----

Person of Importance
Robert Johnson

Robert Johnson (1911–1938) is widely recognized as one of the most influential guitarists who ever lived. Unfortunately, his biographical details are hazy and uncertain due to his shy and reclusive nature. What is known, though, is that in his late teens Johnson was playing in Mississippi Delta in bars, juke joints, and on street corners. Johnson's music at this time wasn't limited to blues; he played to his audience and so his repertoire included jazz, country, and blues. In 1936 Johnson was offered the chance to record in San Antonio, Texas, and it was there that he would record the only twenty-nine known songs written by him. Johnson was playing in a Mississippi juke joint in 1938 when, according to most accounts, he was poisoned by a drink spiked with strychnine. Johnson sweated out most of the poison after a couple days when his already weakened system was struck by pneumonia. He died days later.

Jazz

Jazz started as a blend of various cultural musicalities, including West African, American, and European. Jazz is heavily influenced by West African drumming, improvisation, and intricate rhythms. Another feature of West African music used in jazz is known as "call and response," in which a voice or instrument is answered by another instrument or group of instruments. In the southern United States, African Americans developed work songs, spiritual and gospel hymns, and various dances, a large body of musical works that are direct precursors to jazz.

The American band tradition was another source of jazz. These bands were an important part of American life during the late nineteenth century. The instruments used in these bands—trumpet, cornet, trombone, tuba, clarinet, and drums—would also be used in the jazz bands that followed. Other important influences on jazz were ragtime music and the blues.

Jazz is usually played by a small group of three to fifteen musicians. Larger groups are known as big bands and the smaller groups as combos. A jazz ensemble is made up of a rhythm section consisting of a piano, plucked double bass, percussion, and occasionally guitars or banjos, and melodic instruments like the cornet, trumpet, saxophone, piano, clarinet, vibraphone, and trombone. The percussion used the drum

Repeatable
Quotable

By and large, jazz has always been like the kind of a man you wouldn't want your daughter to associate with.
—*Duke Ellington*

set, newly invented in the late 1800s, which had a snare, cymbals, and a bass drum operated by a foot pedal. Jazz solo musicians utilized brass, woodwinds, and percussions rather than the bowed strings of "classical" music.

Person of Importance
Louis Armstrong

Louis Armstrong (1901–1971) was a famed singer and a trumpeter who had arguably the greatest impact on jazz of anyone from his era. Born in New Orleans, he learned to play the cornet in a reformatory. After his release, Armstrong played various venues where he caught the ear of Joseph "King" Oliver. When Oliver left for Chicago in 1918, Armstrong took his place as the leader of the Kid Ory Band. After four years in that position, Armstrong also left for Chicago to play in the new band run by the man he replaced, King Oliver's Creole Jazz Band. By 1925, Armstrong started recording with his various bands, cementing his place as the leading jazzman. By the 1960s, Armstrong's fame was so great that he was named a goodwill ambassador for the United States.

Armstrong gained recognition as one of the best jazz improvisers of all time; he could invent amazing solos right on the spot and turn ordinary songs into jazz songs. He also helped to popularize scat singing, in which a vocalist sings nonsense syllables in a melodic way. His gravelly voice became his signature.

Types of Jazz

New Orleans Style Jazz

New Orleans was the center of jazz from 1900 to 1917. The city was home to many jazz artists, including Ferdinand "Jelly Roll" Morton, King Oliver, and Louis "Satchmo" Armstrong. New Orleans's port brought in an incredibly diverse population with immigrants arriving from Africa, France, Spain, Portugal, England, Italy, and Cuba. From this social diversity came a rich musical culture that was, and still is, unique to New Orleans. Because of their various backgrounds, many band musicians were classically trained and could read musical notation. However, most played by ear and were master improvisers.

DEFINING MOMENT

Within New Orleans, the main jazz center was in Storyville, a red-light district that provided employment opportunities due to its great number of brothels, saloons, and dance halls. When Storyville closed in 1917, influential jazz musicians moved north to Chicago, Kansas City, and New York City.

New Orleans jazz was played by a group of five to eight performers. The melodic instruments, or front line as they were called, each had a unique role and would improvise several different melodies at once. The cornet would play variations of the main melody. The clarinet would play a counter melody, usually a bit faster and above the main melody. The trombone would play a bass line that was simpler in form than the others but still melodically interesting. These instruments were supported by a rhythm section that provided harmonies for the soloists to improvise over.

New Orleans jazz was based on marches, church songs, or twelve-bar blues. Over time, soloists began to improvise new melodies based on the harmony of the song rather than the original melody of the song. By the 1920s, the trumpet replaced the cornet, and the saxophone was added.

Swing

During the 1920s, a new style of jazz called swing sprung up. It flourished between 1935 and 1945, a decade that was later nicknamed the "swing era." Swing was played mainly by big bands, such as those led by Duke Ellington, Count Basie, and Benny Goodman. These bands featured instrumentalists and occasionally singers such as Billie Holiday, Ella Fitzgerald, and Frank Sinatra.

- - - - - - - -- --- ------ -----------------------------------

Person of Importance
Duke Ellington

Edward Kennedy "Duke" Ellington (1899–1974) was a composer, arranger, and conductor, and is considered one of the most important players in the swing era. Even beyond that, he is widely held to be one of the most influential figures in the history of jazz. He wrote hundreds of three-minute pieces of music for his band and others, as well as for films, television, ballet, theater, and church. During his lifetime, popular music was limited to the three-minute period of the 78 rpm record. Ellington was one of the first jazz artists who wrote longer songs. Ellington wrote music specifically for his band; he knew what his musicians could play and, more importantly, what they couldn't. This made his music richer and more varied than that of his fellow composers.

Swing brought jazz to new heights of popularity and respectability. Due to their size, these bands usually had composed music commonly arranged, or notated, for each musician to read. Because of this, the arranger became almost important as the actual composer. Bands were interested in sounding unique and different, and for the most part they did, thanks to the arranger as much as the actual players. Melodies were played by ensembles rather than a solo player in swing music, and improvising almost disappeared except for some short solo sections.

Bebop

In response to the commercialism and written arrangements of swing bands, musicians in the 1940s started playing a new kind of jazz called bebop. Played by small groups of four to six musicians, bebop was a complex type of jazz meant for listening and not dancing. It had sophisticated harmonies and unpredictable rhythms that were bewildering to people accustomed to the regulated music of swing. Bebop performers were part of an exclusive group of musicians who weeded out other jazz musicians by using strange chord progressions and complex melodies. Bebop performers also used a "hip" language and dressed a special "hip" way with goatees and berets.

In the 1940s, the bebop center was a Harlem club called Minton's Playhouse. Here many young bebop artists such as Charlie Parker,

Dizzy Gillespie, and Thelonious Monk would play in jam sessions. A bebop group would typically consist of a saxophone and trumpet supported by a piano, bass, and percussion. The beat was usually very fast and was marked by the walking bass line and the ride cymbal, instead of the normal snare and bass drum. Also, the pianist's left hand stopped playing the beat and started helping the right hand play complex chords at irregular intervals. The rhythm was more unpredictable than other types of jazz, and the melodies were often a barrage of extremely fast notes with a syncopated rhythm. The harmonies were just as complicated. Just like the other forms of jazz, bebop was usually based on a popular song, or a twelve-bar blues song. As a joke, a bebop musician might change the name of a song, so that only "in" listeners could discern its origin.

- - - - - - - - --- - - - - - - - - - - - - - - - - - - --- - - - - - - - - - - - - - - - - --- ----
Person of Importance
Charlie "Bird" Parker

Charlie Parker (1920–1955) was an alto saxophonist of impressive skill. He was a leading musician during the bebop era, and is still considered one of the best jazz improvisers of all time. When he was young, Parker listened to the sounds of jazz greats Lester Young and Count Basie float out of Kansas City nightclubs. By the age of fifteen, Parker was a fulltime musician working professionally. By the late 1940s Parker was working as soloist in many jazz clubs, and he made his first record in 1944. Parker had become a leading jazz artist even though he was battling drug addiction, alcoholism, ulcers, and emotional illness. By 1950, his playing and health started to fail.

Cool Jazz

By the early 1950s, jazz had started to become calmer and more relaxed, thus the name cool jazz. The movement, led by Lester Young, Stan Getz, Lennie Tristano, and Miles Davis, featured a subdued kind of music that used a gentler approach. Instruments that were not previously used in jazz, such as the French horn, flute, and cello, started to make their appearance. Also, classical works such as those by Bach influenced some groups.

Jazz Form

At the center of jazz is improvisation in which musicians play off each other. Because of this, live performances rarely sound the same from one show to the next. Although not all of jazz is improvised (some is in fact composed), most of the "jazz" sound comes from the spontaneity of the musicians involved. Jazz is mostly polyphonic in texture and features a swing rhythm where the accent comes on the offbeat and some notes are played unevenly in length. For instance, if there's a pair of eighth notes the second one will usually be shorter than the first.

- - - - - - - - --- ----

Person of Importance
Miles Davis

Miles Davis (1926–1991) was one of the most important players in jazz history. He was a leading figure in both cool jazz and the fusion style of jazz that mixed jazz and rock and roll. Davis learned how to play the trumpet at age thirteen. By the time Davis was eighteen he had journeyed to Harlem to study at Julliard and, while he was there, started playing in a group with Charlie Parker and Dizzy Gillespie. Davis claimed that his time at Julliard helped him understand music theory, but he wasn't completely satisfied with his education there because he felt that the classes were too focused on European music. Within the next year Dizzy Gillespie dropped out of Charlie Parker's group, and Davis was brought in as the replacement trumpeter.

By 1948 Davis had left Parker's band and started his own group, one with a more laid back sound that used instruments to emulate a "human voice" sound. In 1957 they released the *Birth of the Cool*, which marked the beginning of the cool jazz era. Davis continued to push the boundaries of jazz and he formed a quintet in 1957 that helped establish Davis as the reigning king of jazz. In the 1960s Davis started incorporating the amplified sound of rock music and using electronic keyboards and guitars, effectively founding the fusion style. He continued his reign even into his last decade of life.

Rock Music

Rock music is a form of popular music that went mainstream in the 1950s. Rock started as a style known as rock and roll, which itself was a fusion of country western, rhythm and blues, and gospel music. As the decades progressed, rock and roll splintered into many different sub-genres and continues to diversify today. While it is hard to clearly define such a broad type of music, it's safe to say that rock music has a hard-edged sound that's driven by guitar or piano accompanied by a bass, drums, and with a singer. Rock music has always been associated with rebelliousness and youth. Early rock artists played basically faster blues music with a more driving beat; they also used great showman tricks like playing guitar with their teeth, jumping around a stage, or playing behind their back. This type of music was heavily sexualized, at least in contrast to the softer, "safer" pop music of the era.

Person of Importance
Elvis Presley

Elvis Presley (1935–1977) is often called the King of Rock and Roll or simply the King. His version of this style skyrocketed the genre to the top of the pop charts. Elvis started with a type of music called rockabilly and soon became a pioneer of rock and roll. In 1954, Elvis recorded his first songs with Sun Records, and by 1955 he had signed with RCA records. His first record was released in 1956 to major success, and later that year Elvis was brought to even wider audiences when he appeared on the Ed Sullivan Show. Elvis enlisted in the Army in 1958 and cut five singles during his service. In 1960 he started making movies, almost all of which were critically panned. Elvis embarked on a comeback tour in 1968 that reinvigorated his career, but by 1972 the King ran into trouble as his marriage dissolved and his health started to deteriorate. The King died in 1977, victim of a heart attack brought on by years of prescription drug abuse.

By the 1960s the rebellion and sexuality of youth was the most prominent subject of most rock songs and gave rock music an even more dangerous edge. In the 1970s rock music started to get heavier with the arrival of bands such as Led Zeppelin and Aerosmith. Other bands during this time went a more psychedelic route, following Pink Floyd's lead. By the 1980s, rock's sub-genres almost outnumbered all other music genres combined. In the 1990s, rock music continued evolving; its more "alternative" sound became mainstream. Rock music continues to evolve and redefine itself.

Types of Rock

Rock and Roll

Rock and roll emerged in the 1940s from blues, rockabilly, jazz, and gospel music. Its instruments included a guitar (either electric or acoustic), a piano, an upright bass, a drum set, and a vocalist. By the later part of the decade, the upright bass gave way to the electric bass guitar, and the piano was phased out in favor of electric guitars. Early artists included Elvis Presley, Buddy Holly, Chuck Berry, and Jerry Lee Lewis, most of whom were heavily influenced by the blues. By the 1960s, British rock bands started gaining popularity and made their way to American charts. These bands brought the English genre of skiffle to the mix. Their arrival was known as the "British Invasion," which lasted from 1964 to 1966 and included the Rolling Stones, the Beatles, and the Who.

Person(s) of Importance
The Beatles

Founded in 1960, the Beatles completely revolutionized rock and roll. Rooted as much in British skiffle as in American rock and roll, the Beatles had an all-new sound. They debut with "Please, Please Me" in 1963, which landed at number one on the pops charts and led to a craze known as "Beatlemania." Their next eleven albums also reached number one on the charts. The Beatles were the leading members of the British Invasion, which displaced virtually all American artists from the top ten and cemented their hold as the world's number one artist. The Beatles continued their stranglehold on the music industry even as their style evolved from a straightforward pop sound to a more sophisticated folk-, psychedelic-, and blues-influenced sound. The Beatles embarked on their final tour in 1966, although they continued making albums after this point. At this time, the Beatles turned to a more studio-oriented sound with many more effects and studio-created sounds. The Beatles released their last album, *Abbey Road*, in 1969, and started to show signs of breaking up. By 1970 the Beatles were effectively over, but their influence on music is still felt even today.

Surf Rock

Surf rock was popularized in 1961 by instrumental bands such as Dick Dale and the Del-Tones. These bands had a rhythm section of a bass and drums, and the solo instrument was either an electric guitar or a saxophone. The guitar sounds were often described as "wet" due to their heavy reverb effect that emulated the sounds of the ocean. By the next year, the Beach Boys exploded onto the scene playing a type of vocal surf music. These songs used complicated vocal harmonies and melodies with relatively simple lyrics and instruments. However, only the Beach Boys were able to survive the British Invasion of 1964.

Blues Rock

In the 1960s, British rock bands started playing older American blues songs. The instrumentation included an overdriven or distorted guitar, an electric bass, a drum set, and a vocalist. Early blues rock was characterized by lengthy guitar solo improvisations, while later songs were heavier and had shorter, more memorable riffs. Early blues rock bands included the Yardbirds, the Animals, and John Mayall's Blues Breakers. Leading guitarists included Eric Clapton and Jimi Hendrix. By the late 1960s, blues rock had traveled to America and bands such as the Doors and the Janis Joplin-led Big Brother and the Holding Company brought it to mainstream.

- - - - - - - - --- - - - - - - - - - - - - - - - - - --- - - - - - - - - - - - - - - --- - ---
Person of Importance
Jimi Hendrix

Jimi Hendrix (1942–1970) is considered the single most influential guitarist of all time due to his innovative use of feedback, distortion, and various other effects. His playing also reinvigorated the blues and laid the groundwork for heavy metal. Hendrix got his start playing in the "chitlin' circuit," the route that many southern blues and rhythm-and-blues artists traveled.

He played with Little Richard, Slim Harpo, and Jackie Wilson, and it was during this time that he honed his guitar skills and technique. By 1966, Hendrix had moved to Greenwich Village, where he was discovered by former Animals bassist Chas Chandler. Chandler brought Hendrix to England and put together a band with bassist Noel Redding and drummer Mitch Mitchell. Together they became known as the Jimi Hendrix Experience.

Hendrix took the British rock scene by storm, blowing other guitarists out of the water with his blazing licks, and changed everyone's conception of how blues could be played. Hendrix released his first album *Are You Experienced* in 1967, which brought them new levels of fame. Later that same year, Hendrix returned to America to only mild success, until he played at the Monterey Pop Festival where he electrified audiences with his performance and awed them by burning his guitar. After the tour, the Experience returned to England to release their album *Axis for Bold as Love*, which was received with positive reviews. In 1968 the Experience released their last album *Electric Ladyland*. This was considered Hendrix's *magnum opus*, but it also led to the groups' breakup. Hendrix then formed a new band called Gypsy Sun & Rainbows, later called Band of Gypsies. Hendrix tragically died in 1970 from suffocation due to a combination of alcohol and barbiturates.

Hard Rock

Hard rock grew out of late 1960s when blues rock bands such as Led Zeppelin and Deep Purple started playing heavier music that veered away from the blues format. By the early 1970s, hard rock had become distinctly different from blues rock, and the prime example of this was Led Zeppelin's album *Led Zeppelin II*. Hard rock continued to use the same instrumentation of blues rock but was played with more distortion and an even more driving beat. By the 1980s hard rock had evolved into a new genre called heavy metal. By the 1990s hard rock had turned into alternative rock, which included genres such as grunge.

Heavy Metal

In the mid-1970s, Black Sabbath helped introduce a style heavier than hard rock and started a movement called heavy metal (which was derived from Steppenwolf's song "Born to be Wild": ". . . heavy metal thunder . . ."). By the late 1970s, the band Judas Priest had done away with its blues influence and was a whole other animal, and in the 1980s a second British invasion occurred, bringing with it a style called New Wave of British Heavy Metal. The new bands practicing this art included Motorhead, Iron Maiden, and Saxon, who went on to influence newer American thrash metal bands such as Metallica. Heavy metal is characterized by its loud, heavily distorted guitars, fast tempos, and shouting, almost screaming, vocals. Heavy metal has almost no perceivable blues influence to it. The bass gained a new importance in heavy metal, providing the low-end rumble that is typical of the genre. During the 1980s, guitarists started incorporating a classical element to their guitar approach, and this was especially used in neo-classical metal. By the mid-1980s the Los Angeles metal scene made its contribution, hair metal, which focused more on glamour and image and style than the actual music.

Punk Rock

Punk evolved as an antithesis to the glamour and glitz that was associated with mainstream rock. It was created in the mid-1970s, and by 1976 it was crystallized in the United States in the form of The Ramones and in the United Kingdom with the Sex Pistols and the Clash. Punk rejected all the flair of the rock musicians, including the solos, the giant stages, the pyrotechnics, and the elaborate costumes. The previously named bands brought punk to new heights of popularity that spawned a second wave of American punk that was much harder, aggressive, and faster, called "hardcore" punk. This wave started in underground California clubs, but sprang up almost at the same time in Washington, D.C., and New York City. In the 1990s a new movement was started, a mix of the Ramones, bubblegum pop influenced punk, and hardcore punk called pop punk. Bands such as Green Day and the Offspring sprouted in California bringing pop punk to new heights of popularity. Punk rock continues to evolve today into new styles such as emo, melodic hardcore, and metalcore.

-------- --- ------ ------------------------------------- ----

Person(s) of Importance
Nirvana

Nirvana was formed in 1987 and signaled the beginning of alternative music's breaking through into the mainstream. Founded by Kurt Cobain and Kirst Novoselic, Nirvana started the grunge music trend, which was like punk rock but with more angst and played at a slower pace. Cobain's use of feedback and his bare bones style of guitar playing also influenced the following wave of hard/alternative rockers.

Despite their success, Cobain felt that the fans weren't getting the right idea of what Nirvana was all about and in fact felt that Nirvana was becoming part of the problem. The band's short run was cut even shorter when Cobain committed suicide. Nirvana's influence is still seen today, and they continue to provide the inspiration and proof that underground, alternative bands can find mainstream success.

Cheat Sheet for Music

The basics of music are pitch, rhythm, dynamics, and timbre or texture.

Gregorian chants are some of the earliest musical forms, dating back to A.D. 400.

During the Renaissance, knowledge of music was considered part of a complete education.

Instrumental music, music without a vocal accompaniment, was not written until the sixteenth century.

The word "baroque" came from the Portuguese word *barroco*, meaning "misshapen pearl."

Johann Sebastian Bach's career is usually used to mark the high point of the Baroque period.

By 1770, the classical style was fully developed with the works of Joseph Haydn, Wolfgang Amadeus Mozart, and Ludwig van Beethoven.

Jazz started as a blend of various cultural influences, including West African, American, and European.

From 1900 to 1917, New Orleans was the major center of jazz due to the melding of various cultures.

Kind of Blue (1959) by Miles Davis is considered by many as *the* definitive jazz album.

Charlie Parker is considered one of the best jazz improvisers of all time.

The blues originated at the end of the 1800s as an amalgam of gospel, work songs, and field hollers.

Chicago blues combines country blues with amplified electric guitar.

Bessie Smith, sometimes called "the Empress of Blues," is considered one of the best blues singers of all time.

Robert Johnson is widely recognized as one of the most influential guitarists who ever lived.

Rock started as a style known as rock and roll, which was a fusion of country western, rhythm and blues, and gospel music.

Rock and roll emerged in the 1940s from blues, rockabilly, jazz, and gospel music.

In the 1960s, British rock bands started playing older American blues songs, giving birth to blues rock.

The Beatle's popular career lasted from 1963 to 1970, but their influence on music is still felt forty years later.

Jimi Hendrix brought music to a new era although his career spanned just four years.

Chapter Three

The Classics

Classical studies is a branch of the humanities that considers the history, literature, language, philosophy, mythology, art, and architecture of the ancient Mediterranean world. This chapter takes a brief look at the contributions of the ancient Greek and Roman civilizations in each of these areas.

Classical Greek History

The classical period of Greek history began in 499 B.C. with the revolt of the Ionian cities on the coast of Asia Minor. The Persians, who controlled the region, defeated the rebels and attacked Athens and Sparta. Athens defeated the Persians at Marathon in 490 B.C., but in 486 the Persians again attacked Athens with a huge armed force and destroyed the city. The Athenians, aided by Sparta, followed and defeated the Persians at Plataea.

In 477 B.C., the Ionian and Aegean cities united with Athens to form the Delian League in defense against the Persians. Athens became the military center of this alliance in 454 and, under the rule of Pericles, started to rebuild the city. Despite the partnership between Athens and Sparta against the Persians, tensions grew between the two city-states, leading to the Peloponnesian War in 431 B.C.

War

The Peloponnesian War, which lasted twenty-seven years from 431 to 404 B.C., involved much of the Mediterranean world. The immediate cause of the war is generally considered to be Sparta's unease with the growing power of Athens, driven by Pericles's expansion of the Athenian navy. Pericles also built alliances with other city-states that were in opposition to Sparta's Peloponnesian League members.

Athens fought a defensive war until Pericles's death in 429 B.C., but after 427 they adopted more offensive strategies. These new assaults were not successful and led to the institution of a truce. The peace was unsatisfactory, and war engulfed the entire region by 418. Sparta held greater resources and understood correctly that Athens could be defeated through economic starvation. Athens surrendered in 404 B.C.

Sparta attacked Athens in 431 B.C., while the latter was involved with a blockade of Potidaea, a city that had revolted against Athens's rule.

The rise to power of Sparta and the invasion of Greek cities by Philip of Macedon in the 350s B.C. marked the end of the Classical Period and the start of the Hellenistic Period.

Classical Greek Contributions

Greece was a collection of city-states with different forms of government during the Greek Classical Period (500–323 B.C.), with Athens dominant. It was a period of great social and political upheaval, as Athens, Sparta, and other members of the Delian League waged war against the Persians, and then with each other in the Peloponnesian War.

Democracy

The first democratic system of government was instituted during this period. In 510 B.C., Cleisthenes, an aristocrat, challenged and overthrew

Repeatable
Quotable

If liberty and equality, as is thought by some, are chiefly to be found in democracy, they will be best attained when all persons alike share in the government to the utmost.—*Aristotle* the rule of Hippias, a brutal Athenian tyrant. He promised citizens the opportunity to participate in government through the power of voting. He in turn was challenged and had to flee the city but later returned from exile and formed a government of representation for citizens and participation by different strata of society.

Drama

The Classical Period saw the development of drama as a genre through the works of Euripides, Aeschylus, and Sophocles. Before this time, drama was an elaborate dance. Under the combined influence of these playwrights, additional actors were introduced who served to enrich the stories and involve the audiences more fully.

Philosophy and Art

In this period, Greek philosophers introduced the idea that rational thinking took precedence over divine influence and people were in control of their own destinies. Socrates, Plato, and Aristotle, who formed the basis of Western philosophical thought, were all active during this period. Art and architecture also saw great advances during the Classical Period. Architecture branched into separate and distinct forms and saw expression in magnificent civic buildings.

Roman History: Foundations of an Empire

The earliest evidence of habitation in the area of Rome dates from about 1500 B.C. This area was occupied by Italic peoples, the Latins and the Sabines, as well as the Etruscans to the north and west of the Tiber River. According to legend, Rome was founded in 753 B.C. by twin brothers Romulus and Remus. Romulus murdered his brother and became the first king of Rome. The Etruscans succeeded the Latins as rulers of the city until they were overthrown and the Roman republic was established near 500 B.C.

The republic replaced the king with a senate controlled by the patrician class and gave some powers to the general population (plebians). After a taste of power, the majority agitated for more, creating great strain between the classes. In 450 B.C., plebians were able to formalize laws in writing, called the Twelve Tables. Even though they were able to obtain greater control, contrasts between the rich and poor continued to cause friction.

Growth of the Empire

By the fourth century B.C., Rome had come into contact with Greek culture and extended its influence in much of the surrounding area. The Romans fought the Etruscans for control of the Tiber during this time and, due in part to the Etruscan conflict with Greece as well as the encroachment by the Gauls, Rome was able to overcome the Etruscan influence. However, the Gauls sacked Rome in 390 B.C. and only left after the remaining Romans were forced to pay a humiliating bribe. Picking up where they had left off, Rome reestablished its dominion over territories in central and southern Italy and set its sights seaward.

By 264 B.C., the first of three Punic Wars pitting Rome against Carthage had started. By the end of the Third Punic War in 146 B.C., Carthage had been destroyed, and Rome had gained control over

Spain, Sicily, Sardinia, Corsica, and the northern shores of Africa; the city-state became the greatest power west of China. This did not stop their conquests however, and the Greeks became subject to Rome at about the same time while Egypt acknowledged their subordination in 168 B.C.

Roman History: *Pax Romana*

Rome's expansion had grave social and political effects at home. Extreme graft by the senators, class dissension, slave revolts, and political infighting kept the city in upheaval until Julius Caesar consolidated power in 48 B.C.

Julius Caesar ruled with wisdom, and this period saw great advances in Roman culture. Greek was spoken in much of the empire, leading to Greek literature and philosophy becoming popular. Rome was plunged into anarchy when Caesar was assassinated in 44 B.C., but Caesar's nephew Octavian was able to gain control in 31 B.C., and his rule as Augustus began two centuries of peace, called *Pax Romana*.

Peace and Prosperity

The Roman Empire was at its biggest during the reign of Augustus, with more than one million citizens. In order to rule its huge empire, Rome built an extensive system of roads, bridges, and aqueducts, developed a postal service, improved commerce and industry, and constructed immense civic and entertainment facilities for Roman citizens. Their expanded world had a great impact on the Romans and influenced their interest in literature and the arts.

Running water and central heating was available, and it was not until the eighteenth century that European cities would again reach this level of sophistication.

Christianity came to Rome in the first century A.D., and Christians were generally persecuted until the religion was recognized in 313. Decline of the Empire is usually said to have started in 180; the Empire was split into Eastern and Western regions in 395, came under attack by invaders, and collapsed, signaling the start of the Dark Ages, in 476.

Ancient Greek Literature

Some of the earliest surviving examples of Greek literature are *The Iliad* and *The Odyssey*, both of which are attributed to Homer. Although these two epic poems served as the basis for Greek education and culture in the Classical age, no reliable biographical information for Homer survives. He is generally believed to have lived in the eighth century B.C.

Hesiod, who lived during the eighth century B.C., was an oral poet and often referred to as the "father of Greek didactic poetry." Two of his epic poems have survived; the *Theogony* provides a history of Greek gods, and his *Works and Days* details the virtue of hard work and the harmony of nature.

PINDAR (ca. 518–438 B.C.) was considered the greatest Greek lyric poet. He primarily wrote epinicia, or choral odes. These odes were celebrations of victories in athletic games and were strongly mythical in character. Forty-five of his odes survive.

AESCHYLUS (525–456 B.C.) was the first of three great Greek tragic dramatists and was noted for his thirteen wins in the Greater Dionysia, Athens's annual dramatic competition. Seven of his approximately ninety plays survive. Before Aeschylus, tragedy was a dialogue between one actor and a chorus; he permitted dramatic conflict by adding an actor, and introduced costumes and stage decoration. His plays were performed in Athens repeatedly after his death.

SOPHOCLES (496–406 B.C.) was a tragic dramatist, general, and priest. Sophocles wrote about 123 dramas, seven of which survive in their entirety in addition to the more than one thousand fragments that remain. He developed the form by adding a third actor, and discontinued the trilogy format for the self-contained tragedy.

- - - - - - - - --- --- ----

Person of Importance
Sappho

Sappho (ca. 610–570 B.C.) was one of the greatest early lyric poets. The ancient library of Alexandria had between seven and nine books of her poetry, but only fragments remain. Her verse was characterized by passion, simplicity, and control of meter. Plato called her "the tenth Muse."

EURIPIDES (ca. 484–406 B.C.) was the last of the three great Greek tragic dramatists. Very little is known of his life; he wrote perhaps ninety-two plays of which nineteen survive. Euripides was less concerned with mythical stories in his work, employing less heroic characters and events. After his death, his plays enjoyed greater popularity than those of his dramatic colleagues.

ARISTOPHANES (ca. 448–388 B.C.) was the greatest writer of ancient Greek comedy. His plays were representative of Greek Old Comedy, in which cutting invective, personal attack, absurd situations, and extravagant burlesque were an important part. Eleven of his plays survive.

The Golden Age of Latin Literature

Latin literature is traditionally broken into two periods, the first of which is the Golden Age (80 B.C.–A.D. 14). Even prior to the Golden Age, however, Latin flourished in the hands of two gifted playwrights: **PLAUTUS** (ca. 254–184 B.C.) and **TERENCE** (185–159 B.C.). Their plot devices and stock characters have influenced the development of comedy up until the present day. Shakespeare himself reworked elements of Plautus's *Menaechmî* in his *Comedy of Errors*.

The first major writer of the Golden Age was **LUCRETIUS** (ca. 98–55 B.C.). Lucretius is best known for his lengthy poem, *De Rerum Natura* ('On the Nature of Things'), which is nothing short of an explanation of the whole universe. His views, known as Epicureanism, form an important philosophical tradition.

The works of lyric poet **CATULLUS** (84–54 B.C.) are in sharp contrast to those of Lucretius. Because of his frank erotic references, many of Catullus's 100 poems remained censored or weren't translated until the twentieth century.

JULIUS CAESAR (102 or 104–44 B.C.) was a famous general and a major literary figure who wrote detailed accounts of his many campaigns (*Bellum Gallicum* and *Bellum Civile*).

VERGIL (70–19 B.C.) is, by most accounts, the greatest poet of ancient Rome. As they did for Cicero's writings, medieval prelates exempted the works of Vergil from their bonfires. He is remembered primarily for his epic poem, *The Aeneid,* whose twelve 'books' recount the human and mythological origins of Rome. In Western literature, only the *Iliad* and the *Odyssey* surpass its sweep, imagery, and universal themes.

A writer of great skill, **HORACE** (65–8 B.C.) eventually became poet laureate of Rome. His satires did much to create the genre of the same name, while his lyric poetry—though often difficult—illustrates enormous range and versatility.

LIVY (59 B.C.–A.D. 17) is the best known and most widely read Roman historian. His mammoth history of Rome ran more than a hundred volumes, but only a small number of them survive.

The reputation of **OVID** (43 B.C.–A.D. 17) as a poet is second only to that of Vergil's. In fifteen books, Ovid supplied a veritable encyclopedia of mythology, much of which was structured around various transformations or 'metamorphoses.'

- - - - - - - - - --- ----

Person of Importance
Marcus Tullius Cicero

The towering figure in all Latin literature is Marcus Tullius Cicero (106–43 B.C.). Trained in rhetoric and Roman law, Cicero was an eloquent orator and advocate who championed republican government. His many essays, letters, and speeches (in written form, the latter were often highly polished versions of what Cicero had actually said) set a prose standard that is still emulated. Much of Cicero's writing survives because he was among the few 'pagan' writers that leaders of the medieval Christian church did not condemn, and his works were therefore preserved by monastic scribes.

The Silver Age of Latin Literature

The Silver Age (14–A.D. 138) was the second major period of Latin literature.

SENECA (4 B.C.–A.D. 65), a stoic philosopher and the emperor Nero's tutor, is the point at which scholars mark the beginning of Silver Age Latin. Seneca wrote widely circulated moral essays and tragedies, as well as a biting satire called *Apocolocyntosis* (gourdification) about the death and deification of Emperor Claudius.

PETRONIUS (?–A.D.) was a courtier whose major work was the *Satyricon*, a satire that, among other things, pokes fun at the newly rich and their pompous attitudes.

QUINTILLIAN (35–A.D. 95) is frequently considered the first pedagogue (one who studies and teaches how to teach). He covered a broad set of Roman educational concerns in his *Institutio Oratoria*. The advice found in that work still rings true to many contemporary teachers.

MARTIAL (45–A.D. 104) was a popular epigrammatist. With more than 1,500 to his credit, Martial certainly gave ancient Romans a large number of short, often satirical poems, to choose from. As with Catullus, some of Martial's poems were considered obscene by many later generations.

PLINY (A.D. 62–133) was an earnest public servant who lived through a tumultuous period in Roman history. His *Epistulae* (letters) offer some of the most revealing first-person accounts that still survive about life in the ancient world.

> ### Fast Fact
> Pliny is often called "Pliny the Younger" to distinguish him from his uncle, "Pliny the Elder."

PLINY THE ELDER (A.D. 23–79) is known for his thirty-seven-volume *Natural History* that served as the basis for scientific knowledge for centuries. Both the Elder and the Younger witnessed the burial of Pompeii in the eruption of Mt. Vesuvius in A.D. 79. The latter lived to tell about it, the former did not.

TACITUS (55–A.D. 117) was a relatively reliable, if sometimes satirical, historian. Only fragments of some of his major works (such as *Histories* and *Annals*) exist, though his treatise on Agriculture (*Agricola*) and description of Germany (*Germânia*) are mostly complete.

JUVENAL (ca. 55–A.D. 117) was perhaps the most gifted satirist who wrote in Latin. His sixteen satires heaped scorn on the vices he perceived in imperial Rome. Regrettably, his gifts for satire were not matched by simplicity in his prose style.

Greek Language

Greek, like Latin, is a member of the Indo-European family of languages. By the sixteenth century B.C., Greek-speaking people had immigrated from the north and established residence in the area known today as Greece.

The history of the Greek language can be divided into four phases with several periods within those phases. The Archaic and Classical periods were marked by the adoption of the alphabet from the eighth to the fourth century B.C., and during this time people spoke a number of separate dialects, including Aeolic, Arcadian, Attic, Doric, and Ionic. As the political power of Athens grew during the Classical period, the Athenian dialect known as Attic dominated the others.

During the rule of Alexander the Great in the fourth century B.C., Koine, which was a standardized version of the language based on Attic, spread through the eastern Mediterranean. Koine became a long-lasting and international language and was used for the New Testament, thereby gaining a wide audience for Christianity.

The earliest surviving documents in Ancient Greek were written in a script known as Linear B. Later texts employed the Greek alphabet, a script borrowed from the Phoenicians around the ninth century B.C. Today's Greek language still uses a variety of the Greek alphabet.

Fast Fact

Greek has the longest documented history of any Indo-European language, dating back to the sixteenth century B.C.

Latin Language

Latin, a member of the Italic subfamily of the Indo-European family of languages, was originally spoken by people living in the central

---

region of Italy where Rome is located. With the increase of Roman power, Latin spread throughout the Roman Empire to western and southern Europe and the coastal regions of northern Africa.

DEFINING MOMENT

The ancient Romans began to develop a literature in the third century B.C., and this marked a divergence between the written form, or classical Latin, and the spoken form, or Vulgar Latin. The elegant Classical Latin drew influences from Greek and served as an appropriate medium for poetry and prose.

Vulgar Latin differed from Classical in its greater use of prepositions, less frequent inflections, more regular word order, and vocabulary. With Constantine's rise to power in the Eastern Roman Empire and his validation of Christianity in the fourth century A.D., Vulgar Latin grew in significance. **ST. JEROME** (347–420) translated the Bible into Vulgar Latin.

Latin was the language of diplomacy in Europe into the seventeenth century and was widely used in scholarly writing for another two hundred years. Today, it remains the official language of communication for the Roman Catholic Church.

Early Greek Philosophy

Philosophy in the Western world began in ancient Greece, most likely in Miletus on the Ionian seacoast of Asia Minor. The first three "pre-Socratic" philosophers were Thales, Anaximander, and Anaximenes. They are often referred to as physicists because of their devotion to *cosmology*—that branch of physics that deals with the "cosmos," or the nature of the orderly universe. In particular, these first philosophers wanted to know the nature of substance, or matter.

THALES (ca. 625–c. 545 B.C.) was a man of broad interests. Thales was different from his Egyptian predecessors because he tried to give a rational explanation of the world. He thought water was the cosmic stuff of the universe, but it's not known why because his writings have not survived. He also believed in the doctrine of *hylozoism*, or that life and matter are inseparable. And according to the Greek historian Herodotus, he predicted an eclipse of the sun in 585 B.C.

ANAXIMANDER (610–545 B.C.) was a student of Thales and is regarded as the second of the Ionian naturalists. He is known for inventing the sundial and provided the first map of the Greek world. Anaximander contended that the original substance of the universe was not matter like water, but must have been immaterial and infinite. From his examination of fossils, Anaximander also offered the first theory of evolution, that living forms evolve from simpler forms.

ANAXIMENES (580–475 B.C.) was a friend and student of both Thales and Anaximander. Anaximenes believed that limitless air, which he called the "Originator," was the principle of all things in nature. He explained that air held all things together, just as the soul is the air that holds us together, and all things arise from it according to whether forces make them expand (rarefaction) and contract (condensation).

Person of Importance
Pythagoras

Pythagoras (ca. 580–500 B.C.), a student of Thales, founded a religiously oriented Pythagorean brotherhood, known for its belief in the purification of the soul. He contributed to the development of mathematics as well as philosophy.

Pythagoras believed in a transmigration (or reincarnation) of the soul from human to human and even from human to animal. He believed that all living things must be interrelated because their souls have each possessed a great number of different bodies during past transmigrations.

Repeatable Quotable

The unexamined life is not worth living.—*Socrates*

The Pythagoreans followed thirty-nine rules, most of which were rules of abstinence. They believed that, whereas physical sensuality contaminates the soul, the noblest means of purification is intellectual activity that liberates the soul. To this group, the greatest intellectual activity is mathematics.

Greek Philosophy—The Greats

The first Greek philosophers were concerned with the cosmos and the origin and nature of life. Later philosophy was directed toward more practical questions and considered much broader questions.

SOCRATES (ca. 470–399 B.C.) is arguably the most important philosopher in the history of Western thought. He virtually invented ethics as a field of philosophy due to his concern for the practical questions of life and values. Socrates believed that goodness and knowledge were inseparable and evil was the absence of knowledge. He is considered the first moralist, and his rigorous method of examination is now known as the "Socratic Method."

PLATO (ca. 428–348 B.C.) was a student of Socrates, and like him believed initially in the harmonious nature of the universe. But Plato ultimately constructed a much broader system of philosophy that examined the relationship between the human soul, the state, and the cosmos. He left a great body of work that included the *Republic*. Most of his work is in the form of dialogues, which are part of the world's greatest literature. Plato founded the Academy in Athens in 387 B.C., which taught philosophy, mathematics, logic, and the sciences long after his death.

ARISTOTLE (384–322 B.C.) followed in the tradition of his predecessors, studied at Plato's Academy, and later founded his own school, the Lyceum. Aristotle was the first to systematize the rules of logic, found in his *Organon*. These principles became the foundation of logic as a discipline until the nineteenth century. He believed that the true philosopher sought knowledge for its own sake, but he was also an empiricist, claiming all knowledge came from experience. Aristotle also believed that the universe was eternal and changes were cyclical.

Repeatable Quotable

It is the mark of an educated mind to be able to entertain a thought without accepting it.—*Aristotle*

Ancient Roman Philosophy

Stoicism, borrowed from Hellenistic Greece, was the most important philosophic discipline of ancient Rome. It advocated duty and the acceptance of all situations with a tranquil mind, and considered the universe as fundamentally rational. Roman citizens considered their agrarian origins as fundamental to their character since Rome began as an agricultural and martial culture. So even after developing and becoming more urban, this worldview gave rise to the concept of *virtus* or "manliness" and was advocated by Roman stoic philosophers.

PANAETIUS (ca. 180–109 B.C.) is considered the founder of stoic philosophy. He was educated in Athens and studied the philosophies of Plato and Aristotle. Panaetius followed the basics of stoic teaching, but softened its rigid severity by introducing humanist ideas. None of the five works attributed to him have survived, although they influenced the work of the Roman statesman and scholar **CICERO** (106–43 B.C.).

SENECA (ca. 4 B.C.–A.D. 65) was a Roman philosopher, statesman, dramatist, and orator. In the first century A.D. he was one of Rome's leading intellectual figures, and was influential during the reign of Nero. Seneca was trained as an orator and received a stoic education. A number of his works survive, including essays on ethics, natural phenomena, anger, divine providence, and the duty of a ruler. His writings are noted for their display of unselfish, stoic nobility.

LUCIUS ANNAEUS CORNUTUS (born A.D. 54) was a Roman stoic philosopher who wrote rhetorical works in Greek and Latin. One of his surviving works, *Theologiae Graecae compendium* (*Compendium of Greek Theology*), is a stoic interpretation of popular mythology.

BOETHIUS (ca. 470–524) was a Roman scholar, statesman, and Christian philosopher who achieved some fame as a translator of works of Greek logic and mathematics. His best known work is *De consolatione philosophiae* (*Consolation of Philosophy*), an imaginary dialogue between himself and philosophy. This work argues that everything is secondary to divine Providence, and the pursuit of wisdom and the love of God are the true sources of human happiness.

Greek Mythology

Classical mythology comprises a group of stories circulated in Greek and Roman cultures in ancient times, starting somewhere around 900 to 800 B.C. and flourishing until Christianity became the official religion of the Roman Empire in the fourth century A.D. The myths served several purposes: to reveal the origins and order of the universe, to explain natural phenomena, to explore human behavior, to praise the deeds of illustrious heroes, and to form the basis of ancient religion and ritual. Even after Christianity replaced Greek and Roman paganism as a religion, the myths themselves lived on.

There are several creation myths with differing details that explain the ancestry of ancient Greek gods. According to Hesiod's *Theogony*, which was their first appearance in the literature, the god Chaos was the foundation of all creation. From Chaos arose Gaia (Earth), Tartarus (the Underworld), Nyx (Night), Erebus (Darkness), and Eros (Love). The union of Gaia and Chaos (or Uranus)

---

resulted in the mountains, the seas, and gods known as the Titans. Twelve Titan gods ruled the earth before being overthrown by the Olympians.

Greek Mythology: The Titans

The first real gods of Greek mythology were the twelve Titans and Titanesses, the six sons and daughters of Gaia and Uranus. The Titans gave birth to another generation of Titans and were eventually overthrown by the Olympians and imprisoned in the underworld. The original Titans include:

COEUS was the father of Leto, who became the mother of Apollo and Artemis.

CRIUS was the father of Astraeus, Pallas, and Perses.

CRONUS, the youngest, was ruler of the Titans and overthrown by his son Zeus.

HYPERION, first god of the sun, later sired Helios, the god most commonly associated with the sun.

IAPETUS is best known as the father of Prometheus, the champion of mankind.

OCEANUS, eldest of the Titans, was the god of rivers.

MNEMOSYNE, the personification of memory, gave birth to the Muses.

PHOEBE, the first goddess of the moon, was the mother of Leto.

RHEA was called the Mother of the Gods because she gave birth to the Olympians.

TETHYS, the first goddess of the sea, gave birth to many children, including 3,000 daughters called the Oceanids.

THEIA is best known for giving birth to Helios, Selene, and Eos.

THEMIS was the goddess of necessity and mother of Prometheus, the Hours, and (according to some myths) the Fates.

Greek Mythology: The Olympians

The twelve Olympians were the principal gods of the Greek pantheon. They acquired their name from their residence, Mount Olympus, and gained their position by overthrowing the Titans. The Olympians include:

APHRODITE was born out of sea foam and is the goddess of love. She was married to Hephaestus.

APOLLO, the twin brother of Artemis, was god of archery, music, and poetry, as well as important to prophecy and medicine.

ARES was the god of war and associated with the dog and the vulture.

ARTEMIS, Apollo's twin sister, was goddess of the hunt, protector of children, wild animals, and the weak.

ATHENA was goddess of wisdom as well as war, crafts, and skills. She is associated with the owl.

HERMES was the god of commerce, travel, and athletics and is best known as the messenger of the gods.

HEPHAESTUS, Aphrodite's husband, was god of fire, smithing, craftsmanship, and metalworking. He is associated with volcanoes.

ZEUS was ruler of the gods and the heavens.

POSEIDON was the god of the seas and was associated with horses.

HERA, Zeus's sister and wife, was queen of the heavens and protector of wives, defender of marriage, and a goddess of childbirth.

DIONYSUS was the god of the vine, wine, and revelry who mingled with mortals.

Early Roman Mythology

While later Roman mythology was literary and consisted of borrowings from Greek mythology, early Roman mythology was quite different. Until they adopted Greek stories, Romans had no sequential narratives about deities.

Instead, Romans had a group of rituals and gods and a wealth of historical myths about the founding and development of their city that involved divine intervention in human activities. For example, Romulus and Remus, the traditional founders of Rome and sons of the war god Mars, exist largely as myth. Romans also had thirty gods associated with fixed festivals and others associated with important activities such as harvesting. The importance of agriculture in the beginning of the Roman Empire is evident in early ritual where each act, e.g., plowing or sowing, had its own deity. Rome's involvement in war was also revealed in their choice of gods.

Practical Beliefs

So, practical needs of daily life were represented by appropriate gods: Janus and Vesta guarded the door and hearth, Lares protected the field and house, Pales watched the pasture, Saturn guarded sowing, Ceres the growth of grain, Pomona the fruit, and Consus and Ops protected the harvest. Mars, god of young men and their interests, particularly war, and Quirinus, believed to be the protector of soldiers in times of peace, were prominent. In early times, these deities and even Jupiter who ruled the gods, lacked the individuality and personal history they would have later.

Development of Mythologies

Local gods were absorbed as Rome expanded into surrounding territories. Romans typically treated the local gods of the conquered areas with the same respect as their native gods and in many cases these new deities were formally invited to residence in Rome. This practice encouraged the growth of Rome, as foreigners could continue to worship their preferred gods. As the influence of Greek philosophy grew and the qualities of Greek gods were transferred to Roman ones in the first century B.C., the old cults and practices dissipated rapidly.

Later Roman Mythology

With the expansion of the Empire, Romans had more contact with the older beliefs of the Greeks. As before, Romans adopted these gods and religious customs, going so far as to give them their own temples in Rome. Castor and Polydeuces were the first Greek gods adopted by the Romans, followed by Apollo.

In certain cases, the threat to Rome of Hannibal for example, a foreign god was adopted as a protective measure; worship of the goddess Cybele was begun in this instance. A driving force behind the adoption and worship of deities was the Roman belief in *numina,* or divine manifestations, that were thought to inhabit everything in nature.

From the large number of gods worshipped in the Roman Empire, twelve were given special consideration and honor: Jupiter, Juno, Minerva, Vesta, Ceres, Diana, Venus, Mars, Mercurius, Neptunus, Volcanus, and Apollo. A gilt statue of each stood in the Roman Forum.

COMPARISON OF GREEK AND ROMAN GODS

Greek Name	Roman Name	Greek Name	Roman Name
Aphrodite	Venus	Hephaestus	Vulcan
Apollo	Sol	Hera	Juno
Ares	Mars	Heracles	Hercules
Artemis	Diana	Hermes	Mercury
Athena	Minerva	Hestia	Vesta
Cronus	Saturn	Muses	Camenae
Demeter	Ceres	Odysseus	Ulysses
Dionysus	Bacchus	Pan	Faunus
Eos	Aurora	Persephone	Proserpine
Eris	Discordia	Poseidon	Neptune
Eros	Cupid	Rhea	Ops
Fates	Morae	Zeus	Jupiter
Hades	Pluto		

Greek Architecture

The basic form of Greek architecture was the megaron, a rectangular structure with a porch on or near the entrance and a pitched gable roof. The megaron could be found in the remains of Troy—dating from 2700 B.C.—and functioned well for the climate and available materials. Between the eighth and sixth centuries B.C., the Greeks added other elements to their architecture influenced by other cultures. The megaron was widened, the roof was extended to create a deeper porch, and a colonnade surrounded the building.

Three Forms

About this time, three orders or forms of architecture were introduced. The Doric style was characterized by straight lines and sharp angles and is believed to have been developed by the Dorians who settled in the Peloponnesus. The Ionic style is much less massive than the Doric, more richly decorated, and was influenced by the Egyptians. It owes its name to the Ionians who lived on the coasts of Asia Minor.

While a Doric column sits on a simple circular base and has a plain rectangular capital, an Ionic column rests on a gently molded base and employs a scrolled or foliate capital that softens the junctures of column and beam above. In the fifth century B.C., Doric and Ionic elements merged and the Corinthian style evolved. Its name is believed to have derived from a Corinthian metalworker who first used the carved-leaf capital.

Greek Architecture: The Buildings

The destruction of Athens by the Persians in 486 B.C. provided the impetus for a great rebuilding of the city and introduced the Classical age of art and architecture.

THE ACROPOLIS combined Doric and Ionic orders in three structures: the Propylaea, the Parthenon, and the Erechtheion. The site of the old Temple of Athena was left in the center of the group, perhaps as a memorial to the wars with the Persians.

THE PROPYLAEA, built between 447 and 432 B.C., was a ceremonial gateway and the only point of access on the steep slopes of the hill. It contained a library where visitors could rest after climbing the hill and a picture gallery, the first known in history.

THE ERECHTHEION was small in scale compared with the Parthenon. It is the site of Poseidon's mythological well, believed to lie far below the building. The Erechtheion is noted for the Porch of the Maidens, six statues of draped females.

THE PARTHENON, built between 448 and 432 B.C., is undoubtedly the ultimate example of Classical Greek architecture. Originally the Parthenon contained a forty-foot-high statue of Athena Parthenos, created by Phidias and covered with ivory and gold. The Parthenon was built of marble with post-and-lintel construction, in which blocks were placed on each other without mortar. The rectangular plan of the building measures 102 × 226 feet and employed many refinements in design to give it a sculptural quality, to reduce its mass, and to make it visually appealing.

Each building is independent of the others and complete in and of itself. They are also arranged to maximize their visual impact. A visitor entering through the Propylaea and walking toward the Parthenon would not approach the building head on but at an angle, which enhances its three-dimensional character.

> ### Fast Fact
> History has not been kind to the Parthenon. During the fifth century, the massive statue of Athena was taken to Constantinople and destroyed during the Fourth Crusade. Stored gunpowder blew up in 1687, considerably damaging the southern side of the building. And in 1806, many of the Parthenon's sculptures were removed and placed in the British Museum.

Roman Architecture

Classic Roman architecture is considered derivative; Romans imitated the Greeks and had no appreciation of Classical aesthetics. However, the Roman approach to architecture and art was similar to their attitudes toward other activities of life and emphasized the practical and realistic.

At the time of emerging Roman power, they had no native artistic traditions, so they chose to adopt Greek ones. They possessed greater engineering skill than the Greeks however; Romans were able to build arches and vaults instead of the simple post-and-lintel system used almost exclusively by the Greeks. This allowed the Romans to build with greater variety and to suit a building's form to its function.

Romans undertook great public works projects, including bridges and aqueducts. They built on an urban scale, sensitive to the use of open space and the relationships between buildings. Some of this vision was made necessary by their success in empire building; as they extended their domain into new areas, they built new towns in their entirety.

The conquest of Greece was completed in 146 B.C., and within fifty years the Romans were applying Classical Greek elements in their construction. The Sanctuary of Fortuna Primigenia, for example, constructed during the first century B.C., demonstrates the Roman's sense of form and space in the way the building fits into its environment.

Fast Fact

One of the earliest examples of the Roman style of architecture, combining Greek and Roman influences, is the Sanctuary of Fortuna Primigenia, constructed in the first century B.C. in Palestrina, east of Rome. It was covered over and forgotten until an Allied bombing raid during World War II revealed the extensive structure.

Great Buildings of Roman Architecture

Roman architecture is noted for its scale. Romans built cites and provided citizens with an extensive infrastructure, civic buildings, and sites of public entertainment.

Rome, from the earliest times, had a forum or open marketplace. The forum had become inadequate by the time of Julius Caesar, so Augustus Caesar built a new, bigger forum in 54 B.C. This forum included a temple to Augustus himself, a tradition that was carried on by enough future Caesars to give Rome a number of open spaces.

Roman Theaters

The Romans' love of pageantry and spectacle gave birth to the construction of giant theaters, amphitheaters, and circuses. The Theater of Marcellus was completed in 11 B.C. and is notable for its use of Doric, Ionic, and Corinthian columns for its three stories. It proved inadequate, however, and so the Colosseum was built between 72 and 80 A.D. At 510 feet in diameter and 157 feet tall, it seated 50,000 spectators and was large enough to host naval battle reenactments.

Even the Colosseum was too small for chariot and horse races, so the grand Circus Maximus was constructed. It was 2,000 feet long, 650 feet wide, and had a seating capacity of 125,000. It too proved inadequate, and by the fourth century had been expanded to a capacity of 385,000.

Roman Baths

In addition to the at least seventy amphitheaters built throughout the Empire, Romans constructed a large number of thermae, or baths. These buildings were complex; they required systems for plumbing and control of air temperature, and contained dressing rooms, gymnasiums, steambaths, small rooms for preparation, and three rooms with pools of water at different temperatures. One of the later and larger thermae was the Baths of Caracalla, completed in A.D. 217. It contained garden courtyards, conference rooms, art galleries, and libraries, and could accommodate 1,600 bathers at a time.

The Pantheon

The masterpiece of Roman architecture is probably the Pantheon. Built between A.D. 120 and 124, the Pantheon was a temple dedicated to all the gods and demonstrates the Romans' engineering skills with concrete, a Roman invention. The building's dome, 142 feet in diameter, was built of concrete supported by wooden forms as it dried. The only light to enter the building comes from a window at the top of the dome. It is one of the best preserved buildings of antiquity.

> **Fast Fact**
>
> The Pantheon, a temple built in Rome during the second century A.D., contains a self-supporting dome 142 feet in diameter, a feat unequaled until the nineteenth century.

Classical Greek Art

After the defeat of the Persians in 479 B.C., Athens became the center of the Greek political, military, and cultural world. The Classical Period (480–323 B.C.) was initiated by the need to rebuild the city that had been destroyed by the Persians and was fueled by the wealth of the Delian League.

Under the leadership of **PERICLES** (ca. 461–429 B.C.), Athens dedicated the Acropolis to Athena, the city's patron goddess. The Parthenon contained a statue of Athena by the Greek sculptor **PHEIDIAS** (ca. 490–430 B.C.) and was decorated by additional sculpture epitomizing the high classical style. These figures demonstrated a new sense of vitality and harmony and required the innovative technique of modeling, in which figures are built up and then copied in stone, to achieve their realistic clarity.

POLYCLITUS OF ARGOS (ca. 450–415 B.C.) devised a system of proportions that made him one of the most significant aestheticians in the history of art. His lost treatise *Canon* presented ideal mathematical proportions for parts of the human body and advances the idea of dynamic counterbalance for representation of the human figure. Two of his greatest statues were the Diadumenus (430 B.C.; "Man Tying on a Fillet") and the Doryphorus (c. 450–440 B.C.; "Spear Bearer").

Person of Importance
Praxiteles

Praxiteles (ca. 370–330 B.C.) was the greatest Attic sculptor of the fourth century B.C., and one of the most innovative of ancient Greek artists. Little is known of his life except that both his father and his sons were also sculptors. His most famous work is Aphrodite of Cnidus, which the Roman author Pliny the Elder considered the best in the world. This statue is notable because the goddess is shown naked, in contrast with previous works in which the female figure had been shown draped.

Only one of his sculptures survives; we know about his work from Roman copies and images reproduced on Roman coins. He departed from the majestic and detached style of his predecessors, effectively humanizing his subjects; his sculptures embody elegant grace and sensuous charm.

Although very few originals survive, bronze became the preferred medium for statues in this period. We know about these sculptures from the literature and later Roman marble copies.

Also during this period, significant advancements were made in techniques of Attic vase painting. The red-figure technique for decorating fine pottery replaced the black-figure technique, and allowed for more natural representation of anatomy, clothing, and motion.

Athens's influence began to decline in the fourth century B.C., and the rise of Macedonia and the end of the reign of Alexander the Great signal the close of the classical period. Alexander was an important patron of the arts, however, and his court sculptor **LYSIPPOS** (ca. 370–300 B.C.) was famous for his natural figures with slender proportions. None of his reputed 1,500 bronze works have survived.

Roman Art

With the expansion of the Roman Empire starting in the late fourth century B.C. and continuing for 300 years, Roman legions came into contact with every Mediterranean culture. Conquering generals returned to Rome with captured works of art that created a great demand among wealthy and educated Roman citizens. A prosperous industry in which Roman artisans created copies of these captured sculptures arose to meet domestic and public need for statuary.

Roman Sculpture

Many sculptures of this time were purely of Roman design, but some were exact copies of Greek works or combined Roman features with

Greek elements. Public sculpture often celebrated an achievement by a military or political figure. A uniquely Roman feature was the addition of a dedicatory inscription to the statue. Private portrait sculpture was most frequently used in tombs or funeral altars by aristocratic families and followed the tradition of displaying death masks.

Augustus Caesar and his imperial family would dominate official public statuary during his reign, using the media as propaganda to advance specific ideas about his leadership and to support the legitimacy of his power. He built temples to himself to display his statues, and had his likeness reproduced on coins circulated in the Empire.

Roman Painting

Although historical literature refers to Roman paintings on wood, ivory, and other materials, the surviving works are wall paintings on plaster. These frescoes were used to decorate private homes in Roman cities and rural areas. Many of the frescoes that have survived were preserved by the eruption of Mount Vesuvius in A.D. 79.

DEFINING MOMENT

On A.D. August 24, 79, Mount Vesuvius, a volcano east of today's Naples, Italy, erupted, burying the cities of Pompeii and Herculaneum and much of the surrounding countryside and killing 10,000–25,000 people. Excavated in the early 1900s, the residences of these areas revealed the lives of the population at that time in incredible detail. Some of the frescoes found in a villa in Boscoreale, an area about a mile north of Pompeii, are among the most important of any found in the Roman world.

Wall painting methods had reached a sophisticated level according to Pliny's *Natural History* (ca. A.D. 78). In preparing their medium, artists inserted lead sheets in the wall to prevent the encroachment of moisture, prepared as many as seven layers of plaster, and used marble powder on the top layers to create a mirror-like surface sheen. Colors came from carbon, elements derived from mines such as ocher and copper, and sea whelks, the source of purple.

Cheat Sheet for The Classics

The classical period of Greek history began in 499 B.C. with the revolt of the Ionian cities on the coast of Asia Minor.

The world's first democratic system of government was instituted during the classical Greek period, about 500 B.C.

The earliest evidence of habitation in the area of Rome dates from about 1500 B.C.

Julius Caesar consolidated power in Rome in 48 B.C., and the period of his reign saw great advances in Roman culture.

The decline of the Roman Empire is considered to have started in 180; the Empire was split into Eastern and Western regions in 395, came under attack by invaders, and collapsed, beginning the Dark Ages, in 476.

Some of the earliest surviving examples of Greek literature are *The Iliad* and *The Odyssey*. Both of these works are attributed to Homer, who is generally believed to have lived in the eighth century B.C.

Vergil (70–19 B.C.) is by most accounts the greatest poet of ancient Rome and remembered for his epic poem, The *Aeneid*.

Pliny the Elder (A.D. 23–79) is known for his thirty-seven-volume *Natural History* that served as the basis for scientific knowledge for centuries.

Greek has the longest documented history of any Indo-European language, dating back to the sixteenth century B.C.

The ancient Romans began to develop a literature in the third century B.C., and this marked a divergence between the written form, or classical Latin, and the spoken form, Vulgar Latin.

Philosophy in the Western world began in ancient Greece, and the first philosophers wanted to know the nature of substance, or matter.

The Pythagoreans believed the noblest means of purification is intellectual activity, which liberates the soul, and the greatest intellectual activity is mathematics.

Plato (ca. 428–348 B.C.) constructed a broad system of philosophy that examined the relationship between the human soul, the state, and the cosmos. He left a great body of work including the *Republic*, which is part of the world's greatest literature.

Panaetius (ca. 180–109 B.C.) was considered the founder of stoic philosophy.

Greek myths served several purposes: to reveal the origins and order of the universe, to explain natural phenomena, to explore human behavior, and to praise the deeds of illustrious heroes.

Until they adopted Greek stories, Romans had a group of rituals and gods and a wealth of historical myths about the founding and development of their city that involved divine intervention with human activities.

In Roman mythology, practical needs of daily life were represented by appropriate gods.

A driving force behind the adoption and worship of deities by the Romans was belief in divine manifestations that were thought to inhabit everything in nature.

The destruction of Athens by the Persians in 486 B.C. provided the impetus for a great rebuilding of the city and introduced the classical age of art and architecture.

The masterpiece of Roman architecture is probably the Pantheon (A.D. 120–124), a temple dedicated to all the gods. It is one of the best preserved buildings of antiquity.

Chapter Four

Modern Languages

Nothing is known about the origin of language, the unique characteristic of the human species, although it was undoubtedly in use as people started to build nontribal communities some 15,000 years ago. Language is critical to our evolution; indeed, humans have a gene that contributes to our ability to use language. Today there are nearly 7,000 distinct languages spoken worldwide, and it's likely that at least that many have disappeared. This chapter includes the most commonly spoken languages arranged alphabetically.

American Sign Language

American Sign Language (ASL) is a complete and complex language that uses hand signs and other movements, including body postures and facial expressions, for communication. It is the first language of many deaf people in North America.

Other than its means of expression, sign language resembles spoken languages in every way. This includes the lack of a universal sign language; even ASL and British Sign Language are so different as to be mutually unintelligible. This situation also demonstrates that sign languages are not dependent on oral languages but have developed on their own.

The exact origin of ASL is not clear. French Sign Language was brought to this country in 1817 and used in the first school for the deaf in the United States, the American School for the Deaf in Hartford, Connecticut. As a result, ASL and French Sign Language share a large vocabulary but despite this are mutually unintelligible.

Fast Fact

In oral languages, only one sound can be made at a time, so complex ideas require longer and more complex phrases.
In sign language, several meanings can be expressed simultaneously through variations in hand and body movement and facial expression.

American Sign Language uses hand shape, movement, and position; body movements; gestures; facial expressions; and other visual cues to form words. The complexity of ASL requires years of study and practice for mastery. Like all languages, ASL contains rules for grammar, punctuation, and syntax. And like all languages, ASL evolves with its users and varies regionally and in its use of jargon and expression.

A deaf child who is born to deaf parents who already use ASL will acquire ASL as naturally as a hearing child picks up spoken language from hearing parents. However, a deaf child with hearing parents who have no prior experience with ASL will acquire language differently. This is important because 90 percent of children born deaf are born to parents who are not.

Person of Importance
Thomas Gallaudet

Thomas Gallaudet (1787–1851) was born in Philadelphia and originally intended to become a minister. He graduated Yale with a degree in education and was asked to teach the deaf daughter of the family doctor. His interest in the special needs of deaf students led him to establish what would become the American School for the Deaf, the first of its kind in the United States.

Because sign languages have a high level of complexity, requiring fingers, hands, and the face or body to often move simultaneously, sign languages are not often written. In most developed countries, deaf signers learn to read and write their country's oral language. However, there have been several attempts to develop a written sign language. In 1965, William Stokoe published *A Dictionary of American Sign Language on Linguistic Principles* that uses a notation system

---

of letters, numbers, and symbols. The Hamburg Notational System, HamNoSys, and SignWriting were developed later and are phonetic systems that can be used for any language.

Arabic

Arabic is a member of the West Semitic group of the Semitic subfamily of the Arfoasiatic family of languages. Arabic is the language of the Qur'an (Koran), the holy book of Islam, and is used widely throughout the Muslim world. It is the mother tongue of more than 180 million people. Classical Arabic, the form used in the Qur'an, has been standardized for use as a written language throughout the Arab world. There are many spoken dialects broken into three principal groups, some of which are mutually incomprehensible.

Fast Fact

Prior to the seventh century, Arabic was limited primarily to the Arabian Peninsula. It spread to the Fertile Crescent and North Africa. Today Arabic is spoken in the Arabian Peninsula, Iraq, Syria, Jordan, Lebanon, Israel, and the African nations of Mauritania, Morocco, Algeria, Tunisia, Libya, Egypt, Sudan, and Chad.

Like other Semitic languages, such as Hebrew, Arabic uses a root system that consists of three consonants separated and surrounded by vowels. The consonant root conveys an idea—the consonants k-t-b convey the idea of writing, for example—and the addition of vowels produces related words such as *book*, *library*, and *office*.

Nouns, verbs, pronouns, and adjectives have gender. Arabic has very few irregular verbs and does not use the present tense of the verb "to be." Normally the verb occurs at the beginning of a sentence.

The Arabic alphabet contains twenty-eight consonants and three vowels. Most of the characters have different forms depending on where they appear in a word. The vowels are indicated by symbols above or below the consonants, but these are optional and infrequently used.

Fast Fact

The Arabic numeral system was first conceived in India, was passed to the Islamic world, and then to Europe in the tenth century. They are referred to as "Arabic numerals" because Arabs in North Africa transmitted them to Europe.

The sounds used in Arabic are very different from those of English and European languages; some are unique. There are a number of distinctive guttural sounds and others requiring changes in the shape of the pharynx and tongue that are unnatural for non-native Arabic speakers.

While Arabic has borrowed very few words from English, it has lent many. English words of Arabic origin include: *alcohol*, *algebra*, *coffee*, *guitar*, *jar*, *mattress*, *orange*, and *sugar*.

Bengali

Bengali is a member of the Indo-Aryan group of the Indo-Iranian subfamily of the Indo-European family of languages. It is native to an eastern South Asian region known as Bengal, which includes Bangladesh, the Indian state of West Bengal, and parts of the Indian states of Tripura and Assam. More than 210 million people speak Bengali as a first or second language with about 100 million in Bangladesh, about 85 million in India, and large immigrant communities in the United Kingdom, the United States, and the Middle East. It is the official language of Bangladesh.

Like Hindi, Bengali descended from Sanskrit. Since 1800, the language has been simplified somewhat by the shortening of verbs and pronouns and other changes. Today there are two literary styles: "Sadhubhasa" is the older form, and "Chaltibhasa" is the simplified, current form.

Sadhubhasa has been the form used in Bengali literature, business, and formal communication since the nineteenth century. Chaltibhasa is the language used in everyday communication.

Fast Fact

During the days of the Raj, many English words were added to the Bengali language.

Bengali is written in its own script although it strongly resembles Hindi, Sanskrit, and other Indic languages. The Bengali script contains twelve vowels and fifty-two consonants. The language is written left to right and the most common word order is subject-object-verb. In spoken Bengali, stress is usually placed on the first syllable of a word, and sentences have a distinctive intonation pattern. Except for the last word in a declarative sentence, virtually every word is pronounced with a rising pitch, lending a song-like quality to speech.

Chinese

The Chinese language, including its numerous dialects, is spoken natively by more people than any other language in the world. It is also distinguished by being one of just a few modern languages with a history that can be documented, unbroken, to the second century B.C. It belongs to the Sino-Tibetan family, which includes more than 300 languages and major dialects. Spoken Chinese includes modern dialects that are as different from each other as they are from the Romance languages.

Mandarin Chinese is the most widespread form of Chinese; more than 800 million people in central and northern China and Taiwan speak it as a native language. Another 100 million people speak it as a second language. Mandarin was originally the language of the imperial court but has since been adopted and simplified and is now the official language of the People's Republic of China and Taiwan. It is also one of the six official languages of the United Nations. The other major forms of Chinese include Wu, Fukienese (Northern Min), Cantonese (Yue), Hakka (Kejia), and Amoy-Swatow (Southern Min), which together are spoken by 230 million people.

The various forms of Chinese are very similar in their grammar; they differ in vocabulary and particularly in pronunciation. While all Chinese forms share a common body of literature, there is no standard of pronunciation, and speakers use the pronunciation rules of their own form. In Chinese, tonal differences distinguish words that would otherwise be pronounced alike; for example, there are four tones in Mandarin for a high tone, a rising tone, a combination falling and rising tone, and a falling tone. Chinese lacks inflection to indicate person, number, gender, case, tense, or voice, and it is strongly monosyllabic.

Fast Fact

It's necessary to understand about 3,000 characters to read most Chinese newspapers and magazines; knowledge of at least 6,000 characters is needed to read Chinese literature or technical writing.

The Chinese system of writing was developed more than 4,000 years ago and consists of individual characters or ideograms, each representing a word or idea rather than a sound. So while spoken languages vary so as to be mutually incomprehensible, the written form is commonly understood. This has not prevented mass illiteracy, however, as it's necessary to know several thousand characters in order to read a newspaper. The government of the People's Republic of China introduced simplified versions of common characters in 1956 and is making a greater effort to standardize the pronunciation of words in Mandarin.

Endangered Languages

Estimates vary for the number of languages involved, but linguists believe that as many as half of the world's nearly 7,000 languages are endangered, that is, parents are not using the language daily nor are they teaching the language to their children. Most of these languages will disappear without being adequately recorded. Although the extinction of languages is not a new phenomenon—half of the world's languages have already become extinct over the last 500 years—the rate of extinction is accelerating. In the next 100 years, as many as ninety percent of current languages may be lost.

Currently, 330 languages are spoken by one million or more people. Yet half the languages in the world are spoken by 6,000 or fewer people, and 450 languages have just a few elderly speakers. There are many factors that contribute to the endangerment of a language: the number of speakers, their ages, whether children are using the language, regular use of other languages, feelings of identity and other attitudes toward the language, displacement of the speaker population, government and religious policies, the languages used in education, economic intrusion, and exploitation. The language may also lack a body of literature or even an alphabet to serve as focus for preservation.

To counter the threat, linguists organized the Endangered Languages Information and Infrastructure workshop with a grant from the National Science Foundation. The workshop, held in November of 2009 at the University of Utah, was the start of an effort to produce an authoritative, comprehensive online catalogue, database, and updatable website of information on endangered languages.

The reasons for preserving languages are many. Each language expresses the nature of the society in which it developed. Languages contain, explain, and transfer the intellectual wisdom of populations of people. Languages demonstrate observations of and adaptations to the world around their speakers. Languages are reflections of cultures and document humanity and what it is to be human.

English

English is a member of the West Germanic group of the Germanic subfamily of the Indo-European family of languages. It is the official language of about 45 sovereign states and is spoken by approximately 470 million people worldwide, making it the third most commonly spoken language. English is the most widely dispersed of languages—it is spoken on six continents—and is the most popular foreign language in most other countries in the world.

Fast Fact
English is not the official language of the United States or the United Kingdom.

English is derived from the language spoken by fifth-century Germanic invaders of Britain. There is no record of any forms of the language before those invasions. French superseded English as an official language after the Norman Conquest of Britain in the eleventh century, but by the fourteenth century English had again become dominant. English can be divided into Old English (prior to the Norman Conquest), Middle English (which extended to about 1500), and Modern English. It changed greatly over the years, affecting sounds, meaning, and grammar. Because pronunciation of English words has changed radically while spelling has changed very little since the fifteenth century, English spelling is not a reliable indication of pronunciation.

Many common words in English are holdovers from Old English; Latin and Scandinavian settlers provided others. Because French became the language of official life and the court following the Norman Conquest, that language provided a significant vocabulary, particularly legal terms and words for social rank and institutions. English has been influenced by classical languages since the time of the Renaissance, with Greek and Latin furnishing many scientific terms. When English speakers reached North America in the seventeenth century, the language took a new track and developed separately from British English. English has continued to expand and most of the world's languages are represented in its vocabulary to some degree.

The following graph shows the relative influences of other languages and sources on the vocabulary of the English language:

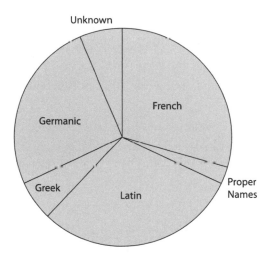

Esperanto

In 1887, Dr. Ludwik Lejzer Zamenhof, a Polish oculist and linguist, introduced Esperanto, an artificial language intended to facilitate communication between speakers of different languages. Zamenhof grew up Jewish in a Russian-speaking family who lived on the Polish-Russian border. There were four distinct populations at the time: Russians, Poles, Germans, and Jews, each of whom spoke their own language and treated the others as enemies. Hoping to promote tolerance, he devoted ten years to developing an international language, and published a textbook explaining the language under the pseudonym *Doktoro Esperanto* (Doctor Hopeful).

Esperanto uses words derived from roots commonly found in European languages, primarily the Romance languages, making it relatively easy to learn for Europeans. The roots can be expanded using a regular process of prefixes and suffixes, allowing speakers to create new words as needed. Words are spelled as pronounced and grammar is simple and regular. Parts of speech have their own suffixes: all nouns end with an *O*, all adjectives end with *A*, and all verbs use a suffix to indicate one of six tenses and moods. Nouns have no gender. Esperanto uses a 28-letter alphabet, dropping the letters *Q, W, X,* and *Y* from the Latin alphabet and adding six letters with diacritics.

Esperanto is arguably the most successful of the artificial international languages. The number of Esperanto speakers is estimated at more than 100,000. The Universal Esperanto Association (UEA) was founded in 1908 and is the largest international organization for Esperanto speakers, with members in 118 countries. The UEA works "not only to promote Esperanto, but to stimulate discussion of the world language problem and to call attention to the necessity of equality among languages."

Most Esperanto speakers currently learn the language through self-directed study, although it has been taught in schools and universities worldwide. And, despite its simplicity and structural regularity, it has not gained a wide enough acceptance to meet the goal of an international language.

Fast Fact

Adolf Hitler saw Esperanto as a threat. In his work *Mein Kampf,* Hitler claims that Esperanto is a language that would be used by the "international Jewish conspiracy" when they had achieved world domination.

French

French is a Romance language, although that's not why it's often called the language of love. In linguistic terms, "Romance" comes from the word Roman and simply means "from Latin." The complete language family classification of French is Indo-European > Italic > Romance. Indo-European is the largest language family and contains most European, American, and Asian languages, including such varied languages as Latin, Greek, Gaelic, Polish, and Hindi. Italic basically refers to Latin. Romance languages are originally from Western Europe, although due to colonization some of them are found all over the world. French, Spanish, Italian, and Portuguese are all Romance languages. French written materials date from the Strasbourg Oaths of 842.

French is an official language in more than twenty-five countries, as well as in numerous immigrant communities in the United States and around the world. French is the second most commonly taught second language in the world after English and is the eleventh most commonly spoken language in the world. There are numerous variations in grammar, vocabulary, and pronunciation, both between and within French-speaking regions. This means that there may be some confusion when you talk to French speakers from different countries, but you should be able to communicate with Francophones (people who speak French fluently and regularly) wherever you go without too much difficulty, even if the French you learned is from another region.

English	French
Hello	Bonjour
Goodbye	Au revoir
My name is	Je m'apelle
I would like	Je voudrais
Please	S'il vouz plait
How much?	Combien?
Thank you	Merci
Excuse me	Excusez-moi
Where?	Où?
Left	Droit
Right	Gauche
One	Un

French in English

French has had a great deal of influence on English, affecting English grammar, vocabulary, and pronunciation. The French influence on English began in 1066 when William the Conqueror led the Norman invasion of England and became king of England. While English was relegated to the language of the masses, French became the language of the court, administration, and culture and would remain that way for 300 years. French and English thus coexisted with no apparent complications; in fact, English was essentially ignored by grammarians during this time and evolved into a grammatically simpler language. As a result of the Norman occupation of England, English adopted about 10,000 French words, of which around three-fourths are still used today.

Fast Fact

More than a third of all English words are derived from French, either directly or indirectly. An English speaker who has never studied French already knows around 15,000 French words.

German

German is an Indo-European language that has evolved over centuries to become part of a larger group of languages called the Germanic languages. German developed on the continent roughly in the territory that is Germany today. Sometime in the fifth century A.D., three large groups from the northern part of modern Germany began to move from their homeland to the island of Britain. These three peoples were the Jutes, the Angles, and the Saxons. They came both as conquerors and as immigrants and had an enormous influence on the culture and language of the large region they occupied. Their Germanic language fused with Celtic-English and made English a predominantly Germanic language.

German is the dominant language in a large area of northern and central Europe. In addition to Germany, Austria, and Switzerland, it is spoken in Liechtenstein, in the Czech Republic near the

German border, and in many cities in Hungary (which was once a part of the Austro-Hungarian Empire). German is one of the languages used in modern European commerce and is the native language of more European Union (EU) citizens than any other language. Only English is spoken by more EU residents than German. It is also a language in which much of the world's great music and literature has been written.

Fast Fact

No matter how long the number gets, German numbers are written as one word: *701* is written *siebenhunderteins,* the year *1776* is *siebzehnhundertsechsundsiebzig,* and *3582* is *dreitausendfünfhundertzweiundachtzig.* For that reason, Germans tend to avoid writing out numbers and prefer to write the numerals.

German has regional pronunciation and even vocabulary differences in some places. These differences are often called dialects, and they are the local variations or peculiarities of the standard language. It is estimated that there are between 50 and 250 dialects (depending on how the term dialect is defined) within the German language. The German alphabet consists of the same letters that make up the English alphabet, with one exception. German has one letter that does not exist in English,

English	German
Hello	Guten Tag
Goodbye	Auf Wiedersehen
My name is	Mein Name ist
I would like	Ich mag würde
Please	Bitte
How much?	Wie viel?
Thank you	Danke
Excuse me	Entschuldigung
Where?	Wo?
Left	Verließ
Right	Richtig
One	Eins

called an "ess-tset," that is often mistaken for a capital "B." It looks like this (ß) and is pronounced like a double "s" (ESS).

There are almost 100 million people who speak German as their first language. Most of them—about 83.5 million people—live in Germany, Switzerland, or Austria, but about 4 million call North and South America home.

Hindi

The Hindi language is a member of the Indo-Aryan group within the Indo-Iranian subgroup of the Indo-European family of languages. It has been the official language of India since 1965, although the Indian constitution recognizes English and twenty-one other languages as official languages. Nearly 425 million people, mostly in India, speak Hindi as a first language and some 120 million more use it as a second language. It's also spoken by large populations in South Africa, Mauritius, Bangladesh, Yemen, and Uganda.

Some linguists consider Hindi (and Urdu) as the written forms of Hindustani; others believe that Hindustani is the spoken version of Hindi and Urdu. Hindi is the version of Hindustani used by Hindus, while Urdu is the variety of Hindustani used by Muslims and is the official language of Pakistan.

Standard Hindi is based on the Kari Boli (Khariboli) dialect spoken to the east and north of Delhi. Braj Bhasha (Brajbhasa) and Bambaiya (Mumbaiyya) are two other important dialects of the more than ten variations of Hindi. Hindi has roots in classical Sanskrit. It is written using the Devanagari alphabet from Sanskrit and is read from left to right. Because Hindi is phonetic, words are pronounced as they are written, making it easier to learn than English. There are no uppercase or lowercase forms of letters in Hindi. Nouns are either masculine or feminine, and many adjectives vary based on the gender of the noun they modify. Verbs also change to indicate the gender of their subjects. Hindi does not use either definite or indefinite articles.

Fast Fact

The British colonization of India is responsible for the introduction of many Hindi words into English. Some of the words English borrows from Hindi include: *bazaar, bungalow, coolie, guru, khaki, loot,* and *pundit.*

International Language

An international or universal language is meant to be used as a means of communication by people who natively speak different languages. An international language is not meant to replace existing native languages but rather to serve as a common means of communication. International languages can include artificial languages, national languages used outside their national boundaries, and national languages that have been modified and simplified from their native form.

The need for improved communication has been apparent since people speaking different languages encountered each other. Since the seventeenth century, it has been estimated that several hundred attempts have been made to create international languages. A number of philosophers, including Francis Bacon (British, 1561–1626), Gottfried Wilhelm Leibniz (German, 1646–1716), and René Descartes (French, 1596–1650), recognized the need and proposed "philosophical" language based on logical systems of classification rather than human speech. Several systems of this type, using representational signs, were constructed but most people found them too difficult to use and unsuited for conversation.

More successful were artificial languages formed from elements taken from existing languages. One of the first of these artificial systems of communications to receive notice was Volapük, a language created by German Roman Catholic priest Johann Martin Schleyer and introduced in 1880. Volapük used an alphabet, grammar, and vocabulary based on Latin, the Romance languages, and Germanic languages. This language enjoyed some popularity, but it too proved difficult to learn and use. In 1887, Dr. Ludwik Lejzer Zamenhof, a Polish-Jewish oculist and linguist, introduced Esperanto (see separate entry). Esperanto is arguably the most successful artificial language; it has had more staying power and is still used by an estimated 100,000 speakers. Words in Esperanto are formed by adding elements to root words and are derived from Latin, Greek, and the Romance and Germanic languages. A simplified version of Esperanto, Ido, was introduced in 1907 but failed to replace Esperanto. Yet another artificial language, Interlingua, was introduced in 1951 by the International Auxiliary Language Association. The grammar and vocabulary of Interlingua is based on English and Romance languages.

Natural languages can also serve as international languages. Latin was the universal language in Europe in medieval times, French was known at one time as the universal language of diplomacy, and English may be said to be the language of commerce today. A greatly simplified version of Latin, *Latino Sine Flexione*, was introduced in the early nineteenth century by an Italian mathematician, but was not simple enough to gain acceptance.

Fast Fact

Between 1925 and 1932, the English scholar C.K. Ogden developed Basic English and proposed it as an international secondary language. Basic English has an uncomplicated grammar and a vocabulary of 850 words: 600 nouns, 150 adjectives, and 100 verbs, adverbs, prepositions, and pronouns.

Italian

Italian, like the other Romance languages, is the direct offspring of the Latin spoken by the Romans and imposed by them on the peoples under their dominion. Of all the major Romance languages, Italian retains the closest resemblance to Latin. In the early fourteenth century, written Italian began to take form through the works of **DANTE ALIGHIERI** (1265–1321). Best known is his allegorical work *La Divina Commedia* (The Divine Comedy), which Dante began circa 1307 and worked on until his death. In 1525, a Venetian, **PIETRO BEMBO** (1470–1547) set out his proposals for a standardized language and style. In 1582, a group of Florentine intellectuals, meeting informally between 1570 and 1580, founded the Academy of the Chaff to maintain the purity of the Italian language.

The unification of Italy in 1861 brought about sweeping social and economic reforms. Amazingly, only 2.5 percent of Italy's population could speak standard Italian at the time of unification. Mandatory schooling and the proliferation of mass communication and mass transit had an enormous impact on the formation of modern standard Italian. Local dialects, characterized as the language of the uneducated, began to fall out of favor in the decades following unification. As Benito Mussolini and his Fascist party rose to power in the early part of the twentieth century, the push toward a common language intensified as he sought to solidify his control over the Italian population.

English	Italian
Hello	Ciao
Goodbye	Arrivederci
My name is	Il mio nome è
I would like	Vorrei
Please	Per favore
How much?	Quanto?
Thank you	Grazie
Excuse me	Scusami
Where?	Dove?
Left	Sinistra
Right	Destra
One	Uno

Fast Fact

L'Accademia della Crusca (Academy of the Chaff) was founded in Florence in 1582 to maintain the purity of the language. Still in existence today, the academy was the first such institution in Europe and the first to produce a modern national language.

Though all Italians receive formal education in modern standard Italian, almost all Italians are bilingual, meaning they speak Italian and their local dialect. There are hundreds of dialects in Italy. For the student of Italian, pure Venetian or Sicilian will be almost incomprehensible. Because of the growing influence of American culture, especially through the media, many English words have found their way into everyday conversation. So many English words have been adopted in Italian that there's a name for them: Itangliano (highly anglicized Italian).

Japanese

Japanese, one of the world's major languages, is spoken by more than 125 million people, ranking it ninth in terms of the number of speakers. Most speakers of Japanese live in Japan, but there are also many speakers in Korea, Taiwan, the Ryukyu Islands, and North and South America. Japanese does not appear to be related to any other language and is of uncertain origin. Some consider Japanese one of the Altaic languages, which includes Turkish and Korean, but other hypotheses link it to language groups from South Asia. It also may be a hybrid, drawing influences from both.

There are three categories of words in Japanese of which native words are the most numerous. Next are words originally borrowed in earlier history from Chinese, followed by the smallest, but rapidly increasing, category of words borrowed from Western languages such as English or other Asian languages. Word order in Japanese is usually subject-object-verb, although words can change position without altering a sentence's meaning. The verb always occurs at the end of a sentence, however. Japanese verbs are also characterized by their lack of number or gender; the same form is used with singular and plural subjects, and no distinction is made for gender.

Japanese is considered an agglutinating language, in which different linguistic elements—particles, auxiliary verbs, and auxiliary adjectives—are joined to form one word. English may require several separate verbs, for example, to express a complete idea, while the Japanese version may use one complex verb. Other agglutinative languages include Korean, Turkish, and Navaho.

Written Japanese

Japanese writing uses two systems for Chinese characters, or kanji, and syllabaries. Chinese characters were introduced to Japan about 1,500 years ago. Because each character is associated with an idea, tens of thousands of characters were in use. In 1946, the Japanese government identified 1,850 characters for daily use and increased the list to 1,945 characters in 1981. Each syllabary, or kana, in the syllabary system represents a sound rather than a meaning. There are two types of kana, however, each containing the same set of sounds. It is not uncommon to find kanji and both types of kana in the same sentence.

Fast Fact

Prior to the introduction of Chinese characters about 1,500 years ago, Japanese was strictly a spoken language.

Portuguese

Portuguese is a member of the Romance group of the Italic subfamily of the Indo-European family of languages. It ranks as the fifth most commonly spoken language, and more than 170 million people, primarily in Brazil, Portugal, the Portuguese Atlantic islands, and former Portuguese colonies in Africa and Asia, speak it natively.

Like other Romance languages, Portuguese developed from Vulgar Latin brought to the Iberian Peninsula by the Romans in the third century B.C. People of Germanic origin invaded Iberia between A.D. 400 and 700 as the Roman Empire was collapsing and Europe entered the Dark Ages. Populations were isolated and languages evolved independently from one another. Evidence of Portuguese distinct from its Latin roots can be found before the eleventh century.

English	Portuguese
Hello	Olá
Goodbye	Adeus
My name is	Meu nome é
I would like	Gostaria
Please	Por favor
How much?	Quanto?
Thank you	Obrigado
Excuse me	Com licença
Where?	Onde?
Left	Esquerdo
Right	Direito
One	Um

There are four major dialects in Portuguese: Northern Portuguese or Galican, Central Portuguese, Southern Portuguese (which includes the dialect of Lisbon), and Insular Portuguese (which includes Brazilian Portuguese). The two officially used dialects are Lisbon and Brazilian. A 1990 act simplified the spelling of European and Brazilian Portuguese and in 2008, the Portuguese government agreed to standardize the language on the Brazilian form.

The language uses an alphabet of twenty-six letters, and *K*, *W*, and *Y* were added by the 1990 Portuguese Language Orthographic Agreement. There are also twelve characters with diacritics, but these are not considered as independent letters. All nouns in Portuguese indicate a gender, as do most adjectives and pronouns.

Spread of Portuguese

Due to Portugal's colonization efforts during the fifteenth and sixteenth centuries, Portuguese uses a large number of loanwords from all over the world—and has provided loanwords to many other languages. However, most of its vocabulary is taken from Latin, and Portuguese uses more verb inflections from classical Latin than any other Romance language.

Fast Fact

There is a movement to encourage the UN to make Portuguese an official language, but the effort faces an uphill battle. Portuguese is the official language of just eight sovereign states, and 80 percent of its speakers live in one country, Brazil. Portuguese speakers are also overshadowed by English- and Spanish-speaking people in the Western Hemisphere. It is not even among the top ten most spoken languages in Europe.

Romance Languages

The Romance languages, also called Romanic, are a group of languages belonging to the Italic (Latin) subfamily of the Indo-European family of languages. They are spoken by approximately 670 million people, chiefly in Europe and the Western Hemisphere. The more important Romance languages include Spanish, Portuguese, French, Italian, Romanian, Catalan (spoken in northeast Spain), Occitan (spoken in Provence), and Rhaeto-Romanic (spoken in Switzerland and northern Italy).

While these languages descended from Latin, the language of the Romans (and the origin of the term *Romance*), they are derived from spoken or popular Latin rather than classical Latin. This vernacular

---

version, known as Vulgar Latin, was spread by Roman colonists and soldiers to every part of the Empire. In some cases, it replaced native languages, although it also mixed with and was influenced by local speech habits and languages of later immigrants. When the Western Roman Empire fell in the fifth century, local dialects developed in isolation and eventually evolved into individual Romance languages, although Germanic invasions had some influence.

Fast Fact

Because France, Spain, and Portugal engaged in aggressive colonial expansion starting in the fifteenth century, their languages spread extensively. Today, 70 percent of all speakers of Romance languages live outside Europe.

Romance languages have many similar features due to their common origin. Instead of differences in structure vocabulary, variations between these languages tend to be phonetical. They also show a common grammatical evolution from Latin: all have dropped one gender, using masculine and feminine rather than Latin's masculine, feminine, and neuter. Except for Romanian, all Romance languages also have just one case instead of Latin's six separate noun cases.

Romance languages are written with the classical Latin or Roman alphabet of twenty-three letters modified and supplemented in various ways. The letter *I* was split during medieval times into *I* and *J* and the letter *V* into *U, V,* and *W.* The Latin letter *K* and the new *W* were rarely used in most Romance languages, and only for nonnative words. Of the Romance languages, only French and Spanish use the letter *Y.*

Russian

Russian belongs to the large and diverse Indo-European language family, a group that includes English, French, German, Hindi, and many others. Specifically, Russian belongs to the Slavic branch of the Indo-European family. Other Slavic languages include Czech, Slovak, Polish, Serbian, Slovenian, Bulgarian, Macedonian, Belorussian, and Ukrainian. Russian, Ukrainian, and Belorussian are considered sister languages because all three of them were developed from the same linguistic stock and have retained many similarities in their sound systems, grammars, and vocabularies. Russian is the most commonly spoken Slavic language in the world; it is the mother tongue of at least 145 million people.

Fast Fact

Alexander Sergeyevich Pushkin (1799–1837) is considered the father of modern Russian literature. He is also remembered as a romantic figure whose life ended tragically in a duel with his wife's alleged lover.

Although Russia's political influence diminished after the fall of the Soviet Union, the Russian language is still widely spoken in Eastern Europe and in the former Soviet republics. The United States, Canada, Israel, and Australia each have sizeable Russian-speaking immigrant communities. Although not all of the immigrants are ethnically Russian, many choose to preserve Russian as the community language. In addition, approximately 100 million people worldwide use Russian as their second language.

Russian is the official language of the Russian Federation and is one of the six working languages of the United Nations. It is written in a script known as the Cyrillic alphabet. The vocabulary of the Russian language consists of native words of Slavic origin and borrowings from Greek, Latin, French, English, and other languages. Most scholars agree that Russian became a distinctive language in the fourteenth or fifteenth century.

With the development of Russian secular literary traditions, regional dialects became more acceptable in oral communication as well as in writing. After the unification of Russia under the leadership of Moscow in the seventeenth century, Russian became the country's national language. The eighteenth century played a significant role both in the history of Russia and in the development of its language, as the country transformed itself from a backwater state on the outskirts of Europe to a powerful empire. Simultaneously, many foreign words (especially French) entered the Russian vocabulary. In fact, French became the unofficial first language among Russian nobility. This set a clear linguistic divide between the masses, who spoke several regional varieties of Russian, and the upper classes, who were often more comfortable in French. French continued to play an important role in the lives of the Russian elite well into the twentieth century.

Spanish

Spanish is a member of the Romance group of the Italic subfamily of the Indo-European family of languages. It is the second most commonly spoken language, the native language of approximately 330 million people and spoken as a second language by another 50 million. Spanish is the official language of Spain and nineteen Latin American countries.

The Spanish vocabulary is of Latin origin, brought to the Iberian Peninsula by soldiers and colonists of ancient Rome. Around A.D. 719, Arabic-speaking Islamic groups from North Africa—who first brought Arabic numerals to Europe—conquered the region, and Spanish still has about 4,000 words of Arabic origin. Over time it also has been enhanced by words from French, Italian, and several indigenous languages of North, Central, and South America. Spanish written materials date from the middle of the tenth century.

- - - - - - - - --- --- - - - -

Person of Importance
King Alfonso

In the 1200s, King Alfonso X of Castile employed scholars to write original works in Castilian as well as translate histories and scientific, legal, and literary works from Latin, Greek, and Arabic. This effort served to spread knowledge throughout Western Europe of the time.

While there are a number of dialects in Spanish, Castilian became the accepted standard by the middle of the thirteenth century due to the political importance of Castile. The Castilian dialect has several pronunciations different from Latin American Spanish, but the differences in pronunciation, grammar, and vocabulary are fairly minor. Two other major dialects include Andalusian, which is spoken in and around Seville, and Catalan, which is spoken in eastern and northeastern Spain. Other dialects survive only is isolated rural areas.

The Roman alphabet is used in Spanish with the addition of several symbols. The tilde (~) used with an *n* changes the pronunciation, and an acute accent (´) can be used to indicate which syllable of a word is stressed when the stress is irregular or to distinguish between homonyms.

Spanish is notable for its use of two forms of the verb "to be." One version indicates a relatively temporary condition, and the other a more permanent state. Another distinguishing characteristic is its use of an inverted question mark at the beginning of a question in addition to a standard question mark at the end. Similarly, an inverted exclamation is used at the beginning of an exclamation.

English	Spanish
Hello	Hola
Goodbye	Adiós
My name is	Me llamo
I would like	Me gustaría
Please	Por favor
How much?	¿Cuánto?
Thank you	Gracias
Excuse me	Con permiso
Where?	¿Dónde?
Left	Izquierda
Right	Derecha
One	Uno

Linguistics

Linguistics is the scientific study of language including its structure, sounds, and meaning. Linguistics also considers the history and development of languages, their relationships to each other, and their cultural place in human behavior. A related but separate field, phonetics, is the study of the sounds of speech.

In the fifth century B.C., Greek philosophers first debated the origins of human language. The first Greek grammar was written in the first century B.C. and served as a model for later Roman efforts. The idea that languages are related was introduced in 1786 by an English scholar who suggested Sanskrit and Persian resembled Greek and Latin and that all diverged from an earlier source.

Linguistics did not become a science until the nineteenth century, when a number of linguists established the existence of the Indo-European family of languages. Structural linguistics, which analyzed speech to discover the underlying structure of language, was developed by Ferdinand de Saussure in the early twentieth century.

Linguistics made another advance, and a diversion, in the 1950s with the work of Noam Chomsky, who challenged structural linguistics. Chomsky introduced "transformational generative grammar," which states that language is a uniquely human, biologically based cognitive capacity. He thought that linguistics should study unconscious knowledge of language.

Fast Fact

A person who speaks many languages is not a linguist, but a polyglot.

The study of linguistics is an analysis of discrete units of language and the rules that govern how these units are put together. The parts of language, morphemes (words or word parts), phonetic features (speech sounds including their distribution and patterns), and syntax (phrase and sentence construction) are seen against the rules and principles that dictate how language sounds are combined and varied and how words are formed and built into larger phrases. Modern linguistic programs are interdisciplinary and combine study in anthropology, classics, philosophy, psychology, statistics, and computer science.

Person of Importance
Noam Chomsky

Born in 1928, Noam Chomsky is an American educator and linguist. In the 1950s, Chomsky introduced revolutionary ideas in the field of linguistics with his theory of transformational (also referred to as generative or transformational-generative) grammar. According to this theory, the sentences formed within every language conform to universal rules common to all languages, so-called "deep structures." These rules show the relationship between an active sentence, "John drove the car," its passive counterpart, "The car was driven by John," as well as interrogative statements, "Who drove the car?" The deep structures of transformational grammar apply to and reveal relationships between these sentences at a more basic and useful level than "surface structures," or the practice of analyzing a sentence by parts of speech.

Transformational grammar also theorizes that the human brain has an innate capacity for language. This theory has been influential in the field of psycholinguistics and the study of language acquisition. Chomsky is a prolific author and has lectured widely on linguistics, philosophy, and politics. As of the publication of this book, he is a professor of linguistics at the Massachusetts Institute of Technology.

Cheat Sheet for Modern Languages

American Sign Language is a complete and complex language not dependent on oral language.

A person using American Sign Language cannot communicate with a person using British Sign Language.

We call our number symbols "Arabic numerals" because North African Arabs brought them to Europe from India where they were first used.

The establishment of Urdu as the official language of Pakistan was one of the causes for the Bengali-speaking Hindus of Bangladesh to establish an independent state.

The family of languages known as Chinese includes more than 300 languages and major dialects that are as different from each other as Romance languages.

There are nearly 7,000 languages spoken in the world today, half of which are spoken by 6,000 or fewer people.

Because pronunciation of English words has changed radically while spelling has changed very little since the fifteenth century, English spelling is not a reliable indication of pronunciation and therefore makes English a difficult language to learn.

Esperanto, the closest we have to an international language, has only an estimated 100,000 speakers.

French is an official language in more than twenty-five countries and provides approximately one third of the English vocabulary.

German is the native language of more EU citizens than any other language, and only English is spoken by more EU residents than German.

Hindi is spoken by nearly 425 million people, mostly in India, and is the version of Hindustani used by Hindus.

There have been many attempts to develop an international language to serve as a common means of communication by people who natively speak different languages; Esperanto has been the most successful.

A standard Italian language was not instituted until 1861; there are still hundreds of local dialects in use in addition to standard Italian.

Japanese does not appear to be related to any other language; it has some characteristics similar to Korean, Turkish, and Navaho.

Due to Portugal's colonization efforts during the fifteenth and sixteenth centuries, Portuguese uses a large number of loanwords from all over the world—and has provided loanwords to many languages.

Romance languages descended from Latin, the language of the Romans, and the origin of the term *Romance*.

Russia, and the Russian language, was greatly influenced by France in the eighteenth century and French became the unofficial first language of the Russian nobility.

The efforts of King Alfonso X of Castile, Spain in the 1200s to have histories, scientific, legal, and literary works translated from Latin, Greek, and Arabic helped the spread of knowledge through Europe.

Linguistics, the scientific study of language, did not become a science until the nineteenth century.

Noam Chomsky, an American linguist, showed that the human brain had an innate, biological capacity to form language.

Chapter Five

History

Our word "history" comes from the Greek *historia* meaning "learning or knowing by inquiry." History as a study or discipline is generally considered a means to understand the past and to record past events. Our recorded history is monumental; this chapter presents a few selected examples.

Ancient Greece

Greece has had an outsized influence on history, particularly cultural history. Its architecture, art, literature, drama, philosophy, and language are still studied and appreciated as providing the roots for later development in those fields. Greece had established civilizations by the time of the Bronze Age (about 2800 B.C.), and its extensive coastline meant that new cultures continually migrated to its islands. Poor soil influenced Greeks to turn to the sea for commerce and expansion, and by the sixth century B.C., Greece had colonies in Italy, France, Spain, and Africa.

Repeatable Quotable

History is the version of past events that people have decided to agree upon.
—*Napoleon Bonaparte*

DEFINING MOMENT

Democracy (Greek for "rule of the people") arose in Greek city-states, small autonomous governments in which politically savvy citizens became involved in the making of their laws. While democratic principles did not extend to resident slaves, and most of these early democracies eventually fell before the greater strength of imperial governments, the idea formed the basis of later, better developed, and more enduring political structures.

Greek Gifts

Greece was the scene of much experimentation with government. The many tribes that had settled on Greek islands formed small, independent city-states, and most went through a political evolutionary process in which monarchies became aristocracies, then tyrannies and oligarchies (power of the few), and eventually the idea of democracy was born. Greek city-states were embroiled in conflict such as the Persian Wars (499 to 449 B.C.) and Peloponnesian War (431 to 404 B.C.) with only limited cooperation, for much of their history. Despite the toll of war, Greek civilization flourished even if the city-states could not maintain their independence. Their influence spread over much of the Western world to Asia and India under **ALEXANDER THE GREAT** (356 to 323 B.C.), king of Macedonia. Having fought with nearly everyone for centuries, the remaining states fell to Roman rule in 146 B.C.

We still consider ancient Greece as a period in which learning and thought were newly elevated by many intellectuals including Sophocles, Euripides, Socrates, Plato, Aristotle, and Hippocrates. Hellenism, the term for the cultural influence and ideals of ancient, classical Greece, derives from the name Greeks gave themselves.

Fast Fact

Logic and the scientific method are two of Aristotle's greatest contributions, but his interests covered many sciences, history, and political and literary theory. His work is vast, yet two-thirds of his original writings may have been lost.

Middle Ages

The Middle Ages is a period in European history that dates roughly from the fall of the Western Roman Empire in the fifth century to the beginning of the Renaissance in the fifteenth century. The Early Middle Ages saw a decline in population as the influence of Rome decayed, unable to protect citizens from increasing barbarian invasions. Many of the improvements that the Roman Empire had introduced, such as water-supply systems, efficient agricultural methods, roads. and shipping routes, fell into disrepair.

While the Middle Ages are sometimes referred to as the Dark Ages and generally considered a period of cultural oppression, ignorance, and the physical suffering of subjugated peasants, this era is now considered to have set the stage for the idea of a modern Europe. Indeed, a period lasting a millennium and undergoing such radical changes in leadership and social pressures must have produced some positives.

The Beginning of the End

CHARLEMAGNE (742–814) was one such figure to step out of the darkness to shed an uplifting light on the lot of his subjects. As ruler of the Frankish Empire, incorporating much of Western and Central Europe, Charlemagne brought many reforms and standardizations to justice. He also oversaw a cultural revival, sometimes known as the "Carolingian Renaissance," that included developments in architecture and the arts and an increase in literacy made possible by his use of a common writing style that allowed for widespread communication.

More dramatic growth occurred during the Central or High Middle Ages as statehoods expanded and consolidated, populations increased, and general economic health improved through greater trade.

Eventually, the period of the Middle Ages gave way to the Renaissance as interest in classical learning and values lifted cultural health throughout Europe. The Renaissance is also the period that saw such important innovations as paper, printing, the compass, and gunpowder.

DEFINING MOMENT

While the exact date of incorporation is unclear, Oxford University was founded sometime in the eleventh century and is the oldest surviving university in the English-speaking world. It is now generally considered one of the world's leading academic institutions.

The Conquest of America

It is believed that the American continents were inhabited by between 70 and 90 million people when Europeans first reached our shores in the fifteenth century. This population, greater than that of Europe at the time, included 30 to 40 million in North America, 11 million in Central America, and another 39 million inhabitants of South America. All were descended from a group or groups who emigrated from Siberia approximately 14,000 years ago and were undoubtedly looking for a more hospitable habitat. They found it in abundance in the Americas and spread quickly throughout the continents.

The Silent Army

One or two hundred years after those first Europeans visited the new world, the indigenous American populations were decimated, reduced by as much as 95 percent, by European diseases against which the natives had no defense. What a concerted and organized military effort would have accomplished only over a long time and at considerable expense and loss of life was achieved with great efficiency by smallpox, measles, influenza, and typhus. The expansion of America might have taken considerably longer had settlers and frontiersmen encountered 20 million hostile natives rather than fewer than 1 million.

DEFINING MOMENT

In 1520, a slave infected with smallpox arrived in Mexico from Cuba. Within one hundred years, the Mexican population had plunged by 92 percent.

The Legacy of Christopher Columbus

Christopher Columbus is celebrated, and in fact has a national holiday named for him, for his achievement in "discovering" America. Although he wasn't the first European to reach North America—the Norse explorer Leif Eriksson reached Newfoundland around 1000—that he was able to pull off the 1492 expedition at all was a great accomplishment.

The effort started badly. His plan to establish spice routes to the Orient by sailing west was denied sponsorship by heads of state in

Italy, France, Portugal, and Spain. Finally, the king and queen of Spain agreed to fund, in part, his expedition and with three tiny ships, the largest of which was just 70 feet long, he set sail in August 1492. The sailor had miscalculated the size of the earth and the distance he would have to travel to reach his destination, by as much as 25 percent. Luckily for Columbus and his crew, North America intervened because no fifteenth-century ship was capable of carrying enough food and water to cover the actual distance between Europe and Asia.

The New World

After a five-week crossing, the fleet sighted land somewhere in the Bahamas. Columbus found no spices, but the natives he encountered were friendly, fortunately, and he continued exploring, landing at Cuba and Hispaniola before kidnapping some of the natives and returning to Spain. It's believed that Columbus's crew also brought back syphilis with them from the New World and later spread the disease across Europe.

DEFINING MOMENT

The volcanic Mount Tambora on the Indonesian island of Sumbawa exploded in 1815, killing 100,000 people and sending thirty-six cubic miles of ash and dust into the atmosphere. The ash filtered the sun and cooled the earth by a mere 1.5 degrees Fahrenheit, yet this was enough to cause the worldwide failure of crops, and the following year came to be known as "the year without summer."

Columbus visited the New World on three more occasions and, although the riches described by Marco Polo had eluded him, was convinced until his death that he had reached Asia.

A New Country

The seeds of the American Revolution were sown during the French and Indian War, the North American campaign of the Seven Years' War, which lasted from 1754 to 1763. It pitted the British against the French and their Native American allies over property rights in North America. While the war ended with a British victory and the acquisition of Canada, all French territory east of the Mississippi, and Florida, its cost doubled Britain's national debt. Now with more territory than it could easily manage, the British king, George III, issued the Royal Proclamation of 1763 establishing a boundary upon westward expansion in the colonies.

Repeatable Quotable

We must, indeed, all hang together, or most assuredly we shall all hang separately.
—*Benjamin Franklin*

Parliament's efforts to raise revenues through various taxes on colonial transactions, as well as restrictive laws, angered the increasingly independent-minded colonists and eventually caused acts of civil disobedience.

The War Begins

Revolution was in the air in early 1775 and a repressive and intractable English government finally pushed back too hard. Hostilities began in April 1775 in Concord and Lexington, Massachusetts, although it wasn't until the following July, after numerous attempts by both parties at reconciliation, that representatives of all thirteen colonies signed the Declaration of Independence and a new nation was born.

DEFINING MOMENT

The French Revolution (1789–1799), a period of horrific violence and bloodshed, replaced the French monarchy with a more democratic form of government. Widespread famine and an inequitable system of taxation combined with the conspicuous consumption of the ruling class led to the uprising. Also, a huge national debt from years of financing wars, including the American Revolution, made it impossible for the monarchy to ease the citizens' suffering. So, it was the French monarchy's support of the American Revolution that contributed directly to its own.

It remained for the fledgling country to establish its independence, an effort that took six years and whose outcome was never a certainty. Surely the military and financial assistance of France, the tactical abilities of George Washington as commander of the Continental Army, and the passion of citizens in defending their newly created nation were instrumental in the conclusion. So too was more than a small amount of luck on several critical occasions, British military arrogance, and finally the huge expense of fighting a war across an ocean that England could not maintain.

The Nineteenth-Century Indian Wars

From 1823 to 1890, the U.S. military engaged in a series of conflicts with Native Americans west of the Mississippi River. They did this with fewer than 15,000 troops in more than 150 forts, posts, camps, arsenals, and armories. Army soldiers acted as advance scouts, settlers, and "improvers" of the wilderness, the area's first scientists and agriculturalists, and protectors of surveyors and railroad and telegraph lines. They are most remembered, however, for their campaigns of extinction, capture and removal, and for destroying the livelihood of the Indians.

The Native Americans, for their part, were battling for survival against whites who saw the frontier as land for the taking. The new American government wanted to prevent foreign powers from recruiting Native Americans against them, as had happened as late as the War of 1812. This prompted President Andrew Jackson to sign the Removal Act in 1830, which permitted the establishment of treaties with Indians and the exchange of tribal lands in eastern areas for reservations on western lands. Not all tribes were compliant with this plan and costly wars resulted.

More than 1,100 individual battles occurred between Indians and Army forces during this period, with estimated casualties of 5,500 and 1,000 respectively. A much greater number died on both sides from diseases such as smallpox, measles, and cholera. Both sides were guilty of unnecessary acts of violence and cruelty. Beyond the immediate loss of life was the destruction of a way of life for many Native Americans, who were forced to live on reservations unsuitable for raising crops and devoid of game.

Repeatable Quotable

There are two classes of people, one demanding the utter extinction of the Indians, and the other full of love for their conversion to civilization and Christianity. Unfortunately the army stands between them and gets the cuff from both sides.
—*William Tecumseh Sherman*

Fast Fact

The Civil War (1861–1865) is also known as the War of the Rebellion (by the Union), the War Between the States (by the South), the War for Southern Independence, and the War of Secession.

The Civil War

The exact causes of the Civil War are still debated by American historians, and it was a conflict viewed by some as unnecessary. The prospect of war was certainly not taken seriously by either side; both were confident that it could be concluded quickly and without significant loss of life. But clearly, the North and South had grown in different economic directions since the founding of the country, with the South largely agricultural and dependent on a plantation system supported by slavery, and the North more invested in commercial trade and industrialism. Conflict became unavoidable as leaders of both sides recognized that there could be no compromise on the issue of slavery.

Abraham Lincoln's election in 1860 prompted seven southern states to secede in February 1861, followed by four additional states two months later. These eleven territories formed the Confederate States of America. Hostilities started on April 12, 1861 when Confederate troops fired on Union-held Fort Sumter in the harbor of Charleston, South Carolina. More than 10,000 military engagements would take place before the war ended when Confederate general Robert E. Lee surrendered to Ulysses S. Grant on April 9, 1985.

Costs of War

At the beginning of the war, the population of the Northern states was slightly more than 22 million, including an estimated 400,000 slaves in five border states. The population of the South exceeded 9 million, which included 3.5 million slaves. The North employed the services of more than 2 million soldiers, or twice that of the Confederate states. The war ended slavery, but the cost for both sides was high with more than 620,000 military casualties, more than all other wars involving the United States combined. The newly reconstituted nation also experienced the loss of Abraham Lincoln when he was assassinated, thereby enduring a more painful period of Reconstruction with its overtones of resentments and lingering intolerance.

Casualties of the Ten Largest Battles
of the American Civil War

The following graph compares Union and Confederate casualties in the Civil War's ten costliest battles. In all cases except one, the battle of Chickamauga, Union forces outnumbered those of the Confederacy; Union casualties exceeded Confederate casualties in these battles and for the war.

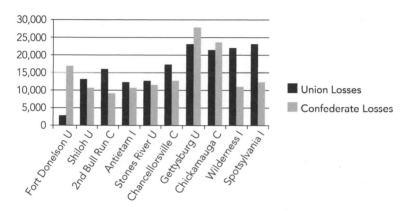

The victor of each battle is indicated with a "U" or a "C" following the name of the battle; "I" indicates an inconclusive outcome. Figures compiled by the United States National Park Service.

The Spanish-American War

Spain was a colonial power into the late nineteenth century, with Western Hemisphere possessions including Cuba and Puerto Rico, and the Philippine, Marshall, Carolina, and Mariana Islands in the

Pacific. In 1868, Cuba started its struggle for independence from Spain and, despite a treaty in 1878, began an armed revolt in 1895. Spain replied with brutal repression of the rebellion, arousing sympathy in the United States and endangering U.S. citizens in Cuba.

February 15, 1898 The road to war was clear after the USS *Maine*, sent to protect U.S. citizens and property, blew up in Havana harbor. A U.S. Naval Court of Inquiry determined that the ship was blown up by a mine and President McKinley ordered a blockade of Cuba in April.

April 21, 1898 The U.S. Congress declared war against Spain.

May 1, 1898 One of the first engagements was in Manila Bay in the Philippines, where American warships destroyed the Spanish fleet. Troops arrived in July to occupy Manila, and on the way obtained the surrender of the Spanish governor in Guam, who was unaware his nation was at war. Planning for an assault on Cuba began in April and in June Marines captured Guantanamo Bay and landed 17,000 troops.

July 1, 1898 African-American cavalry units and the Rough Riders commanded by Theodore Roosevelt charged up Kettle Hill and San Juan Hill, pushing Spanish troops inland.

July 3, 1898 Six ships of the Spanish navy attempted to leave Santiago harbor and were destroyed by U.S. naval forces.

July 16, 1898 Spain agreed to an unconditional surrender.

December 10, 1898 The peace treaty, signed in Paris, ended Spain's colonial presence in the Western Hemisphere. It ceded Puerto Rico and Guam to the United States and allowed for the purchase of the Philippines from Spain for $20 million. While short, the Spanish-American War resulted in the loss of 3,000 lives, 90 percent of these from infectious diseases.

Fast Fact

On April 24, 1898, Spain declared war on the United States after it imposed a blockade on Spanish ports. The following day, the U.S. Congress declared war on Spain, retroactive to April 21.

Antarctic Exploration

At the end of the nineteenth century, scientific societies worldwide became interested in exploring the vast unknown continent of Antarctica. Eight countries sponsored sixteen major expeditions between 1897 and 1922 to explore and map coastlines and interior areas, and to gather scientific data and specimens.

Some expeditions had the goal of being the first to reach the South Pole. Roald Amundsen's expedition of 1910 was one of these. He succeeded, beating the expedition of Robert Scott by thirty-three days. Certainly Amundsen took inspiration for this quest by the accomplishment of Robert Peary in reaching the North Pole in April 1909.

These explorers, some of whom did not survive their experiences, faced extreme hardship and deprivation due to the primitive transportation and communication technologies of the time. Their efforts were later romanticized by reference to the period as the "Heroic Age of Antarctic Exploration."

Further Adventures

Amundsen later turned his attention north and sought to be the first to fly over the North Pole. He failed in this 1925 attempt to reach the Pole in a pair of flying boats, so he collaborated with an Italian aeronautical engineer, Umberto Nobile, to make an attempt in one of his semi-rigid airships. In May 1926, Amundsen's team ran into the American expedition of Richard E. Byrd, who was on the same quest. Byrd took off in a Dutch Fokker, returning later to claim that they had overflown the Pole. Amundsen and Nobile went ahead with their flight and may have accomplished their goal due to the serious doubts subsequently raised about Bryd's credibility.

Fast Fact

Egos were on constant display and may have been prime motivators, during the age of polar exploration. Amundsen and Nobile disagreed, for example, on who should receive more credit for their North Pole flight of 1926. For his part however, Amundsen seems to have put these differences aside, dying in an attempt to rescue Nobile, who had become stranded on the ice in another North Pole expedition in 1928.

The Panama Canal

The idea for a waterway allowing for passage of ships between the Atlantic and Pacific Oceans, thereby avoiding the lengthy circumnavigation of South America, goes back to 1534 when Charles V of Spain ordered a survey of the isthmus. He was looking for a tactical advantage over the Portuguese in their competition to expand their empires. It was the Scottish, however, who tried first, in 1698, to colonize Panama and set up an overland trade route. Unfortunately, both of their attempts failed with great loss of life due to the inhospitable conditions.

A growing United States, which had acquired California in 1848, became increasingly interested in the Panama route and provided funds for a railway link across the isthmus, which opened in 1855. Encouraged by the successful completion of the Suez Canal in 1869, a French company began an earnest effort to construct a sea-level canal in 1880. But poor planning, the loss of nearly 22,000 workers to malaria and yellow fever, and construction difficulties forced them to abandon the project after thirteen years.

Interest Builds

American interest in an interoceanic route increased still further after the United States acquired Puerto Rico in the Caribbean and Guam and the Philippine Islands in the Pacific as a result of the Spanish-American War. A 1901 agreement between the United States and Britain gave the United States the right to create and control a canal with access to the waterway for all nations. A treaty was signed in 1903 with the newly independent government of Panama ceding rights for a canal zone to the United States in return for a payment of $10 million and annual rental of $250,000.

Work began on a canal in 1904, and all the problems that had plagued earlier attempts had been solved. This canal included a system of locks, and most importantly, sanitary and disease-control programs were put in place as mosquitoes had been identified as the carrier of yellow fever and malaria. Even so, 5,600 workers died during its construction. The canal was opened on August 15, 1914, two years ahead of schedule.

Fast Fact

All ships pay a toll to transit the canal based on their type, size, and the type of cargo they carry. In 1928, the American adventurer Richard Halliburton paid a toll of 36 cents to swim the canal.

Taking Flight

The invention and development of heavier-than-air flying machines required a number of advances: the creation and understanding of the science of aerodynamics, developments in mechanics to insure engine reliability, and control of an aircraft once aloft.

The first human flights occurred in France in 1783 when the Montgolfier brothers launched a hot-air balloon. Two other Frenchmen were working simultaneously on balloons filled with the recently discovered gas hydrogen. Hydrogen technology soon gained favor after these flights. In the early nineteenth century, Englishman Sir George Cayley developed some of the basic principles of

---

heavier-than-air flight, and German Otto Lilienthal was the first to successfully make and fly gliders, doing so in the 1890s.

Orville and Wilbur Wright, two mechanics who operated a bicycle repair shop in Dayton, Ohio, built their own controllable biplane glider. The next step, attaching a gasoline engine connected to propellers, led to the first flights in a powered airplane on December 17, 1903, near Kitty Hawk, North Carolina. That first flight lasted just twelve seconds and covered 120 feet but, on the fourth and last flight of the day, Wilbur flew 852 feet in fifty-nine seconds. A modest beginning to be sure, but successful proof of the concept.

Soon, others were competing with the Wrights, and the brothers continued to experiment and make additional flights in the United States and France. In 1909, the U.S. army adopted the Wright airplane for aerial reconnaissance use—the aircraft as weapon of war was not far off—and the Wright Company was founded.

Fast Fact

The first gliders designed by the Wright brothers employed "wing warping," a system of cables and pulleys used to control the shape of a flexible wing structure, and enabled the aircraft to turn. This system was replaced by more rigid wings using ailerons, hinged tabs on the trailing edge of the wing.

Russian Revolution

The Russian Revolution of 1917 consisted of two separate events. The first was the March Revolution, which was precipitated by the catastrophic losses sustained by poorly led and equipped Russian troops in World War I and the collapse of the economy. Food shortages threatened civilians with starvation and workers started demonstrations and strikes in Petrograd. When the local garrison joined the revolt, Tsar Nicolas II was forced to abdicate and a provisional government was appointed. Following months of political unrest by opposing factions, the second event, the November Revolution, replaced the provisional government with the Bolshevik party led by Vladimir Lenin.

Lenin did not have a firm hold on the government and the Russian Civil War broke out in 1918 between the Red Army—Bolsheviks or communists—and the White Army—consisting of conservatives, monarchists, and anti-Bolshevik groups. This war lasted four years and was responsible for the deaths of an estimated 15 million people. Having killed or imprisoned most of his opposition, Lenin and the Bolsheviks triumphed to form the Union of Soviet Socialist Republics in 1922. Lenin died in 1923 and was succeeded by Stalin as the head of the Communist Party.

World War I

Also known as the Great War, World War I lasted from 1914 to 1918 and was fought primarily in Europe. The War pitted Germany, Austria-Hungary, and Turkey against Russia, France, Britain, and eventually the United States.

WWI was brought about by the assassination in June 1914 of Archduke Franz Ferdinand, heir to the Austro-Hungarian throne, but many factors led down the road to war: imperialistic tendencies and associated tensions between Germany, France, Great Britain, Russia, and Austria-Hungary being the most important. There was also a great spirit of nationalism on both sides; the French felt hostility toward Germany after losing Alsace and Lorraine, and Slavic groups with Austria-Hungary yearned for independence. Historians still debate the causes, but it's likely that the leaders at the time believed the war would not escalate as it did, nor prove so costly to its participants.

> **Repeatable**
> # Quotable
>
> The world must be made safe for democracy.
> —*Woodrow Wilson*

DEFINING MOMENT

Austria-Hungary, supported by Germany, declared war on Serbia in July of 1914. Germany then declared war on Russia, which was backing Serbia, and France, fearing that it was about to attack its western border. After Germany violated Belgian neutrality, Great Britain declared war on Germany.

For the first time, poison gas, tanks, and heavy artillery were used against troops, and with disastrous consequences. Germany invaded Belgium, Russia pushed into eastern Germany, and France attacked Germany along their eastern border. But these offensives bogged down and the opposing armies took to trenches with battle lines virtually stationary for the duration of the war. Conditions were more dynamic on the eastern front, but the Russian Revolution in 1917 effectively removed Russia from the war.

In response to Germany's unrestricted submarine warfare, the United States declared war in 1917. The infusion of troops into the war permitted new offensives against Germany and precipitated the collapse of German civilian support for the war, as well as mutiny by the German navy and civil riots. The German Kaiser fled to Holland, and a cease-fire was instituted on the eleventh hour of the eleventh day of the eleventh month of 1918. The cost in lives was high: 16 million deaths, 6.8 million of whom were civilians, and 21 million wounded.

Fast Fact

By the end of 1914, it is estimated that the Allies and Central Powers had dug more than 6,000 miles of trenches. The Allies used four types of trenches: the trenches on the front lines, support trenches containing men and supplies, reserve trenches forming a third line for emergency support, and communication trenches connecting them all.

The Great Depression

The Great Depression was a period of sustained economic slowdown, lasting from 1929 until the outbreak of World War II, that affected North America, Europe, and most of the industrialized world. It was precipitated by the Wall Street Crash of October 1929, during which stock prices collapsed. Prices continued to fall for the next three years to about 20 percent of their pre-crash value.

Besides destroying the value of thousands of individual stock portfolios, the decline strained the asset values of banks and other financial institutions. By 1933, 11,000 of the approximately 25,000 American banks had failed. Consumer confidence in the economy bottomed out and people reduced their spending levels, causing businesses to fail and put people out of work, thus aggravating the cycle. Manufacturing output in the United States had fallen to 54 percent of its 1929 level by 1932, and unemployment reached 30 percent.

Because America was acting as a major financier of European economies, the Depression caused a reduction in investment credits to Europe, impacting fragile economies still recovering from World War I. Most affected were the countries most deeply indebted to the United States: Great Britain and Germany. British industry and export markets were severely depressed and unemployment reached 25 percent in Germany, resulting in the social instability that allowed the rise of Adolf Hitler.

Repeatable Quotable

First of all, let me assert my firm belief that the only thing we have to fear is fear itself—nameless, unreasoning, unjustified terror which paralyzes needed efforts to convert retreat into advance.
—*Franklin D. Roosevelt, from his first inaugural address, March 4, 1933*

Franklin D. Roosevelt's "New Deal" introduced increased government regulation of financial markets, the Social Security Administration, and large public-works projects designed to put people to work. Economic stagnation stubbornly continued, however, although at a somewhat less intense level—unemployment dropped to 15 percent by 1939—and the confidence of Americans improved. It wasn't until World War II started in Europe and U.S. factories started to receive orders for armaments and equipment that the economy fully recovered.

The Nuclear Age

In December 1942, Nobel laureate Arthur Compton achieved the first controlled and sustained nuclear reaction at the University of Chicago. Despite the doubts of many in the scientific community, American scientists had organized a massive and secret research effort, codenamed the "Manhattan Project," to develop an atomic weapon before German scientists could provide one for the Third Reich. In a squash court in one of the most densely populated areas of the country, a chain reaction was achieved.

For the next two and one-half years, scientists working in total secrecy developed two uranium-type and one plutonium-type atomic bombs at a cost of $2 billion. Work took place at an isotope-separation plant in Oak Ridge, Tennessee, a plutonium-production plant in Hanford, Washington, and a bomb laboratory at Los Alamos, New Mexico. Under pressure by a nation eager to conclude World War II, scientists raced against German bomb development efforts (unnecessarily, it was learned later) and to build a means to end the war in the Pacific.

Their efforts were successful; in August 1945, atomic bombs were detonated over two Japanese cities, forcing the surrender of Japan. Development continued, prompted by the Soviet Union's acquisition of the bomb, with bigger, better fusion weapons fueling Cold War tensions. The United States had approximately 32,000 nuclear weapons by 1966, while the Soviet Union reached its peak of 33,000 in 1988.

Since then, the Cold War has ended, and thousands of weapons have been dismantled and destroyed on both sides. Yet the danger of nuclear war is not gone. Today the nuclear club includes the United Kingdom, France, China, India, Pakistan, and North Korea. It is commonly assumed that Israel also possesses nuclear weapons.

World War II

Beginning in 1939 with Germany's invasion of Poland and ending six years later with most of Europe and much of the rest of the world in crumbling chaos, World War II proved to be, in terms of lives lost and cities destroyed, the most devastating conflict in human history. World War II defined an entire generation. For the United States, it was the last "good war," unmuddied by conflicting ideology or uncertain public opinion.

Germany's defeat in World War I was difficult for its people to accept. And by late 1923, the country's economy had bottomed out, crushed by the weight of war reparation payments. Desperate, their economy in disarray and currency worthless, their pride in tatters, the German people in their discontent created a vacuum into which a self-proclaimed hero, Adolf Hitler, entered. All the nation's problems, Hitler told his followers, resulted from unsavory influences and the poisoning of Germany's racial purity. By 1934, Hitler had taken control of the government, allied with Fascist Italy, and set about his plan for a new world order.

Germany invaded Poland in September 1939, prompting Britain and France to declare war on Germany. The following April, Germany invaded Denmark and Norway, and in May invaded France, Belgium, the Netherlands, and Luxembourg. Once the German army forced British forces out of France and France signed an armistice with Germany, the only remaining allied power was Britain, successfully resisting the German effort to bomb it into submission.

The United States remained neutral during this time, although it supported China in its conflict with Japan and sold weapons to the Allied powers. Germany, Italy, and Japan united in September 1940 to form the Axis Powers. Germany invaded the Soviet Union in June 1941, creating an eastern front and an ally for Britain. The United States increased aid to Britain, but it wasn't until the surprise attack on Pearl Harbor by Japan in December 1941 that America entered the war, declaring war on Japan.

Much of the world, Europe, Russia, North Africa, and Asia, was now engulfed in war. The strength of Allied forces, which landed in France in June 1944, the continuous bombing of German cities and industrial centers, and the pressure from Soviet forces in the east wore out the German army and forced their surrender in May 1945. In the Pacific, Allied forces had destroyed the Japanese navy and dropped atomic bombs on two Japanese cites, causing Japan to surrender in August 1945.

Fast Fact

It has been estimated that more than 20 million military personnel and 60 million civilians died over the course of World War II. The Soviet Union lost more than 25 million during the war, nearly half of all deaths from the war, with China accounting for another 11 million deaths. More than 295,000 American servicemen lost their lives. An estimated six million Jews were killed in the Holocaust.

The United Nations

At the end of World War I, a number of prominent citizens advanced the idea of forming a society of nations to promote international peace and security. Although the concept was advocated by President Woodrow Wilson, the U.S. Senate refused to ratify the Treaty of Versailles, which included a covenant creating the League of Nations. The remaining World War I allies, plus most of the neutral nations, founded the League, and by 1935 it had fifty-eight members. The League enjoyed some notable successes in settling disputes, but due to its lack of enforcement power and the indifference of major members, it collapsed in the face of growing conflicts leading to World War II.

The United Nations (UN) was established in October 1945 by fifty-one member nations who desired, as those who had created the League of Nations before them, to maintain international peace and security, develop friendly relations between nations, and cooperate to promote social progress, better living standards, and human rights. The General Assembly first met in London in January 1946, but it was decided to locate the UN headquarters in the United States, and facilities opened there in 1952.

The General Assembly, composed of representatives of all members, is the main deliberative organ of the UN. It deals generally with political, social, or economic issues and meets in regular session annually. The Security Council is chartered with primary responsibility for maintaining international peace and security. Five of the fifteen members are permanent—the United States, Great Britain, France, China, and Russia—and the remaining ten are elected for two-year terms by the General Assembly and are chosen to ensure an equitable geographic representation. The Security Council may make recommendations to disputing parties or, in more serious cases, take enforcement action. Other main bodies of the UN include the Economic and Social Council, which investigates economic and social questions and reports to the General Assembly; the International Court of Justice, which settles legal disputes; the Trusteeship Council, which was formed to supervise Trust Territories; and the Secretariat, which handles administrative functions.

Fast Fact

By the late 1990s, the United States was so far behind in paying its dues to the United Nations—owing $1.3 billion—that it was in danger of losing its vote in the General Assembly.

The power of the United Nations has waxed and waned over the years. New membership was blocked by tensions between the Soviet Union and the United States in the early 1950s, and some countries refused to pay for UN actions they did not approve of. Yet today, with its 192 members, the UN has played a part in international matters such as the Gulf War and has been effective in working with less developed countries. It has been less successful with its peacekeeping missions in Somalia, Bosnia, Haiti, and Sierra Leone.

The Korean War

As World War II was raging, the Allied powers agreed that Korea would become an independent state once Japan was defeated. After

Japan's surrender, General Douglas MacArthur's plan called for the creation of an artificial line at the 38th parallel in Korea, splitting the country in half. The Japanese forces above the parallel surrendered to the Soviet Union, and those to the south to the Americans. In June 1950, the Communist government of North Korea launched a full-scale military invasion of neighboring South Korea. The UN Security Council voted 9-0 to hold North Korea accountable for the attack. The resolution sent a peacekeeping force, virtually all of which was made up of U.S. troops.

The Korean "Police Action"

President Truman termed the conflict a police action and put General MacArthur in command of the UN forces. In one of his boldest military operations, MacArthur and American forces recaptured the capital of Seoul on September 27, 1950. Many thought the war was over with, the UN goals having been achieved and the Communists contained behind the 38th parallel. The Americans had done so well, however, that the South Koreans believed they could push farther to expel Communism from Korea completely. South Korean troops crossed the 38th parallel and attacked the North Koreans with UN forces (the majority of them U.S. soldiers) following. A little too arrogant and confident, MacArthur violated his instructions and advanced too close to the Chinese border. By November, it was evident that China was invading on a much larger scale. Washington feared that the Soviet Union would view the Korean conflict as a global struggle, sparking another world war. President Truman's anxiety over this eventually led him to replace MacArthur. Though peace negotiations had begun in 1951, the newly elected Eisenhower administration inherited the war, and fighting continued for two more years until an armistice was signed on July 27, 1953. In the final analysis, the war cost everyone in lives and materials, and left no country satisfied—certainly not the United States. Americans had to accept something less than victory in this, the first limited U.S. war. The Cold War continued, while the United States committed more funds to the North Atlantic Treaty Organization (NATO) and stepped up aid to another capitalist government in danger of Communist takeover in South Vietnam.

The Vietnam War

Following World War II and occupation by the Japanese, the French reoccupied their former colony in Southeast Asia. Ho Chi Minh led his communist army in a revolt, known as the French Indochina War, against French rule starting in 1946. Chinese communists became involved in 1949, and the conflict escalated from a minor insurgency to a conventional war. This conflict, very unpopular in France and termed the "Dirty War," reached an unhappy conclusion in the disastrous defeat at Dien Bien Phu in 1954. The Geneva Conference of 1954 divided the country into the Republic of Vietnam (South Vietnam) and communist North Vietnam. Ho Chi Minh's attempts to reunify Vietnam through legitimate political elections were thwarted by the South Vietnam government.

The leaders of South Vietnam were closely aligned with the West and the number of U.S. advisers there grew through the 1950s. In 1961, the United States and South Vietnam entered into a military and economic aid treaty. Instability and a military coup in South Vietnam led to the Tonkin Gulf Resolution of 1964 authorizing military action in Southeast Asia. Active combat units were introduced in 1965, air raids began on North Vietnam and communist-controlled areas of the South, and by 1969 there were more than a half million troops in Vietnam.

The War Grows

While the United States was supplying and fighting in Vietnam, the Soviet Union and China were supporting the North with weapons, supplies, and advisers. The United States and South Vietnam were unable to make any progress against the insurgent Viet Cong fighting in the South. The Tet Offensive of 1968, in which the Viet Cong and North Vietnamese army attacked more than 100 cities and towns in the South, clearly demonstrated enemy strength.

DEFINING MOMENT

U.S. casualties in the Vietnam War were 58,000 dead and missing. It's estimated that approximately 2 million civilians, another million North Vietnamese and Viet Cong fighters, and as many as 250,000 South Vietnamese soldiers perished. The United States fought the Vietnam War to prevent the spread of communism in Southeast Asia but had seriously underestimated the nature of the conflict.

The war dragged on, but casualties and the discontent of citizens in the United States and worldwide was growing. Negotiations

---

with the North started in 1968 but had no results. President Nixon started a program to withdraw American troops and turn over fighting responsibilities to South Vietnam while conducting bombing raids against communist forces in Cambodia. North Vietnam was tiring of hostilities also and, despite (or perhaps because of) saturation bombing of Hanoi, signed a peace agreement on January 27, 1973. By the end of March, the last U.S. military personnel were withdrawn. On April 30, 1975 what was left of the government of South Vietnam surrendered to a North Vietnamese invasion and the country was reunified one year later as the Socialist Republic of Vietnam, thus ending a thirty-year struggle.

Cheat Sheet for History

Greece had established civilizations by the time of the Bronze Age, about 2800 B.C.

Democracy (Greek for "rule of the people") arose in Greek city states, small autonomous governments in which politically savvy citizens became involved in the making of their laws.

The Middle Ages dates roughly from the fall of the Western Roman Empire in the fifth century to the beginning of the Renaissance in the fifteenth century.

Approximately one-quarter of the entire European population died from outbreaks of the plague from the fourteenth to eighteenth centuries.

One to two hundred years after the first Europeans visited the new world, the indigenous American populations were reduced by as much as 95 percent by European diseases against which they had no defense.

The French and Indian War (1754–1763) doubled England's debt and prompted Parliament to raise taxes in the American colonies, fueling anti-British revolutionary feelings.

The Revolutionary War began in April 1775, although it wasn't until the following July after numerous attempts by both parties at reconciliation, that representatives of all thirteen colonies signed the Declaration of Independence and a new nation was born.

The 1815 explosion of volcanic Mount Tambora in Indonesia cooled the earth enough to cause the worldwide failure of crops.

There were more than 10,000 military engagements during the four years of the Civil War.

In February 1898, the USS *Maine* exploded, very possibly due to an accident in Havana harbor, and precipitated the Spanish-American War.

A French company began an effort to construct a sea-level canal in Panama in 1880. They lost 22,000 workers to malaria and yellow fever, and abandoned the project after thirteen years.

World War I was the first time that poison gas, tanks, and heavy artillery were used against troops. Nearly 10 million soldiers died during the conflict.

During the Great Depression of the 1930s, manufacturing output in the United States fell to 54 percent of its 1929 level, and unemployment reached 30 percent.

Britain and France were fighting Germany for nearly two years before the United States entered World War II.

World War II proved to be, in terms of lives lost and cities destroyed, the most devastating conflict in human history. It defined an entire generation.

The United Nations was established in October 1945 by fifty-one member nations who desired to maintain international peace and security.

In June 1950, the Communist government of North Korea invaded South Korea. The UN Security Council voted to hold North Korea accountable and the Korean War began.

At the end of the Korean War in 1953, Americans had to accept something less than victory in this, the first limited U.S. war.

By 1966, the United States had 32,000 nuclear weapons, while the Soviet Union reached its peak of 33,000 nukes in 1988.

On April 30, 1975 the government of South Vietnam surrendered to a North Vietnamese invasion and the country was reunified one year later as the Socialist Republic of Vietnam, ending a thirty-year struggle.

Chapter Six

Language Arts

Language arts traditionally include the skills of speaking, composition, reading, spelling, and dramatics. It is a field rich and diverse. This chapter considers selected topics of speech, composition, and literature.

Language Learning in the United States

In many areas of business and government in the United States, there is an acute need for individuals who speak and understand a language other than English. Language was identified as the intelligence community's single greatest need in a report issued in September 2001 by the House Permanent Select Committee on Intelligence. The late Senator Paul Simon declared in 2001 that "some eighty federal agencies need proficiency in nearly one hundred foreign languages . . . . Only eight percent of American college students study another language."

The Problem

Of the small number of Americans who study a foreign language, very few attain any proficiency. The Foreign Service Institute, the Federal Government's primary training institution for officers and support personnel of the U.S. foreign affairs community, estimates that a minimum of 1,320 hours of instruction is necessary to acquire language proficiency at the superior level. (According to the American Council on the Teaching of Foreign Languages, a person at the superior level can "communicate in the language with accuracy and fluency in order to participate fully and effectively in conversations on a variety of topics in formal and informal settings.") However, undergraduate college programs in languages in the United States typically provide three hours of instruction per week. At that rate, it would require fifteen years of study for an individual to acquire a superior level of language proficiency.

Bilingualism

An increasing number of parents in the United States believe in the importance and value of raising bilingual children. They may wish to maintain ties to heritage, language, and culture; to provide academic advantages for their children; or to promote cross-cultural communication and understanding.

Research indicates, however, that raising children to be bilingual is uncommon in the United States, and most children ultimately become English dominant or even exclusively English speaking. This is the result of social status placed on mastery of English and the limited opportunities available to children in the United States to learn and use languages other than English. Parents' beliefs and attitudes as well as their interaction with their children also play an important part in their children's bilingual proficiency.

Parental Beliefs

Many parents believe, for example, that teaching bilingualism can result in language delay, although there is no research to support this contention. Some parents also believe that their children would experience confusion if exposed to two languages. This also is not borne out by the evidence. The ability to switch back and forth between languages is not a sign of confusion, as parents may conclude, but rather a sign of competence in the languages.

Another common belief of parents is the notion that children will receive a general cognitive benefit from bilingualism. Research shows that certain specific cognitive skills may be strengthened, but bilingualism does not lead to general improvement in intelligence or academic performance.

> **Fast Fact**
>
> Language dialects arise because languages change over time, and people who live in the same geographical area or share a social identity tend to speak in a similar way. Major changes may occur on a large scale to many speakers of a language, while other changes are localized and accumulate in the form of dialectical variations over time.

Official English

The founders of the United States decided not to declare a single language as official. Many languages were spoken in the North American colonies at the time and, energized by their commitment to freedom and liberty, the Founding Fathers advocated a tolerance for linguistic diversity. As a result, the United States does not have an official language.

In 1981, Senator S.I. Hayakawa of California introduced a Constitutional amendment in Congress to make English the official language. The amendment would have the effect of striking down any state laws requiring programs, policies, or documents to use a language other than English. Concern over the results of such an amendment on the lives of non-English speaking U.S. citizens and residents led to the establishment of the English Plus language advocacy coalition.

Changes to Language

Languages are continually changing. Most changes start subtly and unconsciously among middle-class speakers and, once established, spread to other classes. Middle-class groups have the strongest connection to the local community and are the most attuned to language innovations. Social context, the social evaluation of language variations, is as important to language changes as the mechanisms of language. Socially based resistance has prevented the term *oxen*, for example, from evolving into *oxes*. It also may explain why the term *mouses* is acceptable for use as a plural for the computer input device but not for the rodent. Higher-status groups, while acting as innovators, can also serve a gatekeeper role by repressing changes originating in lower-status groups.

The Spread of Change

There are several paths of language change. The cascade or hierarchical model is a dominant pattern in American culture. In this model, change starts in densely populated metropolitan areas recognized as cultural focal points and having extended social networks. The change then spreads to medium-sized cities under the influence of the larger centers, and then to smaller cities, and so on, finally reaching rural and backwater areas. Although less frequent, the contra-hierarchical model, in which change spreads from rural origins to larger urban areas, can be seen in places such as Oklahoma. Here, urban natives adopt rural language constructions to distinguish themselves from outsiders. Another path of diffusion can be explained by simple radiation: innovation flows outward over time.

> **Fast Fact**
>
> The media have less of a homogenizing effect on language than is commonly assumed. Dialects are distinct and growing stronger and show that people don't tend to model their speech on media personalities; they prefer to talk like others in their social groups.

New Words

The American Dialect Society voted *tweet* as the 2009 word of the year and *google* the word of the decade. Members in the 119-year-old organization include linguists, lexicographers, etymologists, grammarians, historians, researchers, writers, authors, editors, professors, university students, and independent scholars. Previous winners included: *bailout* in 2008, *subprime* in 2007, *to be plutoed* or *to pluto* (to be demoted or devalued, as was the former planet) in 2006, *truthiness* (courtesy

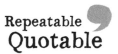

Repeatable Quotable

Literature enlarges our being by admitting us to experiences not our own.—*C.S. Lewis, from An Experiment in Criticism*

of Stephen Colbert's "Colbert Report") in 2005, *red/blue/purple states* in 2004, *metrosexual* in 2003, *weapons of mass destruction* or *WMD* in 2002, *9/11* in 2001, and *chad* in 2000. The society chose *web* in 2000 as word of the decade, *jazz* as word of the century, and *she* as word of the millennium.

How Languages Change

All languages change over time, just at different rates. English has evolved so rapidly in just a few hundred years that most readers find the sixteenth-century writing of Shakespeare difficult to understand, and earlier works impossible to get through. On the other hand, Japanese has changed very little over a millennium.

Why Languages Change

Major changes in languages occur in response to economic, political, and social pressures. When peoples migrate or invade new lands, their own language and that of their new home may undergo radical shifts. One of the most dramatic changes in the development of languages came with the extension of the Roman Empire throughout Europe. As soldiers and settlers introduced Latin, the language of the Romans, local dialects were influenced and gave rise to the romance languages.

Language also can change without these radical events, however, as the development of new technologies, products, and industries requires a new vocabulary. But probably the most influential pressures on language stem from social interactions. Every individual has built a language brand—words, phrases, and constructions—that is dependent on one's social status, education, age, place of residence, background, and a host of other factors. We share our brands when we come into contact with others, and each party may adopt aspects of the other.

The Components of Change

Three components of language vary over time: vocabulary, sentence structure, and pronunciation. Vocabulary changes most rapidly as words are borrowed from other sources or are internally modified. Words can also enter the language by mistake. The Linguistic Society of America notes that *pease* was a term used for one or more peas until 400 years ago. Because people thought that *pease* was the plural of pea, they invented a new word, and the plural was modified in the bargain. Sentence structure changes more slowly, yet dramatic shifts do occur. Lastly, changes in sound, while harder to document, contribute to the dynamics of language. In the fifteenth century, for example, English speakers changed their pronunciation of certain vowels, a change linguists refer to as the "Great Vowel Shift."

Because of the way humans learn language, as children hearing spoken words and phrases, each individual internalizes sounds and meanings uniquely. Children then share those variants with others, transmitting changes through the language population.

The Art of Translation

It is easy for English speakers to forget that non-English speakers outnumber them, and that a vast amount of the world's literature

---

is written in other languages. In order to share literature, skilled translators are essential. Yet, artful translation is not simple or as straightforward as it may seem.

Correct word choice is critical to preserve the original author's intent; a single, poorly chosen word may start a narrative in a new and unwanted direction. There is simply no such thing as a literal translation. Sound also plays an important role in translating meaning, particularly in poetry. And differences in dialects or regional variations can impact the translation dramatically.

Learning to Speak

As a child learns to speak during childhood, extensive brain development takes place. Instead of coming into the world with a specialized mind fitted to a specific environmental function, a child has a brain with the ability to grasp complex patterns and associations. The brain grows and is shaped by interaction with the environment.

The brain of a child at birth (even before birth, in fact) is equipped with the resources necessary to acquire the means to communicate. The ability to acquire speech appears to play an important evolutionary role in humans and sets us apart from other animals.

Brain Development

The areas of the brain responsible for learning speech start with extra cell connections. Those used are retained and strengthened, while unused cells are eliminated. The elimination process occurs early in sensory areas and later in parts of the brain controlling higher functions. As a result, typically one-third of brain cells are lost by the time a person reaches adulthood. The level of complexity in the environment is directly related to brain development. In both children and adults, an enriched environment promotes a greater number of synapses (connections) per neuron.

The region of the brain known as Wernicke's area is responsible for speech comprehension. It develops quickly, reaching a peak in the number of cell connections during the first six months of life. The number of cell connections in this region also is directly related to the individual's education level. The Broca's area of the brain controls speech. It develops somewhat less rapidly with the density of cell connections peaking around fifteen months.

Fast Fact

At birth the human brain is approximately 25 percent of its adult weight. It grows rapidly, reaching about 80 percent of its adult weight in the first few years of life. Much of this growth is the result of speech and language learning.

Another region of the brain, the inferior parietal lobule or "Geschwind's territory," was recognized in the 1960s for its role in language acquisition. This structure matures more slowly and may explain why children do not read and write until they are five or six years old.

Another part of the brain important to speech is the hippocampus, which develops primarily during the second year of life. This structure is crucial to working memory, and so plays an important part in word retrieval

---

Middle English

Middle English is a term used to refer to the English language as spoken from the twelfth to sixteenth centuries. With the Norman invasion of England in 1066, Old English began to feel the influence of French. This begat a long period of great political unrest during which Middle English was in a state of constant flux.

Middle English differs most profoundly from Modern English in vocabulary and spelling. In Middle English, consonants are pronounced that are now silent (*g-nat* and *k-nave*) and many words have disappeared (*thou* and *ye*, and verbs ending in *est* and *eth*). However, the similarities with Modern English in construction are great enough to make Middle English largely understandable to the modern reader.

Old English

Old English is the term applied to the language spoken by the inhabitants of England from the sixth century to the Norman invasion in 1066. This language is characterized by the Germanic tongues of the invaders of that time from Denmark and northern Germany. Old English is distinct from Modern English both in vocabulary and grammar. Verbs in Old English are inflected for gender, case, and number; verbs often occur at the end of sentences; and prepositions are placed after, not before, the object. Although Modern English has derived many common words from Old English, it is largely incomprehensible without translation.

Ancient Manuscripts

Ancient manuscripts and examples of writing are one of the best sources of information about the past. Paleography, the study of ancient writing, is a painstaking and time-consuming process. It is a technical analysis of the script, or handwriting, and involves the angles of strokes, density of ink, and the style of handwriting as compared with other examples. Paleographers also study the material used for the writing and the format of the writing itself.

In the ancient world, people wrote on such items as clay tablets, stone, bone, wood with a layer of wax, leather, various metals, potsherds, papyrus, and parchment. The most widely used materials were papyrus and parchment. In dry climates and under favorable conditions, these materials could last for a very long time; one of the oldest known examples dates to 2600 B.C.

Early Copy Centers

However, the materials were not immune to wear or damage, and if their contents were to be preserved or if additional copies were required, a scribe was employed to make a copy onto a new surface. The scribe was paid on the basis of the quality of his work and his output. A single scribe might work alone, reading to himself as he copied the original. Under certain circumstances, a group of scribes would work in a scriptorium, each making a copy as a person read from the original.

It was possible, and perhaps inevitable, that copies would vary from the original document. Some of these variations may be errors introduced by the scribe, and some are corrections to the original text. And some of the corrections may actually introduce new errors.

Writing as Profession

Edgar Allan Poe was the first well-known American writer who tried to earn a living strictly through writing. He first published a volume of poetry and then took jobs at various magazines to earn a livelihood. His unswerving dedication to this goal of being a professional writer destined him and his family to a life of poverty.

In 1831, Poe entered five stories in a contest sponsored by the Philadelphia *Saturday Courier*. Poe did not win the $100 prize, but the newspaper published his stories later that year—they were the first of Poe's tales in print—without paying him. Perhaps this experience influenced Poe to take up the cause of protecting writers against losing the rights to their work. Unfortunately, he had been dead for fifty years by the time the International Copyright law was enacted in 1898.

The Novel

The novel, which currently attracts more writers than any other literary form, is believed to have come into existence around 1200 B.C. Two notable examples from Egypt at that time are *The Predestined Prince* and *Sinube*. Following a number of novel-like stories written in Japanese in the early part of the first millennium (including, most notably, *The Tale of Genji*), the stories that eventually became the *Arabian Nights' Entertainments,* or *The Thousand and One Nights,* were begun. These stories were eventually grouped together between the fourteenth and sixteenth centuries and were read widely in Europe early in the eighteenth century. Miguel Cervantes published the first part of *Don Quixote* in 1605. By the time Daniel Defoe's *Robinson Crusoe* came into the world in 1719, the modern novel had come into its own. By the end of that century, it had become a major literary form.

Literary Theory

Literary theory is the study of the principles of literature and the means of analyzing literature's relationships with authors, its audience, and the world at large. Literary theory attempts to answer such questions as: What is literature? What distinguishes literature from communication? How do we judge literature? What are the differences between various forms of literature? Some of these questions were asked by Aristotle in his *Poetics*, but it was not until the twentieth century that literary theory and criticism became formalized.

One of the most influential literary scholars of the twentieth century, M.H. Abrams (b. 1912), served as editor of the *Norton Anthology of English Literature*, a standard text in U.S. undergraduate survey courses. In 1953, he published *The Mirror and the Lamp,* in which he identified and explained four types of literary theory.

Four Theories

In **MIMETIC THEORIES**, literature is analyzed by its ability to represent the real world. Plato was a mimetic theorist, for example, because he criticized poetry for distorting reality by showing gods as petty tyrants or presenting appearance as truth. More recently, Marxist critics admired works of social realism in their honest depiction of class relations. Mimetic theories are concerned with the relationship between the work and the world and by measuring accurate representations distinguish the quality of literature.

PRAGMATIC THEORIES judge the effects of a work on the audience. Didactic theorists, viewing literature as a means of teaching, fall into this category. These didactic principles were concerned with uplifting instruction, and literature needed to advance morality and ethical behavior to have value. Pragmatic theorists also may be looking for social or political instruction by portraying a historical condition. Most pragmatic theorists assume that literature has a direct influence on the reader. Some would argue the opposite: that depictions of violence, for example, ultimately have a curbing effect—which is Aristotle's theory of *katharis* (catharis).

EXPRESSIVE THEORIES, the third type, examine literature as an expression of the author; it views the relationship between the work and the author. Expressive theories consider literature as an externalization of private experiences and memories, traumatic events, and viewpoints. Expressive theories are seen in romantic interpretations of art and in surrealism as the artist represents inner unconsciousness and disregards the outside world.

Repeatable
Quotable

The end of writing is to instruct; the end of poetry is to instruct by pleasing.
—*Samuel Johnson*

OBJECTIVE THEORIES examine literature apart from the author, the reader, or the world. Elements such as language, plot, and events in the work are seen in isolation, only as part of the work itself. Formalist criticism is part of this category; it focuses on formal properties of literature and advances those qualities that distinguish a work.

Person of Importance
M.H. Abrams

Meyer Howard Abrams, born in 1912, is an American literary critic who became editor of the *Norton Anthology of English Literature*. His work, *The Mirror and the Lamp* (1953) is a seminal history of literary criticism, which states that literature before the Romantics was viewed as a mirror reflecting the real world and with the Romantics became a lamp serving to illuminate the world.

Literary Terms

Following is a list of some of the more important literary terms and definitions with which everyone should be familiar:

Allegory
A literary work with a meaning other than its literal meaning

Alliteration
The repetition of beginning sounds in words (e.g., *sweet Sue* or *March Madness*)

Allusion
A reference to a well-known person, place, or thing

Antonym
A word that is the opposite of another (e.g., *happy* is an antonym of *sad*)

Aphorism
A short statement of a truth

Assonance
Repetition of similar vowel sounds successive or proximate words, as in the phrase "live wire"

Cliché
An overused expression (e.g., *over the hill* and *always been there for me*)

Connotation
Emotions a word brings to mind (e.g., *Mother* has a connotation that includes nurturing and protection). (See *denotation*.)

Consonance
Repetition of consonant sounds in words (e.g., *strong* and *thing*)

Denotation
The dictionary definition of a word (See *connotation*.)

Denouement
Resolution at the end of prose or drama

Euphemism
The use of a gentler word or phrase in place of something explicit or harsh (e.g., "buy the farm" instead of "die")

Hyperbole
Conscious exaggeration to make a point (e.g., "I'm so hungry I could eat a horse.")

Malapropism
The unintentional misuse or distortion of a word or phrase

Metaphor
A comparison without using *like* or *as* (e.g., "Time is a thief, stealing moments we wish would last forever."; time is compared to a thief, with no *like* or *as*)

Metonymy
Use of a word or phrase that's substituted for another with which it's closely related (e.g., in "The pen is mightier than the sword," *pen* is represents any written matter; *sword* represents any hostile action)

Onomatopoeia
Words or phrases that sound like what they mean (e.g., *buzz* and *kerplunk*)

Oxymoron
A phrase in which seemingly incompatible or contradictory terms are combined (e.g., *definite maybe*)

Palindrome
A word or phrase that is spelled the same backwards and forwards (e.g., *kayak* and *a Toyota*)

Parody
A work that makes fun of or imitates the style of another work, either affectionately or harshly

Personification
Giving human qualities to places or things that aren't human

Simile
The comparison of two unlike persons or objects, using the word *like* or *as* (e.g., "overcooked meat as dry as the Sahara")

Symbol
Something that represents something else

Synecdoche
A figure of speech in which a part represents a whole (e.g., "I like your new wheels"; *wheels* is a synecdoche for the whole car)

Synonym
A word that means the same or nearly the same as another word

Person of Importance
Noah Webster

Noah Webster (1758–1843) was an American teacher, clerk, and lawyer who recognized the need for educational materials directed toward the new and growing American culture. In 1783 he published *A Grammatical Institute of the English Language*, a work containing rules for spelling, reading, and grammar. The first part of this publication, *The American Spelling Book*, was universally adopted and annual sales reached one million copies by 1850. His *American Dictionary of the English Language* (1828) included definitions of 70,000 words and established Webster as the chief authority on American English.

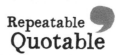

Repeatable Quotable

No one man's English is all English.

—*Sir James Murray*

His primary achievement and lasting contribution to the language was his simplification of spelling and standardization of American pronunciation. He introduced radical changes to the American dialect and, although most of his innovations were not adopted, Webster can be thanked for making the spelling of many words in American English more logical.

Person of Importance
Sir James Murray

Sir James Murray (1837–1915) was a Scottish lexicographer and the first editor of what would become *The Oxford English Dictionary*. In 1879 Murray undertook the compilation of a comprehensive dictionary of English words used since the mid-twelfth century. He was able to complete about half of the dictionary by the time of his death, having invested thirty-six years of exhaustive work in the project by that time.

The dictionary was expected to be completed in ten years and require four volumes; when it was finished, forty-nine years had been invested in the publication of a work of twelve volumes. Its essential feature and value to the language is its historical documentation of more than 400,000 words.

Literary Criticism

Literary criticism is the evaluation, analysis, interpretation, and judgment of literature. Most literary criticism is in the form of a critical essay and considers a particular author's work individually or as a whole. There are a number of varieties of criticism based on different approaches. Biographical criticism derives a literary work's meaning from an examination of the author's life. While technically not biography, and written with the understanding that a creative work stands independently, a biographical criticism may illuminate aspects of an author's life that can generate greater understanding by the reader. Scholars frequently disparage this form of criticism due to its lack of sound methodology.

Schools of Criticism

DECONSTRUCTIONIST CRITICISM is based on the work in the 1960s by French philosopher Jacques Derrida. It combines aspects of

---

linguistics, psychoanalysis, and especially philosophy in a complex and critical dismantling of traditional modes of thought.

FORMALIST CRITICISM stresses the importance of form and technique in literature rather than content. Its focus stresses ways to separate literary works from other forms of communication. This approach is the opposite of historical criticism.

GENDER CRITICISM developed from the feminist movement of the 1960s and examines the role of sexual identities in the creation, evaluation, and interpretation of literary works. Its purpose is to reorient the literature of a patriarchal culture and provide a more balanced understanding of gender influences.

HISTORICAL CRITICISM involves the study of social, cultural, and historical contexts in the evaluation of literary works. Historical critics argue that our understanding of a work is incomplete without an understanding of its setting.

MYTHOLOGICAL CRITICISM employs an interdisciplinary examination of repeating patterns of plot and character in relation to experiences common to all cultures.

PSYCHOLOGICAL CRITICISM traces its roots as a school of thought to the work of Sigmund Freud. It attempts to analyze the mental state of the author or that of elements, like characters or settings, in a literary work to determine meaning.

READER-RESPONSE CRITICISM assumes that literary works exist only in the context of the reader's reaction and that there is no single interpretation of a work. It examines the effect on the reader and considers reading a creative process.

SOCIOLOGICAL CRITICISM applies a sociological interpretation to literature and examines the social conditions prevailing at the time a work was created. This method can reveal new dimensions of a work, but can also be limited by applying social prejudices.

Aestheticism

Aestheticism was a nineteenth-century artistic movement centered in Europe that proposed art was the highest human achievement and existed for its own sake; no other social or political purpose was necessary. Proponents of aestheticism denied that literature had a moral commitment or obligation to follow certain guidelines. The aesthetic movement began in reaction to utilitarian social philosophies of the time and the unpleasant characteristics of the developing industrial age.

Repeatable Quotable

There is no such thing as a moral or an immoral book. Books are well-written or badly written. That is all.
—Oscar Wilde

Immanuel Kant laid the philosophical foundations of aestheticism in the eighteenth century by claiming the independence of aesthetic standards. The center of aesthetic thought moved to Paris, where the philosopher Victor Cousin coined the phrase *l'art pour l'art* (art for art's sake).

Their concentration on art made aesthetes focus on form, manner, and style and rebuke natural norms, sometimes adopting their beliefs as a lifestyle with unorthodox dress, sexual deviance, and antisocial tendencies. They admired artists such as Edgar Allan Poe, whose intense sensations permeated his work.

Aestheticism ended as a movement just after the turn of the century, but its influence was felt much longer. Ezra Pound and T.S.

Eliot were defenders of culture, and the beat generation practiced impetuous, antisocial behavior. Also, James Joyce and many other writers expressed the aesthetic sense of alienation and detachment.

Expressionism

Expressionism is an aesthetic movement that occurred in art, literature, and drama in which the artist strongly expresses inner experience through emotions. The movement originated at the beginning of the twentieth century in European, specifically German, painting, finding a voice in the United States in the literary works of T.S. Eliot and other poets.

Fast Fact

Expressionism was more influential in the theater and was associated with the works of August Strindberg and Bertolt Brecht.

In contrast to realism's emphasis on surface details and external reality, expressionism, an extension of impressionism, focuses on an intense, subjective, and often extreme, experience. Expressionism features chronological plots, rapturous characters, distorted and exaggerated lines and shapes, unusual movement, and concise speech. Its subjects can range from a discredited, materialistic world saved by new systems of belief, to pessimistic pictures of ultimate disaster. Dominant themes involve alienation from materialistic society, disillusionment with progress toward an enlightened state, and forebodings of catastrophe.

Impressionism

Impressionism is a term originally applied to a school of late nineteenth century French painters including Edgar Degas, Claude Monet, Edouard Manet, Pierre Auguste Renoir, and Camille Pissarro. This movement is characterized by the artist's attempts to represent the effects or impressions of objects rather than the objects themselves. Initially dismissed by the scholars in the art world, impressionism became the dominant style in visual arts within two decades, and its influence reached into the literary realm.

European poets adopted impressionistic themes by developing reflective emotion and refined word use. For their part, novelists explored their characters' inner lives rather than their outer reality. Impressionistic qualities are found in the works of Edgar Allan Poe and symbolists such as Stéphane Mallarmé, who attempted to capture the transitory impressions of a moment.

Modernism

Modernism is a broad term with many complexities, but generally describes a movement in the arts that took place in the first three decades of the twentieth century. It is characterized by experimentation in form, it describes an outlook on life, and it expresses an aesthetic. The writings of T.S. Eliot, Ezra Pound, James Joyce, Virginia Woolf, W.B. Yeats, and Joseph Conrad are strongly associated with modernism.

The technical experimentation of modernism is seen in Eliot's *The Waste Land* (1922) as verses jump from one form to another, diverse allusions are introduced, and narrative voices change. Modernist works serve to test the expressive capacity of structural forms and are notable for their discontinuity with earlier practice.

Social changes at the opening of the twentieth century, particularly World War I, caused modernists to see a world in crisis. Some, such as Pound, attempted to overcome the loss of tradition and art, fighting the vulgarities of culture by reviving a sense of beauty and history. Others looked for new meanings in the revised cultural landscape.

The aesthetic of modernism contrasts with romanticism's emphasis on self and instead builds a world of distinct, concrete images. Eliot advised writers to escape from emotion and personality and adopt a dispassionate attitude. The result was a literature notable for its well-defined imagery.

EXAMPLES OF MODERNIST LITERATURE
Mrs. Dalloway by Virginia Woolf
The Sound and the Fury by William Faulkner
The Sun Also Rises by Ernest Hemingway
Ulysses by James Joyce
The Waste Land by T.S. Eliot

Person of Importance
William Faulkner

William Faulkner (1897–1962) was one of the greatest authors of the twentieth century. Faulkner's early years were undistinguished; he never graduated from high school and attended the University of Mississippi for just three semesters. He worked at odd jobs—as an assistant in a bookstore, postmaster at the university post office, and scoutmaster. Later in life he would need to hire himself out as a screenwriter in Hollywood to make ends meet.

Yet it was Faulkner's literary output, largely ignored and often out of print during his lifetime, that would make his reputation. In a little more than a decade, he published ten novels including *As I Lay Dying*, *Light in August*, and *Absalom, Absalom!*, an accomplishment greater than most novelists' achievements during a lifetime. He won Pulitzer Prizes for *A Fable* (1954) and *The Reivers* (1962) as well as the 1949 Nobel Prize for Literature.

Most of Faulkner's novels were set in an imaginary county in Mississippi, a microcosm of the South, and concern the decay of social values in different levels of Southern society. His themes include the mistreatment of blacks by whites, struggles of the poor and uneducated, and the disintegration of tradition and authority.

Faulkner believed in the strength of the human spirit and created powerful and compelling expressions of "problems of the human heart in conflict with itself . . . ." He went on to say in his Nobel Prize acceptance speech that it was the poet's "privilege to help man endure by lifting his heart, by reminding him of the courage and honor and hope and pride and compassion and pity and sacrifice which have been the glory of his past."

> **Repeatable**
> # Quotable
>
> The poet's voice need not merely be the record of man, it can be one of the props, the pillars to help him endure and prevail.—*William Faulkner*

Postmodernism

Postmodernism was originally an artistic movement in the 1950s and 1960s, but is now a term applied to a set of broad, loosely defined cultural beliefs spanning aesthetic, artistic, philosophical, and social practice that come after the twentieth-century movements constituting modernism. Postmodernism has become a liberally applied term for many aspects of art, society, and theory. While lacking a single definition, postmodernism embodies several common threads.

In general, the postmodern view harbors a skepticism or coolness toward traditions of truth, value, and history. Postmodernists are relativists, believing that truth is relative to time and place and that values are relative to its culture. The postmodern irreverence toward artistic tradition is demonstrated by the mixing of different styles of art and the use of parody and kitsch in creative works. Postmodernists discard the idea of traditional authority from government, educational institutions, or religion. These have been replaced by forces of consumerism, capitalism, media, and technology.

Postmodern influences can be seen in architecture and in the literature of Thomas Pynchon and Kurt Vonnegut.

EXAMPLES OF POSTMODERNIST LITERATURE
Fear and Loathing in Las Vegas by Hunter S. Thompson
Gravity's Rainbow by Thomas Pynchon
Naked Lunch by William S. Burroughs
One Hundred Years of Solitude by Gabriel García Márquez
Slaughterhouse Five by Kurt Vonnegut

Naturalism

Naturalism describes a movement primarily found in French prose fiction and drama in the final third of the nineteenth century. It is also applied to groups of writers or similar movements taking place in other countries at the end of the nineteenth century and early part of the twentieth century.

Naturalism does not idealize experience but rather presents characters as products or even victims of heredity and environment, subject to strict natural laws. Naturalism was influenced heavily by evolutionary theory and adopts the belief that human behavior is driven by the same urges affecting all living creatures. Below a thin layer of social nicety, people act on base needs and their behaviors and conflicts are portrayed with scientific objectivity. These qualities show how the movement was influenced by the biological determinism of Darwin and the economic determinism of Marx.

ÉMILE ZOLA (1840–1902) was the first to formally develop naturalism. He promoted naturalism as a theory of human behavior and urged scientific case study as a model for naturalist literature. American naturalist novelists include Jack London, Stephen Crane, and Theodore Dreiser.

EXAMPLES OF NATURALIST LITERATURE
The Call of the Wild by Jack London
Ethan Frome by Edith Wharton
L'Assommoir by Émile Zola
The Return of the Native by Thomas Hardy
Sister Carrie by Theodore Dreiser

Realism

Realism is applied to literary composition that faithfully reproduces the actualities of life as they are observed, especially of ordinary people in common situations. Realism portrays recognizable characters, everyday settings, and events in ways that readers will consider credible, free from prejudice, idealistic interpretation, or romantic shadings. Unlike naturalism, determinism and amoral attitudes are not part of realism. Nor does it depend upon involved factual description or documentation, but rather on conventional plots within realistic frameworks. Unusual characters and plots, as well as emotional extremes common in romance, are rejected.

There is no defining creative moment for realism as a literary movement, but the works of nineteenth century French authors such as Stendhal, Gustave Flaubert, and Guy de Maupassant are considered the beginnings. The middle-class characters and their ordinary behaviors provoked critics to label realism as tedious and limited. Ambrose Bierce called realism "The art of depicting nature as seen by toads."

American authors transitioned from romance to realism as well, with Whitman's descriptive poems an example. Later, novelists such as Upton Sinclair used realism for humanitarian protest by exposing the social evils that frustrated his characters' happiness.

EXAMPLES OF REALIST LITERATURE
Bel-Ami by Guy de Maupassant
Great Expectations by Charles Dickens
The Jungle by Upton Sinclair
Madame Bovary by Gustave Flaubert

Romanticism

Romanticism was a literary movement that took place in Britain and Europe between approximately 1770 and 1848, although romantic qualities can be part of literature from any period. It was politically inspired by the revolutions in American and France as well as the wars of independence in Spain, Poland, Greece, and other countries. It expressed itself emotionally in the value of self, individual experience, and personal freedom and tended to champion progressive causes. Romanticism contrasts with classicism, in particular its qualities of reason and restriction. Typically, romanticism could be gloomy and despairing when thwarted.

In Britain, romanticism got its start in the works of William Wordsworth, Samuel Taylor Coleridge, Robert Burns, and William Blake. Other writers, such as Lord Byron, Percy Bysshe Shelley, and John Keats, expressed their romantic vision through poetry, letters, and life stories. In America, romantic characteristics such as the celebration of natural beauty and the simple life and introspection could be seen in the works of James Fenimore Cooper, Ralph Waldo Emerson, Henry David Thoreau, and Edgar Allan Poe.

EXAMPLES OF ROMANTIC LITERATURE
The Complete Poems by John Keats
Frankenstein by Mary Shelley
Les Misérables by Victor Hugo
"The Fall of the House of Usher" by Edgar Allan Poe
Wuthering Heights by Emily Brontë

Surrealism

Surrealism was founded in 1924 in Paris with the publication of André Breton's *Surrealist Manifesto*. Surrealism attempts to reach a higher plane of reality by rejecting logic for the world of absurd dreams and unconscious mental activity. Surrealists rejected standard ways of thinking about the world, instead believing in, as a precursor to surrealism Arthur Rimbaud wrote in a letter about poetry, "the reasoned disorder of all the senses."

Surrealists reacted against what they believed were bourgeois social restraints and rational conventions. They called on Freud's theories about the unconscious and its relations to dreams in order to understand human psychic needs. Breton attracted a group of writers and painters who experimented with automatic writing in order to produce surreal poetic images. Surrealists also believed in the political and revolutionary nature of their literature and allied themselves with the thinking of Marx and the French Communist Party.

Fast Fact

Surrealism was a major intellectual force in literature and the arts in the period between the wars, although its influence was greater in the arts. It produced such artists as Max Ernst, Salvador Dalí, Man Ray, and Joan Miró.

EXAMPLES OF SURREALIST LITERATURE

Death to the Pigs by Benjamin Peret

Hidden Faces by Salvador Dalí

Kafka on the Shore by Haruki Murakami

Mad Love by André Breton

The Metamorphosis by Franz Kafka

DEFINING MOMENT

In June of 1936, London's International Surrealist Exhibition introduced surrealism to Britain. More than 30,000 people viewed works by Max Ernst, Salvador Dalí, and Joan Miró over three weeks, and lectures on the theories of surrealism drew large crowds. During one, Salvador Dalí attempted to deliver his speech dressed in a full deep-sea diving suit, but needed to be pried out of the helmet as he began to suffocate.

Comedy

Comedy, a work designed to amuse an audience, has had a complex and varied meaning over time. Comedy is rooted in the fertility rituals of ancient Greece in which named persons were the subject of crude satire. As this form of criticism came to be considered unacceptable, fictional characters were substituted. This classical comedy was replaced by mime in the time of the Roman Empire. During medieval times, the definition of comedy changed to become a movement of the plot from complication and difficulty to clarity and contentment.

Classical comedy reappeared in Italy in the fifteenth century and was combined with farce in the sixteenth and seventeenth centuries by playwrights such as William Shakespeare, Ben Jonson, and Molière. After the Romantic period, serious comedy tended to blend with realist drama, and only light comedy survived as a separate genre.

Drama

Dramatic compositions, unlike fiction and poetry, are written to be performed on a stage by actors playing the roles of characters through action and dialogue. The issue of realism in drama has proposed problems for dramatists, audiences, and critics. Critics have wondered why bloody violence and horrific conclusions were appealing on stage to audiences who were repelled by them in real life. When realism is carried too far, Oscar Wilde complained, drama becomes wearisome and pointless. The Renaissance and seventeenth-century dramatists were troubled by how to represent time and space on stage. Samuel Johnson dismissed this issue in his *Preface to Shakespeare* (1765) by pointing out that changes in time and place did not hamper the audience's comprehension if the changes were logical.

Repeatable **Quotable**

The truth is, that the spectators are always in their senses, and know . . . that the stage is only a stage, and that the players are only players.
—*Samuel Johnson*

Yet the twentieth-century philosopher Ernst Cassirer holds that "Dramatic art discloses a new breadth and depth of life." This simultaneous involvement and detachment of the audience results in an experience more intense than one gained from reading a play from a book.

Tragedy

Tragedy is a form of drama that presents sorrowful or disastrous events encountered or caused by a heroic individual. The term also can be applied to other literary forms, such as the novel. The three periods of classic tragedy took place in three separate locations: Attica, in Greece, in the fifth century B.C., Elizabethan and Jacobean England (1558–1625), and France in the seventeenth century.

Aristotle developed the concept of tragedy in the *Poetics* as a genre that evokes pity and fear in the audience, but not solely by means of a plot that ends in the suffering of the protagonist. The hero must be good but not perfect so the audience can identify with the world he inhabits. The hero's fall must be caused by an unwitting error or an unavoidable encounter with fate, not due to an immoral act. In fact, the hero often invokes his own ruin by acting honestly. Finally, the drama must resolve in a way the audience deems sensible and rational.

The large issues of human life and frailty, freedom, virtue, and failure were carried into later dramatic works, although Shakespeare's tragedies *Othello* (1604), *Hamlet* (1601), *King Lear* (1605), and *Macbeth* (1605) effectively ignored some of Aristotle's rules.

Macbeth, for example, intentionally commits evil acts so that we don't pity his fall. The motives of Othello and Iago are never justified, and Macbeth's demise is his own fault, not fate's. While not filling the requirements set forth by Aristotle, these plays express tragic themes and evoke pity in the audience.

Shakespeare

When **WILLIAM SHAKESPEARE** (1564–1616) died, the news journals of the day did not herald his passing. He was, after all, just a writer of popular plays. It wasn't until more than 150 years later when director David Garrick held the First Shakespeare Jubilee in the Bard's birthplace, Stratford-upon-Avon, to showcase his plays that Shakespeare's genius began to be recognized. He is now considered the greatest writer in world literature.

Authorship Doubts

Despite several hundred years of scholarship, doubts still remain among some that the man from Stratford wrote the works that are commonly attributed to him. The nonbelievers include the likes of Walt Whitman, Mark Twain, Sigmund Freud, and Ralph Waldo Emerson. Most of these doubters point to Shakespeare, the "Stratford rustic," as lacking education and worldly knowledge. As alternatives, fifty-eight candidates have been put forth, including Sir Francis Bacon; Edward de Vere, seventeenth Earl of Oxford; and Christopher Marlowe.

Sir Francis Bacon's supporters have looked for, and claimed to have found, secret messages and ciphers hidden in Shakespeare's plays identifying Bacon as the author. But, this line of argument ultimately proved more wishful thinking than reasoned proof. As for de Vere, his claim rests on his fitting the right profile as someone who *could* have written Shakespeare plays, but there is no evidence that he actually did. He also died before some of last and greatest of the plays were produced.

No one has produced evidence showing anyone other than Shakespeare was the author of the works attributed to him. The dispute still rages in certain circles, but most Shakespearian scholars are content that Shakespeare's style is unique to him and is therefore convincing evidence of his sole authorship.

Cheat Sheet for Language Arts

Language was identified as the intelligence community's single greatest need in a report issued in September 2001 by the House Permanent Select Committee on Intelligence.

Raising children to be bilingual is uncommon in the United States, and most children ultimately become English dominant or even exclusively English speaking.

The founders of the United States decided not to declare a single language as official.

Dialects are distinct and growing stronger and show that people prefer to talk like others in their social groups.

English has evolved so rapidly in just a few hundred years that most readers find the sixteenth century writing of Shakespeare difficult to understand, and earlier works impossible.

Of the three components of language that vary over time—vocabulary, sentence structure, and pronunciation—vocabulary changes most rapidly.

The brain of a child at birth (even before birth, in fact) is equipped with the resources necessary to acquire the means to communicate.

The human brain grows rapidly, reaching about 80 percent of its adult weight in the first few years of life. Much of this growth is the result of speech and language learning.

Paleography is the study of ancient writing.

Edgar Allan Poe was the first professional American writer, publishing a volume of poetry and then taking jobs at various magazines to earn a livelihood.

The novel, which currently attracts more writers than any other literary form, is believed to have come into existence around 1200 B.C.

Noah Webster's *American Dictionary of the English Language* (1828) is responsible for standardizing the pronunciation and making the spelling of many words in American English more logical.

The Oxford English Dictionary provides an historical documentation of more than 400,000 words.

Aestheticism was a nineteenth-century artistic movement centered in Europe that proposed art was the highest human achievement and existed for its own sake; no other social or political purpose was necessary.

Expressionism, an extension of impressionism, focuses on an often extreme, intense, and subjective experience.

Realistic literature faithfully reproduces the actualities of life as they are observed, especially of ordinary people in common situations. Realism portrays recognizable characters, everyday settings, and events in ways that readers will consider credible and free from prejudice, idealistic interpretation, or romantic shadings.

Romanticism expresses itself emotionally in the value of self, individual experience, and personal freedom, and tended to champion progressive causes. Romanticism contrasts with classicism and its qualities of reason and restriction.

Aristotle developed the concept of tragedy in the *Poetics* as a genre that evokes pity and fear in the audience.

In a little more than a decade, William Faulkner published ten novels, including *As I Lay Dying*, *Light in August*, and *Absalom, Absalom!*, an accomplishment greater than most novelists achieve during a lifetime.

William Shakespeare (1564–1616) wrote forty-two plays and 154 sonnets and is generally considered the greatest writer in world literature.

Chapter Seven

Religion

While the exact number of religions is not known with any certainty, the best estimate is about 4,200. The longing for religion seems built into human nature; according to Voltaire (1694–1778), "If God did not exist, it would be necessary to invent him." The religions considered in this chapter are organized alphabetically.

Defining Religion

The word "religion" derives from the Latin *religio,* meaning "to be bound to" or "to tie fast." Believers are bound to their faiths. Religion is commonly described as a set of beliefs, values, and practices based on the teachings of a spiritual leader, or defining a person's relation to God or spirits. Yet advancing a single definition satisfactory to all is difficult.

Religions constitute an enormous set of traditions, practices, ideas, faiths, and claims. Whether a supreme being even exists, whether a soul exists and, if so, whether it's immortal—these are questions that can be debated endlessly. There has rarely been unanimity about the nature of the subject among scholars, partly because believers see different things in religions and because the subject itself has been so involved in controversy throughout its history.

Fast Fact

The Concise Oxford Dictionary defines religion as "the belief in a superhuman controlling power, especially in a personal God or gods entitled to obedience and worship." This is a broad and loose definition encompassing many beliefs and traditions.

Bahá'í Faith

The Bahá'í Faith was founded in Persia in the nineteenth century. It is a monotheistic religion emphasizing the unity of the human race and the need for a single global society. There are approximately five million Bahá'ís, and they hail from most of the world's nations, races, and cultures.

History

BAHÁ'U'LLÁH (1817–1850) was a member of a wealthy Persian family. On May 23, 1844, in Shiraz, Persia, a man known as the Báb announced the imminent appearance of the Messenger of God, who was awaited by all the peoples of the world. Despite the Báb's arrest and execution, and the deaths of some 20,000 of his followers, Bahá'u'lláh announced his support for the message of the Báb. Bahá'u'lláh himself was imprisoned, tortured, and banished. In Baghdad in 1863, he declared he was the Báb's Promised One. His teachings were spread by his son, Abdu'l-Bahá.

Beliefs

Bahá'u'lláh teaches that there is one God and the revelations of his will have been the chief civilizing force in history. Divine Messengers, founders of the world's great religions, have been the agents of this process due to their common purpose of bringing spiritual and moral maturity to the human race. The principles of the Bahá'í Faith vital to the unification of the human family and the building of a peaceful, global society include: abandonment of all prejudice, women's equality with men, recognition of the unity and relativity of religious truth, elimination of extreme poverty and wealth, universal education, the individual's independent search for truth, a global commonwealth of nations, and recognition that reason and scientific knowledge are in harmony with religion.

The Bahá'í World Center in Haifa, Israel, serves as the administrative center of the Bahá'í Faith. In the United States, the center of faith is located in Wilmette, Illinois. Because world unity is one of the fundamental goals of the Bahá'ís, they are strong supporters of the work of the United Nations.

Buddhism

Buddhism was founded by Siddhartha Gautama, called the Buddha, in the fourth or fifth century B.C. as an alternative to Hinduism. Gautama lived the life of a prince until age twenty-nine when he became aware of the suffering of others and gave up his life to become a wandering ascetic, searching for enlightenment. He reached enlightenment while meditating beneath a fig tree and was henceforth known as Buddha, "the enlightened one."

Beliefs

The core of Buddhist doctrine is the Four Noble Truths and the Eightfold Path. The Truths are life is suffering; suffering is caused by desire for pleasure, comfort, or immortality; suffering can be eliminated by eliminating desire; and there is a path that leads to release from desire. The path is called the Eightfold Path and consists of right views, right aspirations, right speech, right action, right livelihood, right effort, right mindfulness, and right meditation. These eight aspects of the path fit three attributes: wisdom, ethical conduct, and mental discipline. Buddha also taught that the supreme good of life is nirvana: "the extinction" or "blowing out" of suffering and desire and awakening to what is most real. All in all, Buddha's core philosophy is a practical and spiritual approach to living.

Buddhism does not accept the Vedic literature and rites or the caste system of Hinduism, although it does retain the concept of reincarnation. Buddhism's vision of salvation is based on the actions of the individual and fueled by effort. And, contrary to the orthodoxies of Jainism and Hinduism, Buddhism taught that women, too, could experience enlightenment.

Whereas Jainism was extreme in its ascetic precepts, Buddhism prescribed a more moderate path, or "middle way," between the desire for worldly indulgence and self-mortification. Due to this middle path, Buddhism drew more followers and held great appeal in India for several centuries. It is practiced by approximately 376 million people.

Fast Fact

Buddha is not a proper noun but rather a title. There have been many Buddhas in the past, and there will be many in the future. When the term "the Buddha" is used today, it's assumed to mean Buddha Gautama, the Buddha of the present era.

Catholicism

Catholicism is a branch of Christianity. Today, Roman Catholics throughout the world outnumber all other Christians combined.

History

Christianity became an accepted religious belief in A.D. 323 when Constantine emerged as the political power of the Eastern Roman Empire. As Christianity spread throughout the empire, theological interpretations began to differ in the East and West. The divide between Rome and the Eastern churches became permanent in 1504. The Eastern part became the Eastern Orthodox Church; the Western part became the Roman Catholic Church, with headquarters eventually located in the Vatican in Rome, Italy. One issue was the authority of the papacy, but the most important disagreement between the churches centered on the nature of Jesus Christ: the Eastern Church emphasized his divinity, while the Western church emphasized that plus his humanity. On October 31, 1517, the German priest and theology professor **MARTIN LUTHER** (1483–1546) tacked his famous "Ninety-five Theses" on the door of the castle church in Wittenburg, Germany, and thereby started the Protestant Reformation.

Church Hierarchy

Jesus Christ is the invisible head of the church and the Pope, by Jesus' authority, is the visible head. Over the centuries, the Bishop of Rome became the leading authority in both civil and religious matters and assumed the title "Pope." The pope is the successor to St. Peter and thus the shepherd of all Christians and the representative (or vicar) of Christ.

Each local church is attached to a district called a parish which is run by a priest. A group of parishes in a region is called a diocese and is presided over by a bishop. Bishops are priests nominated by other bishops and appointed to their office by the Pope. The Pope chooses and elevates 120 bishops to the position of cardinal.

Beliefs

The Virgin Mary is revered as the mother of God and holds a unique devotional position in the Catholic Church. The Catholic Church teaches that penance is a sacrament instituted by Jesus Christ. The church recognizes two kinds of sin: venial and mortal. It used to be that Catholics were instructed to observe a weekly rite of confession of sins. While this sacrament has declined in ritual observance, it still remains an important part of a Catholic's spiritual life. The Roman Catholic Church bases its teachings on the Holy Bible, which differs from the Protestant version of the Bible, and the Ten Commandments hold an important place in Catholic teachings. The Catholic Church has extensive rules including Precepts of the Catholic Church and the Canons, which includes 1,752 rules.

Christianity

Christianity is a monotheistic religion that arose from Judaism and rapidly developed as a faith with a separate identity, one based on the teachings of Jesus of Nazareth, referred to as the Christ. There are many different denominations within Christianity. These have evolved over the years, often because of disagreements about teachings or through different ways of worshiping. Most, however, agree on the basic tenets of the faith. The story of Jesus Christ's ministry and an early history of Christianity are contained in the New Testament of the Holy Bible.

Beginnings

The founder of Christianity, **JESUS OF NAZERETH** (4 B.C.–A.D. 30) lived in Palestine during the height of the Roman Empire. Following his baptism, Jesus began to preach, teach, and perform miracles throughout Judea. As he did so, he recruited many disciples, including a core group of twelve referred to as the Apostles. As Jesus' fame and reputation grew, so did the resentment of the authorities. Approximately A.D. 30, Jesus was executed on a cross in Jerusalem. After his death, his followers believed he had risen from the dead and viewed him as Christ, the Messiah.

One of his apostles, Paul, helped spread Christianity, and by the fourth century it was practiced from Spain to India.

Fast Fact

Christianity is practiced by approximately 2.1 billion people in most parts of the world.

Beliefs

The belief that Jesus rose from the dead is central to Christians. As the Son of God, Jesus represents the person that all Christians must strive to be like. Christians believe that he came to earth to teach

God's plan and died for their sins. Christians, as well as Jews and Muslims, believe in one all-powerful creator—God. Thus, the most important belief for Christians is that the world and everything in it is an expression of God's power and love.

The holy book of Christianity is the Bible. It is divided into two segments: the Old Testament and the New Testament. Generally, the average Christian looks at the Old Testament as the part that concerns the Jews, their history, and their prophecies, and at the New Testament as the part that concerns Jesus and the Apostles. Christian ethics derive in large part from Jewish teachings of the Old Testament, especially the Ten Commandments.

DEFINING MOMENT

The resurrection of Jesus after his crucifixion, as told in the Gospels, is the central idea of Christian religion. It validated Christ's mission and the possibility of redemption, and signified the resurrection of all men.

Confucianism

Confucianism, which means "teaching of the scholars," is an ethical code and spiritual philosophy founded on the teaching of CONFUCIUS (551–479 B.C.), the best known and most influential thinker in Chinese history. He was honored in Chinese chronicles as the Great Master K'ung or K'ung Fu-tzu. In the West, he is simply known by the Latinized "Confucius." Confucianism is more a worldview than a world religion; it is a social ethic, a political ideology, and a scholarly tradition.

- - - - - - - - --- ---

Person of Importance
Confucius

Confucius was born in the small state of Lu in 551 B.C., in what is now Shantung Province. As a thinker and teacher, Confucius made important contributions to political thought, especially with his insistence on the connection between ethics and politics.

History

Confucius believed everyone could benefit from self-education and defined learning as not only the acquisition of knowledge but also the building of character. It is said he initially attracted over 3,000 students, some of whom became close disciples.

The most important Confucian literature comprises two sets of books. The Four Books—the Analects, the Great Learning, the Mean, and the Book of Mencius—introduced Confucian literature to students who then progressed to the more difficult texts, the Five Classics: the Book of History, the Book of Poems, the Book of Change (I Ching), the Spring and Autumn Annals, and the Book of Rites.

Teachings

A major point in the teachings of Confucius was filial piety, the virtue of devotion to one's parents. He considered it the foundation of virtue and the root of human character. Confucius concentrated his teachings on his vision, *Jen*, which has been translated in the most complete way as love, goodness, and human-heartedness; moral achievement and excellence in character; loyalty to one's true nature; righteousness; and, finally, filial piety. All this adds up to the principle of virtue within the person. Proper social behavior and etiquette were considered essential to right living. An ethical view is set forth in the Analects, a collection of moral and social teachings that amount to a code of human conduct. Many of the sayings were passed on orally.

Influence

The influence of Confucianism on China was largely due to the power of its disciples and of the written works of Confucius and his followers. But in modern times it began to wane, due to the rise of Marxism-Leninism in 1949 as the official ideology of the People's Republic of China. However, the traditions and moral standards of Confucianism are still an important component of the culture of China and other East Asian countries.

Fast Fact

Between 1313 and 1905, Chinese students studying for civil service examinations were required to study the Five Classics of Confucius.

Eastern Orthodoxy

Together with Roman Catholicism and Protestantism, Eastern Orthodoxy is one of the three principal traditions in Christianity.

Orthodoxy evolved in 1054 following the Great Schism, the climax of the major cultural, intellectual, and theosophical differences between the Roman Catholic Church and the Orthodox Church.

History

Constantine became emperor of the Eastern Roman Empire and accepted Christianity in A.D. 323. In 1054, the differences in religious practices and beliefs led to the excommunication of the leader of the Eastern Church, the patriarch of Constantinople, by Pope Leo IX. In turn, the patriarch condemned the Pope. Thus, the Christian church has been divided into the Roman Catholic and the Eastern Orthodox ever since.

Fast Fact

Today, the Eastern Orthodox Church numbers about 225 million adherents.

Beliefs

Members believe that Jesus Christ founded the Orthodox Church and that it is the living manifestation of his presence. Orthodoxy further believes that the Christian faith and the church are inseparable. They believe that it is impossible to know Jesus Christ, to share in the life of the Holy Trinity, or to be considered a Christian apart from the church. It is through the church that an individual is nurtured in the faith. The Orthodox Church stresses "right belief and right glory." Essentially, Orthodox adherents' beliefs are very similar to those of other Christian traditions: they recognize seven sacraments—baptism, confirmation, holy Eucharist, confession, ordination, marriage, and holy unction—but express them slightly differently than other faiths.

The Role of Scripture

Scriptural authority is stressed, and there is an insistence upon the gospel, which is considered the foundation of the faith. It has been quoted that "scripture is fixed, it is the ground and pillar of our faith." The Bible, therefore, is highly regarded by the church; a portion of it is read at every service. The church sees itself as the guardian and interpreter of the scriptures. The content of the Old Testament is seen as preparation for the coming of Jesus. The New Testament, with its four gospels, twenty-one epistles, the Acts of the Apostles, and the Book of Revelation, is also an accepted part of the church.

Egyptian Religion

The religious life in ancient Egypt is of interest partly due to the imposing structures that remain as a testament to their peoples' faith, and partly because of the faith's age since Egypt is the scene of one of the earliest civilizations of humankind. Unfortunately, the records we have today, while abundant, are inconsistent and incomplete and so many of our conclusions are based on hypothesis.

Early Egypt

In predynastic times (prior to approximately 3200 B.C.), religious belief was fragmented with individual tribes worshiping their own

---

gods, who usually appeared in animal form. Cats were sacred in one ancient city, and a bull was worshipped at Memphis. Over time, deities developed human bodies while retaining animal heads.

Ancient Egyptians believe the earth to be a disk, with the flat plains of Egypt in the center and mountains surrounding and supporting the disk. The deep waters of the underworld were below the disk and above was the sky. There were several systems of deities that explained this universe: ram-god Khnum was said to have constructed the world on his potter's wheel, or Ptah conceived the world through divine thought. The most widely accepted divine explanation involved the sun-god Ra or Atum, who created the air-god Shu and his wife Tefnut. Their offspring were the sky-goddess Nut and the earth-god Geb, who bore Osiris, Isis, Set, and Nephthys.

A National Religion

A combined state was created ca. 3200 B.C., and a national religion grew out of the various local beliefs, although variations continued. Amon became the prominent deity with Suchos, Bast, and Neith also rising in importance. There seems to be a politically based conflict between the gods as cities and regions changed in influence.

Cults

The cults of Osiris and Ra were the most important to Egyptians. Osiris was judge of the dead, and deity of the Nile, grain harvest, and the moon. Osiris protected rich and poor alike, and his murder and restoration made him symbolic of eternal life. Horus, his son and successor, demonstrated the triumph of good over evil by defeating Set, god of evil and darkness. The worship of Ra, said to be

---

the direct ancestor of the kings of Egypt and closely related to the fate of royalty, was paramount in Egyptian belief. Ra lived out a daily cycle of birth, journey, and death, a foundation of Egyptian life.

Fast Fact

There are about 1,500 ancient Egyptian gods and goddesses that have been identified by name.

Beliefs

Egyptian religion had no set of written teachings; it was the duty of the king to translate the will of the gods and to bring order to the universe through the idea of *maat*, or justice. Egyptians believed in the afterlife, and it was essential to prepare and care for the dead to ensure immortality. These beliefs gave rise to the ritual and practice of mummification and were manifested by the construction of huge pyramids to preserve royal remains and honor the gods.

Hinduism

Hindus see their religion as a continuous, seemingly eternal, existence—not just a religion, but a way of life. It includes customs, moral obligations—known as *dharma*—traditions, and ideals.

The word "Hindu" has been in the language ever since Greek times, although some Hindus did not take to the word Hinduism, preferring the ancient name Vedic. The Vedic texts, or Vedas, provide the only textual source for understanding the religious life of ancient India. "Veda" means "sacred knowledge" or "learning" in

Sanskrit, the oldest written language of India. Originally the Vedas consisted of 1,000 hymns; the Veda of Chants followed, with musical notations for the performance of sacred songs.

Vedanta philosophy consists of three propositions. First, that real nature is divine; second, that the aim of human life is to realize this divine nature; and third, that all religions are essentially in agreement. Hinduism has neither a single prophet nor one god to worship; rather, it offers a plethora of ideas—a metaphor for the gods. Hinduism has no beginning, no founder, no central authority, no hierarchy, and no organization.

Fast Fact

Hinduism is practiced by some 900 million people, approximately 14 percent of the world's population.

Beliefs

Though they do not worship one ultimate god, Hindus do believe in a supreme being who has unlimited forms. The search for the worship of the "One that is All" is made through a favorite divinity, of which there are many. However, there is no exclusivity in the choice of the divinity to worship during the search. Hindu teachings revolve around a vast series of interlocking narratives with the purpose of drawing the audience into a discourse.

In Hinduism, the law of *karma* states that all actions produce effects in the future. Linked to karma is the concept of *dharma*, one's duty or station in this life. Essential to Hinduism is the idea of reincarnation and the belief that previous acts are the factors that determine the condition into which a being is reborn. People are born over and over again (transmigration) into a state of suffering. One's *atman*, or self must become one with *Brahman*, the Being, to be released from the cycle of rebirth.

The ultimate spiritual goal, *moksha*, is the individual soul's release from the bonds of transmigration—to get out of the endless cycle of reincarnation.

Islam

Islam is the religion of Muslims, revealed through Muhammad, the prophet of Allah. In effect, Muhammad, as God's messenger, was to the origins of Islam what Moses was to Judaism. An Arabic term meaning "submission to God," Islam originated in Arabia in the seventh century. There are now some 1.5 billion Muslims.

Fast Fact

Muslims believe in the resurrection of the body. Accordingly, they bury their dead quickly, giving all due care to treat the body with respect. On the Day of Judgment Allah will raise all the dead and judge them. The good will go to Paradise, the others to the fire.

History

The founder and prophet of Islam, **MUHAMMAD** (A.D. 570–632) was born in Arabia. He was selected by God (Allah) to be the prophet of true religion. He heeded the command to preach and spread the word, preaching openly against idolatry and of the oneness of Allah, or God. Muhammad traveled widely and studied with followers of other tribes and the many religions that were practiced in Arabia of the time. He and his followers established the first Islamic community in Medina, created a federation of Arab tribes, and made the religion of Islam the basis of Arab unity.

Beliefs

Islam is a monotheistic religion—Allah (God) is the sole god, the creator, sustainer, and restorer of the world. The overall purpose of humanity is to serve Allah, to worship Him alone, and to construct a moral lifestyle. The Five Pillars of Islam, set down as the anchor for life as a Muslim, are profession of faith, prayer (five times a day facing Mecca), the *zakat* (an obligatory tax), fasting, and *hajj* (pilgrimage to Mecca). The Qur'an, or Koran, is the holy book of Islam and the primary source of every Muslim's faith and practice. It deals with the subjects that concern all human beings: wisdom, beliefs, worship, and law. However, it focuses on the relationship between God and his creatures. It also provides guidelines for a just society, proper human relationships, and

World Religion	Adherents
Christianity	2.1 billion
Islam	1.5 billion
Secular/Nonreligious	1.1 billion
Hinduism	900 million
Chinese Traditional	394 million
Buddhism	376 million
Primal/Indigenous	300 million
African Traditional	100 million
Sikhism	23 million
Judaism	14 million
Bahá'í Faith	5 million
Jainism	4 million

equal division of power. The Qur'an also posits that life is a test and everyone will be rewarded or punished for their actions in the next life.

The Qur'an forbids the worshiping of idols, which means Muslims are not permitted to make images of either Allah or of the prophet. The Qur'an stresses that God does not share his powers with any partner. Blasphemy, or shirk, is a great sin in Islam, and different grades of shirk have been identified in Islamic law, such as shirking of custom or shirking of knowledge. Islam absolutely forbids the use of alcoholic beverages.

Jainism

Two new schools of thought emerged in the sixth century B.C. Buddhism taught that enlightenment came from the monkish existence of renouncing the world. The other school of thought was Jainism, which practiced reverence for life, celibacy, and moral conduct. It stressed a life of the mind and turning away from a life of bodily pleasures.

History

Jainism is a religion and philosophy of India that, along with Hinduism and Buddhism, is one of the three most ancient religions still in existence in that country. Tradition holds that there were twenty-four Tirhankaras, or spiritual leaders. The last was Mahavira who, like Buddha, was born to wealth and eventually became unhappy. Mahavira's unhappiness led to his joining an order of wandering ascetics. For practicing the most extreme forms of asceticism, Mahavira earned the title of *jina* (conqueror). He had obtained *moksha* (release) and was freed from the bonds that tied his soul to the endless cycle of birth, death, and rebirth.

Beliefs

According to Jainism, spiritual progress is made through accomplishments in one's own life. Jains reject the idea of a caste; in addition, like Buddhism, Jainism emphasizes that, no matter what a person's station in life—no matter what level of the caste he occupies—living properly provides release. Jainism rejects the idea that a person achieves release from life by offering sacrifices to the gods or other forms of worship. Jainism redirects the focus from attention to the gods to a personal philosophy, such as asceticism.

Fast Fact

With slightly more than 4 million followers in the world today, Jainism doesn't claim many adherents. Perhaps the strict requirements of Jainism keep it a minority religion.

Jainism teaches that, the more one denies pleasures and satisfactions of the body, the more one is able to achieve freedom from the endless cycle of birth and rebirth. The founders of Jainism went beyond the traditional Indian moral concern for cattle to teach that all forms of life are sacred and should be loved and preserved wherever possible. This doctrine of love and nonviolence toward all things is known as *ahimsa*. The notion of *ahimsa* is applied toward animal life primarily, but in Jain philosophy it is recognized in the case of plants as well. Mohandas Gandhi admitted that his regard for all life was inspired by the Jains' practice of *ahimsa* toward all things.

Mahavira

Nataputta Vardhamana (599–527 B.C.) is usually identified as the founder of Jainism. He became a Tirthankara or spiritual leader, attracting all of the Jain community to him, and is now known as Mahavira or "Great Hero."

Judaism

Judaism traces the origins of its traditions to God's covenant with Abraham and his descendents, God's chosen people. Their history, starting as early as the twentieth century B.C., is a story of their struggle to overcome centuries of persecution. Judaism is more than just a religion; Jews have been regarded as a "people," a "nation" (though, for most of its existence, one without a homeland), a "race," and a "culture."

Beliefs

Judaism is a religion of ethical monotheism; it holds that God is omnipotent (all-powerful), omniscient (all-knowing), and omnipresent (filling all places at all times). God is eternal. Since God is incorporeal, Jews are forbidden to represent God in a physical form.

Judaism also emphasizes the significance of the individual. God is unique and the ultimate authority, but the essential backbone of the entire religion is the Torah, consisting of the first five books of the Bible that are attributed to Moses. The Torah, the most important section of the Jewish Bible, is a series of narratives and laws that chronicle the beginning of the world through the death of Moses. The Talmud refers to the interpretations of the Torah and is used to decide all matters of Jewish law.

Person of Importance
Moses

According to the Biblical account, Moses was protected and guided by God from infancy. He became a Jewish prophet and led his people out of bondage in Egypt in the thirteenth century. God revealed to Moses the Ten Commandments, which form the ethical foundation of many religions.

Festivals are the backbone of the Jewish faith; they reflect Jewish history and the religion's teachings. There are five major festivals. Rosh Hashanah, or Jewish New Year, ushers in a ten-day period of self-examination and penitence. Yom Kippur is the most solemn Jewish religious holiday when Jews seek purification through the forgiveness of others and sincere repentance of their own sins. Passover celebrates God's deliverance of the Israelites from captivity in Egypt. Shavuot originally marked the beginning of the wheat harvest and Sukkot, known as the Feast of Tabernacles, celebrates the end of the harvest.

Present-day Judaism is practiced in three main forms. Orthodox Jews follow the traditional faith and practice with great seriousness. Conservative Judaism, which developed in the mid-eighteenth century, follows most traditional practices, yet tries to make Judaism relevant for each generation. Reform Jews do not hold the oral traditions of the Talmud to be a divine revelation, and they emphasize ethical and moral teachings.

Fast Fact

There are about 14 million people in the world who practice the Jewish faith.

Newer Faiths

There are a number of newer faiths, most of which have derived from other, established religions. While not major religions, they are well dispersed throughout the world and illustrate the wide mosaic of faiths that exist.

Hare Krishna

Hare Krishna, also called the International Society for Krishna Consciousness, was founded by Srila Prabhupada in the United States in 1966, making it one of the world's youngest religions. Krishna is the eighth and principal avatar of Vishnu in the Hindu religion, and this religious sect has strong Hindu affiliations. The faith proposes moving society toward a more natural economy with smaller, self-sufficient economic units based on simple living (vegetarianism, abstinence from alcohol and drugs) and high thinking. To achieve peace and happiness, adherents are urged to seek Krishna. The original Bhagavad-Gita forms the basis of Hare Krishna's required study, and followers are advised that chanting "Hare Krishna" is a way of seeking Krishna directly.

Pentecostalism

Pentecostalism is a movement that likely began in Los Angeles in 1906. Now a worldwide Christian movement, Pentecostalism emphasizes the experience of spirit baptism, evidenced by spiritual healing and ecstatic speaking in "tongues." Pentecostalists endorse a more literal interpretation of the Bible than mainstream Christians and seek a direct experience of God that would produce a sense of ecstasy, known as the baptism of the Holy Spirit. Pentecostalists believe in exorcism, speaking in tongues, faith healing, and seeking supernatural experiences. Three main movements have evolved: Pentecostalism, Fundamentalism, and Evangelicalism. Other sects, particularly throughout the rest of the world, are still emerging.

Rastafarianism

Rastafarianism originated with **MARCUS GARVEY** (1887–1940), who preached that members would be going back to Africa led by a black African king. In 1930, Ras Tafari Makonnen was crowned king of Ethiopia, claimed the title Emperor Haile Selassie, and Rastafarianism came into being. Rastafarians accept the Bible, but with reservations. They have no holy scriptures apart from the Rastafarian interpretation of the Bible. Dreadlocks symbolize the Rasta roots and represent Haile Selassie. Ganja, the Rasta name for marijuana, is used for religious purposes. The movement spread mainly to black youth throughout the Caribbean, helped along by the popularity of Jamaican reggae artist Bob Marley.

The Church of Scientology

Scientology is a philosophical religion without a god or deity, developed by **L. RONALD HUBBARD** (1911–1986) as an extension of a bestselling book, *Dianetics: The Modern Science of Mental Health* (1950), which detailed his new form of self-help psychotherapy. His Church of Scientology was formally established in the United States in 1954. Scientology urges that a person can get "clear" by overcoming physical and mental stress by a process called "auditing." The process clears the person of past painful experiences that block their achievement of happiness and self-realization.

Fast Fact

Scientology may be considered the most persistently controversial of all of the newer religious faiths. Despite the publicity, some of which has been negative, Scientology has grown steadily and, according to the Church, has been ministered to some 8 million people.

Protestantism

The term "Protestantism" refers to various forms of Christianity originating during the Reformation. Essentially a movement for theological and moral reform in the Western Christian Church during the sixteenth and seventeenth centuries, the Reformation was an incomparable catalyst for change that gave birth to a number of different types, such as Lutheranism, Calvinism, Anglicanism, Presbyterianism, Methodism, Congregationalism, and Baptism.

History

The traditional beginning of the Reformation occurred when Martin Luther, a German Roman Catholic priest, posted his Ninety-five Theses for debate on the door of the Castle Church in Wittenberg, Germany, on October 31, 1517. In his theses, Luther attacked what he saw as the theological root of corruption in the life of the Church.

Luther insisted that the Pope had no authority over purgatory and that only the scripture was authoritative. He also said that the Church was acting as a mediator or filter between the individual and God and exerted excessive control over people. Luther was excommunicated in 1521.

Two distinct branches of Protestantism arose from the Reformation. Lutheranism spread through Germany and Scandinavia, and Calvinism extended to many other parts of Europe including Scotland, the Netherlands, France, Hungary, and Poland.

Lutheranism

Martin Luther's act of defiance in 1517 provoked a general revolt against the Papacy. Luther believed the church had lost sight of its central teachings, the most important of those being justification— God's act of declaring a sinner righteous by faith alone, not though any act or work.

Lutherans believe that all human beings are sinners, in bondage to the power of Satan because of original sin. Their faith, therefore, is the only way out. Worship is firmly based on the teachings of the Bible, which Luther insisted was the only way to know God and his will. The Bible was the divine word, brought to man through the apostles and prophets. Worship was conducted in the vernacular.

Calvinism

JOHN CALVIN (1509–1564) was the leading French Protestant reformer and the most important second-generation figure of the Reformation. In the mid-1560s, he produced *Institutes of the Christian Religion*, his masterpiece, that systematized Protestant thought and became the single most important statement of Protestant belief.

What has come down as Calvinism is a philosophy that expressed the sovereignty of God's will in predestination. Calvinism held that those God specifically elects are saved and that individuals can do nothing to effect this salvation. The term "Calvinism" is also used as a system of doctrine accepted by the Reformed churches, such as Presbyterianism.

Shinto

Shinto is the religion of Japan. The word "shinto" came from the Chinese words *shin* and *tao* ("the way of the gods/spirits"), a translation of the Japanese phrase *kami-no-michi*. *Kami* is the spiritual

---

essence that exists in gods, human beings, animals, and even inanimate objects. Followers of Shinto believe that the world is created, inhabited, and ruled by kami.

History

Shinto was influenced by the arrival in Japan of Confucianism and Buddhism in the sixth century, although it has neither a founder nor sacred scriptures. Both religions melded into the culture and a cross-fertilization of religious and cultural influences took place. During the first century of Buddhism in Japan, the religion had a great influence on the arts, literature, and sciences and was the dominant faith of the upper classes. Buddhism evolved and merged with many aspects of Shintoism to incorporate the worship of kami. From the earliest recorded times until the later part of the nineteenth century, Shinto and Buddhism coexisted without incident.

During the reign of **EMPEROR MEIJI** (1868–1912), State Shinto, in which the emperor is divine, became the national religion. It was banned after World War II, and Sectarian Shinto, Folk Shinto, and other sects developed and continue to thrive.

Fast Fact

In 1587, Christian missionaries were banned from Japan. For the next fifty years, many initiatives were enacted to abolish Christianity from the islands of Japan.

Beliefs

Shinto is an optimistic faith, believing that all humans are fundamentally good and that evil is caused by wicked spirits. Its rituals are directed toward avoiding evil spirits through rites of purification, offerings, and prayers. Shinto lacks a fully developed theology; it has no concepts that compare to Christian or other beliefs concerning the wrath of God or the dogma of separation from God due to sin. All humanity is regarded as children of *kami*, so all life and human nature is sacred.

The absolute essence of Shinto philosophy is loyalty. It is of greater importance for a follower of Shinto to demonstrate loyalty than to do good deeds for others. A follower is absolutely loyal to the family, his superiors, his job, and so on. Traditions are preserved through the family. A love of nature is sacred; close contact with nature is equated to close contact with the gods. Natural objects are worshiped as sacred spirits.

Sikhism

Sikhism is a major religion of India and the fifth-largest faith in the world. Sikhs reject the assertion that Sikhism is a reform movement of Hinduism and Islam.

History

Sikhism was founded by Guru Nanak in Punjab (Panjab), India, in the late fifteenth century. He and a friend would meet together to compose and perform their own hymns. Many of his Hindu and Muslim audiences became followers of the fledgling religion (Sikh means "follower" in Sanskrit). As he gathered followers around him, his spiritual ideas bore fruit, and his composed hymns, all of which were written down, eventually became the core of the Sikh sacred text, the Adi Granth ("original book"). Guru Nanak was the first of the Ten Gurus who influenced and contributed to Sikhism until the late 1600s.

Person of Importance
Guru Nanak

Guru Nanak was born a Hindu in 1469. Just as many predicted that Siddhartha Gautama would become a Buddha, so did people predict that Nanak would praise God and teach many others to do the same. In his late twenties, Nanak received enlightenment and traveled in search of truth and wisdom. After about twenty years, he acquired farmland and settled in central Punjab, where he founded the town of Kartarpur and became Guru Nanak. The Sikh religion was born and Nanak was its first guru.

Beliefs

Sikhism is monotheistic: Sikhs believe in one God called Waheguru (great teacher). Sikhism is based on the discipline of purification and the overcoming of the five vices: greed, anger, false pride, lust, and attachments to material goods. At the end of a person's life, the good and the bad conduct are balanced out, and the result determines the family, race, and character of the person when reborn. There is no direct belief in heaven or hell as places, but those who have been selfish or cruel in the current life will suffer in their next existence. Those who acted with compassion and honesty will be better off in their next incarnation. The soul develops as it passes through the many incarnations until it becomes united with the infinite one.

Sikhs are opposed to the idea of austere asceticism; rather, they emphasize the ideal of achieving saintliness as active members of society. Sikhism prohibits idolatry, the caste system, and the use of wine or tobacco. Stress is placed on the importance of leading a good moral life that includes loyalty, gratitude for all favors received, philanthropy, justice, truth, and honesty.

The history of the development of the Sikhs over the past 500 years has at times been tumultuous and bloody. The involvement of the British only propagated the violent fighting between the Sikhs and the Hindus. There are approximately 23 million Sikhs today.

Fast Fact

The Khalsa (saint-soldiers) was established in 1699 to defend Sikhs against Muslims. The Khalsa had five tenets, known as K's: *kesh* (uncut hair), *kangha* (comb), *kirpan* (sword), *kara* (steel bracelet), and *kachch* (short pants for use in battle).

Taoism

The word *Tao* signifies "path" or "way." Taoism is a Chinese system of thought and, until the twentieth century, was one of the three major religions of China, along with Confucianism and Buddhism. The Tao is a natural force that makes the universe the way it is. It has also been referred to as "the way of heaven."

History

The foundation of Taoism is attributed partially to Laozi (Lao Tzu) and his written material called the Dao De Ding or Tao Te Ching ("The Way and its Power"). Little is known about the life dates of Lao Tzu; he is sometimes placed in the sixth century B.C. and sometimes in the fourth. The work of the philosopher Chuang Tzu is also considered important to the ideas of Taoism. Taoism wasn't a religious faith when it began; it was conceived as a philosophy and had evolved into a religion with a number of deities by the second century A.D.

Beliefs

Taoism is generally seen as a balance to Confucianism rather than in opposition to it. Taoism seeks harmony with the nature of things through a humble submission to the Way Tao, which for Taoists is the ultimate metaphysical principle of being. Confucianism also seeks a harmony with nature, but with Confucianism this is achieved by enacting rituals and ceremonies deemed conducive to it. Where Confucianism is ceremonial, Taoism is intuitive and meandering. A key Taoist concept is that of non-action, or the natural course of things. It is a direct link to yin and yang, complementary duality. The basic feature of Taoism is restoring balance. Extremes produce a swinging back to the opposite. Therefore, there is a constant movement from activity to inactivity and back again.

The idea of a personal deity is foreign to Taoism, as is the concept of the creation of the universe. The Tao—a natural force—constrains the universe to act as it does. Yet nature is full of deities; the most familiar are those connected with childbirth, wealth, and health. However, a Taoist does not pray as the Christians do, for they believe there is no god to hear their prayers or act upon them. The way to seek answers is through inner meditation and outer observation.

Taoists have an affinity for promoting good health. They believe that there are five elements: water, fire, wood, metal, and earth. You are healthy when the five elements are balanced within your body, and you will experience disease of some kind if they out of balance. Each person should nurture the *chi* (breath), which refers to the spirit, energy, or life force within everything.

Fast Fact

Taoist thought permeated the Chinese culture the same way Confucianism did, and the two are often linked. Taoism became more popular than Confucianism, even though Confucianism enjoyed state patronage. There are between 20 and 50 million people practicing Taoism today.

Tribal Native American Faiths

It is almost impossible to generalize about Native American religions because of their amazing diversity. Knowledge about the development of religion in the Native American tribes is imprecise. In fact, the word "religion" had no equivalent in any of the 300 Native American languages that existed at the time Columbus arrived on the continent.

Origins

The origins of Native American religions have been traced back to the beginnings of human habitation in the New World, but there is little in the way of early written material to provide reliable data. The various teachings, ways of life, and stories were passed on orally and fell prey to the drawbacks inherent in that form of communication. In other words, they became tainted and more unreliable with each telling. There are common elements, though. Religions (used here in the sense that the immigrant Christians and Roman Catholics knew) were closely related to the natural world, which included supernatural and sacred spiritual worship and power.

Fast Fact

The Native American Church, which became institutionalized in the twentieth century, has accepted some of Christianity's beliefs as it spread from coast to coast. The church includes some 100,000 adherents from over fifty North American Indian tribes, including American Indians and Eskimos.

Central Beliefs

Many tribes recorded events. The known method was to use a specially prepared buffalo hide. Each year a figure or symbol illustrating the most memorable event would be painted on the hide. In time, the hide would become filled, and it would be maintained as long as there were people who could remember what the figures and symbols meant. For one year, there might have been a very good harvest of berries; in another the tribe might have moved to another location.

The majority of Native American rituals revolved around the calendar and lunar and solar observations. Others were allied to the various subsistence needs; for example, hunting and harvesting. The Native American environment was symbolized by the ritual of the six directions: north, south, east, west, the zenith, and the nadir. The zenith was Grandfather (day). Sky was represented by Father Sun and the Thunderbirds. The nadir is Mother or Grandmother Earth, and Grandmother Moon was female.

Many Native Americans still hold on to and express the values and traditions they were taught by their forefathers. Original languages are virtually extinct, but the Native American Church and its congregations are endeavoring to keep them alive and re-establish a culture that has been virtually destroyed by its invaders.

Cheat Sheet for Religion

The word "religion" derives from the Latin *religio,* meaning "to be bound to" or "to tie fast" and commonly refers to a person's relation to God, gods, or spirits. There are approximately 4,200 religions practiced today.

Most religions may be classified as monotheistic, in which there is one god (e.g., Christianity, Judaism, and Islam); polytheistic, in which there are many gods (e.g., Hinduism); dualistic, having good and evil deities (e.g., Zoroastrianism); supratheistic, in which the participant experiences a union with the deity (e.g., Hindu Vedanta); or pantheistic, identifying the universe with God.

The Bahá'í Faith, founded in Persia in the nineteenth century, is one of the newest religions but still has about 5 million followers in most of the world's nations.

Buddha is a title; there have been many Buddhas in the past and there will be many in the future.

Catholicism is the largest Christian organization and is practiced in most countries in the world.

Approximately 2.1 billion people practice Christianity.

The teachings of Confucius have had a profound influence on Chinese culture and were studied by civil service applicants for nearly 600 years.

Eastern Orthodoxy grew from the establishment of the Eastern Roman Empire in the fourth century.

Egyptian religion offers examples of religious beliefs as practiced by one of the oldest of humankind's civilizations. Highly localized and fragmented at first, a belief system was organized into the united efforts to construct the pyramids.

Hindus consider their religion as a way of life with customs, moral obligations, traditions, and ideals that touch all facets of existence.

The purpose of Muslims in practicing Islam is to serve Allah, to worship him alone, and to construct a moral lifestyle.

Jainism emerged in the sixth century B.C. Its core belief is the practice of love and nonviolence to all living things.

Judaism is one of the three great monotheistic world religions, incorporating the fundamental belief that the people of Israel are God's chosen people who must serve as a light for other nations.

A worldwide Christian movement, Pentecostalism emphasizes the experience of spirit baptism, evidenced by spiritual healing and ecstatic speaking in "tongues."

Protestantism refers to various forms of Christianity originating during the Reformation, a movement for theological and moral reform in Europe during the sixteenth and seventeenth centuries.

Shinto was influenced by the arrival in Japan of Confucianism and Buddhism in the sixth century, with both religions melding into and cross-fertilizing with Japanese culture.

Sikhism, founded in the late fifteenth century in India, is based on the discipline of purification and the overcoming of the five vices: greed, anger, false pride, lust, and attachments to material goods.

Taoism originally was conceived as a philosophy between the sixth and fourth centuries B.C. and had evolved into a religion with a number of deities by the second century A.D.

The study of Native American religions has been hampered by the lack of written records; most information has been handed down through generations of oral tradition.

Chapter Eight

Social Sciences

The social sciences are a group of academic disciplines that apply scientific methods to the social relations of humans. Many of these studies had their roots in a desire for social betterment of society but now employ quantitative methods and statistics in their analysis of theories and trends. This chapter takes a brief look at the fields of psychology, economics, sociology, political science, anthropology, and archaeology.

Psychology

Psychology is a scientific approach to understanding the thought processes and behaviors of humans in their interaction with the environment. The term *psychology* has its origins in the Greek words *psyche* (soul or self) and *logos* (logic and, in turn, science). Psychologists study the processes of thinking and cognition, sense perception, learning, emotions and motivation, personality, abnormal behavior, and interactions between individuals and with the environment.

History

Aristotle's *De anima* (350 B.C.; *On the Soul*) is considered the ancient foundation of psychology. In three books, Aristotle discusses the nature of living things and the different kinds of souls they possess. He concludes that the mind exists without the body, cannot be corrupted, and therefore is immortal.

It is generally agreed that **WILHELM WUNDT** (1832–1920) founded psychology in 1879 when he established the first "psychological" laboratory at the University of Leipzig in Germany. Wundt set out to study the human mind using a method called *introspection*. In this approach, specially trained individuals attempted to look inside their minds and describe what went on in response to "events," such as lights and sounds, they were exposed to.

Introspection was also the approach used by **WILLIAM JAMES** (1842–1910) in the United States, when he wrote *Principles of*

Repeatable Quotable

We have lost the art of living; and in the most important science of all, the science of daily life, the science of behavior, we are complete ignoramuses. We have psychology instead.
—*D. H. Lawrence*

Psychology (1890)—which for most psychologists marks the beginning of modern psychology. James firmly believed that psychology should be the "study of mental life." He also proposed—in agreement with the views of **CHARLES DARWIN** (1809–1882) on physical evolution—that the human mind evolved as a result of successive adaptations by our ancestors. This view, called *functionalism,* would soon fall into disfavor, but it resurfaced in the latter twentieth century as an increasingly popular line of theory and research now known as evolutionary psychology.

Person of Importance
Sigmund Freud

Sigmund Freud (1856–1939) developed his psychoanalytic theory in Austria over forty years. The prevailing view in the late nineteenth century was that humans are rational beings, but Freud believed that people are anything but rational, instead driven by selfish "animal" impulses. Freud alleged that these impulses are biological in origin, and they demand satisfaction even though they are part of what he called the unconscious mind. His was a hedonistic view, stating that we exist entirely to seek pleasure and avoid pain. Freud developed his theory through his treatment of typically mildly disordered patients, which eventually yielded the treatment approach he called psychoanalysis. Some of Freud's ideas have survived, but much of his theorizing has been discounted. However, he is still regarded as one of the most influential figures in all of psychology, and he was the first to attempt a comprehensive theory of personality.

Psychology Disciplines

Behaviorism

Behaviorism is a school of psychology that attempts to explain behavior in terms of observable and measurable responses to environmental stimuli. Biological processes are only reactions, and behaviorism discards such concepts as consciousness, ideas, and emotions. Behaviorist theories dominated psychology in the 1920s and 1930s, due largely to the work of U.S. psychologist John B. Watson. In his *Behaviorism* (1924), Watson breaks with previous introspective psychologies. The conditioned-response experiments of Russian Ivan Pavlov and American Edward Thorndike were influential in the development of behaviorism. Behaviorist thought has led to behavior modification therapies employing such techniques as conditioning, desensitization, and modeling.

Cognitive Psychology

Cognitive psychology studies human internal mental processes such as problem solving, memory, and language, particularly as they affect learning and behavior. The field grew out of Gestalt psychology and the work of Jean Piaget on intellectual development in children. Cognitive psychology took off in the 1960s, having been launched by the information-processing model developed by **ALLEN NEWELL** (1927–1992) and **HERBERT SIMON** (1916–2001) some years earlier. This model studies the similarities between the human brain and the computer in the ways information is received, processed, stored, and retrieved.

Humanist Psychology

Humanist psychologists, in reaction to the mainstream trends of behaviorism and psychoanalysis, argue that humans are individuals and should be treated as unique beings. The best-known humanist psychologists were **CARL ROGERS** (1902–1987) and **ABRAHAM MASLOW** (1908–1970). They held that, although we certainly have needs in common with other animals and can be quite selfish at times, there's more to being human. We have goals in life, we have a need to grow and fulfill ourselves psychologically and feel good about it all, and we have a need to find happiness that goes beyond the satisfaction of basic needs. To the humanists, the positive thinking and hoping that both the psychoanalysts and strict behaviorists ignored are the most important aspects of human behavior.

Biological Psychology

Biological psychology is the study of physiological bases of behavior, or the mind-body phenomenon. Researchers use highly sophisticated brain scanning and monitoring equipment to study what goes on the brain in response to external events or the performing of certain tasks. They attempt to assess which areas of the brain are active in a given situation and how the flow of information through the brain takes place.

Fast Fact

Biological psychology is being applied to areas such as understanding the physiological bases for learning and memory, emotionality, and mental and behavioral disorders.

Clinical Psychology

Clinical psychology has become a significant focus within psychology in the United States, and the number of clinical psychologists has grown steadily. Clinical psychologists study and treat mental and behavioral disorders and typically deal with the more serious illnesses. Clinical psychologists often specialize in working with people of different age ranges or who have specific disorders, and psychotherapy and psychological testing are a large part of the work they do.

History

In 1896 at the University of Pennsylvania, Lightner Witmer, a student of Wilhelm Wundt, established the world's first psychological clinic and originated the field of clinical psychology. Witmer started the first journal in the field in 1907, *The Psychological Clinic*, in which he coined the term "clinical psychology." World War II provided a major impetus to the field as psychologists were called upon to treat returning service men suffering from "shell shock."

Trends

Although clinical psychology is rooted in experimentation and the scientific method, it has moved away from science despite strides made in complementary areas such as neuroimaging, molecular and behavioral genetics, and cognitive neuroscience. Research has shown that a number of psychological interventions are efficacious and cost-effective, important considerations in the face of rising healthcare costs. However, these therapies are not used as often as they could be because practitioners often value their personal and subjective clinical experiences more highly than scientific evidence.

-------- --- ------ ------------ --- --------------------- ----

Person of Importance
Alfred Binet

Alfred Binet (1857–1911) was a French psychologist who went in to medicine due to his interest in the work of neurologist Jean-Martin Charcot. As head of a research laboratory at the Sorbonne, he studied experimental techniques to measure reasoning ability and intelligence. He founded the first French journal of psychology in 1895.

Binet adapted the standardized testing methods developed by English psychologist Sir Francis Galton for the purpose of studying intellectual development in his two daughters. As a result of this work, he published *L'Étude expérimentale de l'intelligence* (1903; "Experimental Study of Intelligence"). He collaborated with Theodore Simon to develop scales for measuring intelligence, which were revised by American psychologist Lewis M. Terman to become the Stanford-Binet IQ tests, still a mainstay of intelligence evaluation.

In order to promote scientific psychology, representatives of top research-focused graduate-training programs formed the Academy of Psychological Clinical Science (APCS) in 1994. This movement could be encouraged by following the British model; there the National Institute for Health and Clinical Excellence evaluates therapies for effectiveness and approves programs for coverage by state insurance. There is a critical need for effective psychological care: the number of Americans receiving mental healthcare has doubled in the last twenty years.

Economics

Economics is the study of how people and societies allocate resources to produce goods, how they decide what goods and services will be produced, how goods will be produced, and how they will be distributed for consumption among people in the society. Economics is based on the fact that resources tend to be scarce, or at least finite, and all the needs of society cannot be met. Economists are principally concerned with fair and efficient means of distributing goods and resources, and the balance of wealth in and between societies.

Two Fields
Economics is typically divided into microeconomics and macroeconomics. Microeconomics seeks to understand the operation of markets on an individual level, or in a single group within a society. Macroeconomics studies the functioning of complete economic systems and concerns itself with major trends such as the rate of economic growth, inflation, and unemployment.

Econometrics
Yet another branch of economics, econometrics, has developed from the use of complex mathematical techniques and statistical data in

economic forecasting. Accurate economic modeling leads to better policy planning. In the mid-twentieth century, Norwegian economist Ragnar Frisch worked in this area and founded the Econometric Society. Despite further development of econometric techniques, criticism of the field increased due to its lack of predictive ability. In the 1990s, advertisers began using econometrics to measure and predict sales performance.

Later Changes

The 1980s saw the growth of supply-side economics, the theory that economic health could be obtained by influencing the supply of labor and goods and by using tax cuts as incentives. The theory was applied in the economic programs of the Reagan administration, and supply-siders pointed to their positive effect on economic growth. Critics charged that supply-side economics created massive federal deficits, penalized the middle class, and prompted damaging speculation.

History of Economic Theory

As they did in many fields of human endeavor, the ancient Greeks considered the issues of economics in their early writings. Plato's *Republic* recognized that social life had an economic basis and proposed a system for the division of labor. Aristotle also understood the importance of economic security to the political health of individuals and society.

In the fifteenth through eighteenth centuries, mercantilism was the economic system of major trading nations. It held that national

---

economic health was based on the export of goods and the accumulation of precious metals. Physiocrats, the first economists, argued for free markets unencumbered by government intervention and regulation. They also considered land as the single basis of wealth and a tax on land as the only justifiable tax.

Person of Importance
Adam Smith

Adam Smith (1723–1790), a Scottish philosopher and economist, was a professor of moral philosophy. During travels in France, he met with some of the physiocrats and began work on *An Inquiry into the Nature and Causes of the Wealth of Nations*, published in 1776.

Wealth of Nations is considered the first comprehensive explanation of a system of political economy. In it, Smith advanced his theory of an economic system based on individual self-interest that would lead to the greatest good for all. He also designated the division of labor as the most important component of economic growth, and that value arises from the labor involved in the process of production.

Smith wrote before the Industrial Revolution, and some of his theories did not hold up. He was, however, one of the most influential economic thinkers in history.

The most important development of the eighteenth century was Scottish economist Adam Smith's *An Inquiry into the Nature and Causes of the Wealth of Nations* (1776), a work that many consider as the first example of a complete economic theory. Smith believed that self-interest was the basic economic force, and his treatment of the division of labor and economic institutions established economics as a legitimate field of study.

In the nineteenth century, English economist Thomas Malthus published his study of population, in which he predicted population growth would always exceed the means of subsistence, ensuring poverty and suffering. In 1817, English economist David Ricardo's "iron law of wages" maintained that wages would always stabilize at the subsistence level. The rise of socialism and the work of Karl Marx challenged classical economics by questioning the morality of capitalism and predicting its ultimate collapse.

In the 1930s, John Maynard Keynes published his influential work *General Theory of Employment, Interest, and Money*, which emphasized the importance of government intervention in the economy. Since that time, the economics of growth and development has dominated economic thinking. A relatively new school of thought is monetarism whose advocates, like Milton Friedman, believe that the money supply exerts an important influence on the economy.

Person of Importance

John Maynard Keynes

John Maynard Keynes (1883–1946) was an English economist, journalist, and financier. He worked in the British treasury during World War I and accompanied Prime Minister Lloyd George to the peace conference in Versailles at the end of hostilities.

He resigned in protest over what he considered unrealistically high war reparations levied against Germany, and in his *Economic Consequences of the Peace* (1919) accurately prophesized Europe's economic ruin.

His chief work was *The General Theory of Employment, Interest, and Money* (1936). The book, published in the middle of a worldwide depression, argues against laissez-faire economic policies and promotes government involvement in controlling unemployment through spending programs.

The Great Depression

The Great Depression, the decade of the 1930s during which unemployment in the United States reached 25 percent, is often called a defining moment in U.S. history and in economic thinking. The widespread and relentless economic hardship prompted many Americans to expect a much greater role of government in the workings of the economy. The federal government established Social Security to care for the elderly, started an unemployment compensation program, created the U.S. Securities and Exchange Commission to regulate the securities industry, and founded the National Labor Relations Board to ensure fair labor practices.

Causes

Many economists blamed inadequate demand for the Depression, and Keynesian theories advocating government involvement became dominant in economic thinking for the next forty years. Economists now discount this view, although the public still supports it. Recent research points to the actions of the United States and other countries that were still tied to the international gold standard, and wished to remain so, as the main factor that brought about the Great Depression. During World War I, many European nations went off the gold standard to print money and then attempted to return to the standard, causing huge deflationary pressure. The United States and others initiated policies to prop up the gold standard, which reduced economic activity and induced the Depression.

The Picture Worsens

Because the Herbert Hoover administration urged businesses not to lower wages, as they normally would given the reduced levels of production, massive layoffs occurred. As corporate profits fell, the value of their securities also fell, leading to the significant reduction in the portfolios of banks. Panicky Americans withdrew all their funds from banks, thereby causing widespread bank failures. Income taxes were raised to balance the budget, further reducing disposable income, spending levels, and economic activity. By 1933, newly elected president Franklin Delano Roosevelt found it necessary to declare bank holidays, stopping all financial activity, in order to prevent further banking failures. Unfortunately, nearly half of U.S. commercial banks had already disappeared by that time.

More Mistakes

Roosevelt's New Deal held much promise for a beleaguered nation, but many new policies had the opposite of their intended effects. The Agricultural Adjustment Act and the National Recovery

---

Administration aimed to raise wages and prices by reducing production. Wages did rise as a result, but reduced production and lack of demand caused more layoffs. Monetary policy, unfortunately, reduced the money supply.

Sociology

Sociology is a social science that studies human social behavior, societies, their interactions, and the processes that affect them. Sociology is concerned with economic, political, social, and religious activity, and all component parts of societies including communities, institutions, specific populations, and various groups as defined by gender, age, or race. Sociologists study social status and stratification, deviant or criminal behaviors, social movements, and revolution. Sociologists also attempt to determine how laws or rules govern human social behavior.

Sociology is concerned with social forces that constitute other separate disciplines: economics, political science, psychology, anthropology, and history. In sociology, these factors are considered as a whole, rather than independently. Contemporary study of sociology combines an examination of classical theories and modern qualitative and quantitative methods.

Because humans lack the instincts that direct the actions of most animals, people largely depend on social institutions to provide the norms that regulate human behavior. Sociology attempts to determine the role of these institutions, how they are established and dissolve, how they interact with each other, and how they gain or lose influence. Basic organizational structures include economic, educational, religious, and political institutions.

History of Sociology

Many philosophers and political theorists, going back to the time of Plato, have considered broad social issues in their writings.

AUGUSTE COMTE (1798–1857) was a French philosopher influential in the founding of sociology. Primarily a social reformer, Comte founded the school of philosophy known as positivism, which maintains that the only knowledge is scientific knowledge. He believed that sociology combines all the sciences and, through the methods of positivism, could achieve a society in which people lived in harmony and comfort.

HERBERT SPENCER (1820–1903), an English sociologist and philosopher, believed in the natural basis of human action and, along with Charles Darwin, was an early supporter of the theory of evolution. Spencer, however, believed that evolution was a progressive force directed toward good. He applied his ideas in *The Principles of Sociology* (3 vols., 1876–1896) to show how the individual evolves relative to the group.

ÉMILE DURKHEIM (1858–1917), a French social scientist, is traditionally considered to be the father of sociology. He brought the scientific methodology of empirical research to the study of sociological theory and established sociology as an academic discipline. One his most important works, *De la division du travail social (The Division of Labor in Society*, 1893) argues that commonly held values maintained order in primitive societies. In more complex societies, the division of labor orders society but is unstable due to the lack of moral regulation.

MAX WEBER (1864–1920) was a German sociologist, economist, and political scientist. He developed an objective methodology for social science that considerably influenced twentieth century sociologists. Rejecting the Marxian view that economics was the main social motivator, Weber argued for the role of belief systems, including religious values and ideologies, in shaping societies. His *Protestant Ethic and the Spirit of Capitalism* (1920) explored the relationship between the Calvinist aesthetic ideal and the rise of capitalistic institutions.

KARL MARX (1818–1883), the German social philosopher and socialist, was an important influence on sociological thought. Marx advanced his theories of the primacy of class struggle in the *Communist Manifesto* (1848) written with Friedrich Engels. Marx felt that the organization and development of society was economically motivated and class struggle the primary factor of social progress.

Sociology in America

Some of the earliest American sociological work on record comes from **GEORGE FITZHUGH** (1806–1881) and **HENRY HUGHES** (1829–1862) who, improbably, offered a defense of slavery based on their belief that society needed a hierarchical structure of superiors and dependents. The Civil War put an end to this line of reasoning. Two later and more influential pioneers of the study of sociology were Graham Sumner and Lester Frank Ward.

GRAHAM SUMNER (1840–1910) was born in Englewood, New Jersey, and taught at Yale from 1872 to 1909. He advocated extreme laissez-faire economics and individual liberties, strongly opposing any government interference with free-market trade. His sociological thought followed the same paths of self-determination: the forces of competition eliminated poorly adapted individuals and preserved cultural soundness. He believed that the middle-class work ethic, thrift, and sobriety would lead to a wholesome, moral society. Sumner disparaged any social reforms in overcoming poverty because of the burden it would place on the middle class. His best known work, *Folkways* (1907), charted the evolution of folk customs. He started work on *Science of Society*, which was not published until 1927, seventeen years after his death.

Person of Importance
Jane Addams

Jane Addams (1860–1935) was an American reformer who worked for legal protection for women and children, women's suffrage, a juvenile court system, labor laws, and education. She also founded Chicago's Hull House settlement in 1889 to provide social services for poor immigrants. The community provided an early research model for sociologists from the nearby University of Chicago.

She was criticized as a pacifist and socialist, but many of the reforms she advocated became federal policy. She was awarded the Nobel Peace Prize in 1931.

LESTER FRANK WARD (1841–1913) was born in Joliet, Illinois, and would become one of the most important of American sociologists. Ward developed the theory of *telesis*, which is the idea of planned social progress made possible by an active government. This type of society employed social scientists to provide a nationally organized education. Ward believed that human intelligence rather than nature guided social evolution. A prolific writer, his important works include *Dynamic Sociology* (1883), *Psychic Factors of Civilization* (1893), *Pure Sociology* (1903), and *Glimpses of the Cosmos* (6 vol., 1913–1918). In 1893, the University of Chicago established the first American chair in sociology and appointed Albion Woodbury Small (1854–1926) to it. The first issue of the *American Journal of Sociology* appeared in 1895 under Small's editorship. In 1905, Small and others founded the American Sociological Society, later renamed the American Sociological Association (ASA).

Fast Fact

An early classic in the field of sociology was the series of *Middletown* books authored by the husband-and-wife team of American sociologists Robert Lynd (1892–1970) and Helen Lynd (1894–1982). The first volume, *Middletown: A Study in Contemporary American Culture* (1929) was a treatise on social stratification of the community of Muncie, Indiana, using anthropological study techniques. They published a follow-up study in 1937, *Middletown in Transition: A Study in Cultural Conflicts*, which analyzed the social changes brought about by the Great Depression.

Person of Importance
Talcott Parsons

Talcott Parsons (1902–1979) was an American sociologist who taught at Harvard from 1927 until 1974. He is best known for introducing structural-functional theory; a single, general theoretical system in which general and specific characteristics of societies could be analyzed and classified. He also promoted a realignment of sociology with social psychology and cultural anthropology in order to better define sociology's subject matter.

Parson helped sociology move away from the dominant fields of economics and political science. His writing includes *The Structure of Social Action* (1937), *The Social System* (1951), and *Structure and Process in Modern Societies* (1960).

A Future of Sociology

In the 1980s, the field of sociology was in decline due to conservative antipathy and reduction in research funding. A few universities closed their sociology departments; even Yale almost lost its department. Graduate student enrollment recovered in the 1990s, however, and by 2000 their numbers rivaled those studying economics. Some of the more important directions in recent sociological thought include conflict theory, structural-functional theory, and symbolic interaction theory.

Conflict Theory

Conflict theory emphasizes the importance of conflict in driving social change and draws upon the work of Karl Marx. One conflict theorist was British sociologist **RALF DAHRENDORF** (1929–2009), who published *Class and Class Conflict in Industrial Society* in 1959. He went beyond Marx's narrow view that class is defined by property ownership and claimed that modern struggles are between those with authority and those without. Capitalism, changed from the times of Marx, has institutionalized conflict through the creation of unions, collective bargaining, the court system, and political debate.

Structural-Functional Theory

In addition to Talcott Parsons, structural-functional theory was greatly influenced by the work of American sociologist **ROBERT MERTON** (1910–2003). He attempted to explain the function of social structures as well as their dysfunctions and balances. Instead of analyzing society as a whole, Merton examined different social structures, such as groups, organizations, or communities. His published works include *Social Theory and Social Structure* (1949).

Symbolic Interaction Theory

The study of symbolic interaction was begun by American social psychologist **GEORGE HERBERT MEAD** (1863–1931). This theory posits that the world people inhabit is built on the interpretation given to objects, and interpretations vary from one group to another. Even the way we look at ourselves is based on our interpretation of how others see us. Mead's work was further developed by American sociologist **HERBERT BLUMER** (1900–1987). He coined the term "symbolic interaction" and defined the three premises on which the theory is based. First, human beings act toward things, be they objects, people, institutions, or ideas, based on the meanings the things have for them. Second, the meaning of such things derives from social interaction. And third, these meanings are handled in and modified by an individual's interpretive process.

Political Science

Political science is a social science concerned with the study of the state, government, and politics. Topics investigated by political scientists include the nature of states, the functions performed by governments, political culture and parties, the behavior and opinions of voters, and political economy. Political science has a number of subfields, with the most important being political theory, comparative government, national government, and international relations. It also shares certain areas with other social sciences such as sociology, psychology, and economics.

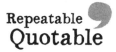

Repeatable
Quotable

History is past politics and politics present history.—*Edward A. Freeman*

History

As long ago as ancient Greece, thinkers and philosophers such as Aristotle and Plato were considering the relationship between citizens and the state. In 1741, the Scottish empiricist philosopher and historian **DAVID HUME** (1711–1776) foresaw the looming debate in his pamphlet *That Politics May Be Reduced to a Science.*

Yet political science as a discipline was not taught until 1880 when the School of Political Science was established at Columbia University. This institution served a formative role, drawing elements of history, economics, geography, and sociology in the development of political science theories. Johns Hopkins published the *Johns Hopkins Studies in Historical and Political Science* in 1882, and Columbia began the *Political Science Quarterly* in 1886. Other universities established departments and political science became a recognized academic discipline.

The American Political Science Association was formed in 1903 and launched the *American Political Science Review* three years later. More American institutions developed political science curriculums; both instruction and research took on more of an American focus. **CHARLES E. MERRIAM** (1874–1953) called for "a new science of politics" that would bridge the gap between theory and practice, although some in the field questioned the possibility of scientific objectivity.

After World War II, political science was colored by Cold War conflicts and other changes in the profession. Mathematics and statistics became commonplace in research, and behaviorist methods became popular in the 1950s and 1960s, only to be replaced by "positive political theory" in the 1970s and 1980s. Comparative politics and area studies developed as fields. Political science had become entrenched as an academic discipline with programs available at all major U.S. universities.

Repeatable Quotable

Nothing is more surprising than the easiness with which the many are governed by the few.—*David Hume*

John Rawls

John Rawls (1921–2002) was an American political philosopher whose *Theory of Justice* (1971) is considered the major work in twentieth-century political philosophy. In it, Rawls argues against the idea of utilitarianism, the philosophy that the maximization of happiness is the ultimate aim of all human activity and that an action is right only if it promotes the greatest happiness for the greatest number of people. Instead, Rawls developed a theory of justice appropriate for a democratic society. He believed that agreement forms the principles of justice, that individual rights trump those of the group, and that a rational society protects the rights of those who are the worst off.

Political Science Movements

Political scientists debated their methodological preferences in the twentieth century. Some believed that it was important to establish objective, scientific methods that were useful in explaining events. Behaviorism was the methodology that became dominant and was subsequently replaced by rational choice theory as advocacy of behaviorism declined in the 1970s.

Behaviorism
Behaviorism is a movement in political science that is based on analyzing only observable behaviors of political agents. It was developed

from the same school of thinking that gave birth to behavioral psychology and stresses the relationship between stimuli and responses. Behaviorism arose in the 1940s and was prominent in the United States through the 1960s. Using newly developed survey research methods, it was less an explanation of history and theory and more a study of the behaviors and statements of political actors. Behaviorists focused on areas that could be supported by quantitative data.

Rational Choice Theory

Rational choice theory, or positive political theory as it is also known, is a political science movement that uses individuals as the basic unit of analysis and models outcomes based on the assumption that those individuals behave in a self-interested, rational manner. Proponents take a narrow view in defining rational individuals and behaviors; the theory depends on an almost mathematical progression of thoughts and a strict consistency of choice. Rational choice has two subdivisions: public choice and social choice.

Politics of Globalization

Globalization can be broadly defined as the process of uniting—politically, economically, and culturally—nations and populations into a larger community. It involves and affects more elements than this definition implies, however. Some of these factors are the international flow of goods, services, and capital; the deregulations of markets; the increasing mobility of work forces and work; the growth of multinational corporations that view the world as a single market; developments in financial and information services; and the melding of customs and cultures.

The Challenge

These factors require political scientists to analyze forces beyond the normal concepts of the nation-state. The changes brought about by globalization have created new domestic politics and new agents, such as anti-globalization movements that are well organized and, somewhat ironically, globalized in their reach. Political scientists face revised questions about the place of government in a world of mobile resources, about new political affiliations and fragmentations, about the future of nations struggling for survival in a global economy, and about the role of democracy.

While globalization can bring about new opportunities for groups of people who would otherwise be limited by their local economies, they are often powerless to invoke the changes that result in growth and prosperity. The forces underlying globalization are volatile, unpredictable, and their benefits can be transitory. Worse, globalization can produce economic and social dislocation and, due to reduced accountability of global agents, effects can also include damage to the environment and harm to cultures.

Different Viewpoints

There are many who see the globalization glass as half full and claim free market and technology advances will provide a boon as the world enters a period of unity. Others have a half-empty view and decry the politically destabilizing effects and economic dangers for nations and cultures. Clearly, globalization presents unparalleled opportunities and challenges that demand objective understanding and effective political leadership.

Military Expenditures in 2008

This graph shows the total military spending for each country or area of the world in billions of U.S. dollars in 2008. The United States and its strongest allies (NATO, Japan, South Korea, and Australia) spent a combined $1.1 trillion on their military budgets.

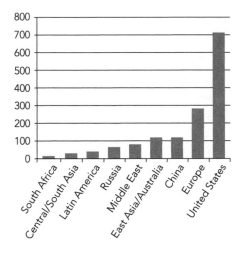

Figures were compiled by the Center for Arms Control and Non-Proliferation.

Nuclear Politics

In January 2009, eight countries possessed nearly 8,400 active and operational nuclear warheads. The table lists the countries and the estimated number of warheads owned by each (as of January 2009).

Five countries, the United States, Russia, the United Kingdom, France, and China, were recognized as nuclear-weapon states by the 1968 Treaty on the Non-Proliferation of Nuclear Weapons. By all indications, these five are determined to remain nuclear powers. Indeed, all are in the process of modernizing their nuclear forces or have immediate plans to do so. Coincidentally, the United States and Russia are in the process of reducing their operational nuclear weapons from previous Cold War levels due to the 1991 Treaty on the Reduction and Limitation of Strategic Offensive Arms (START Treaty) and the 2002 Treaty on Strategic Offensive Reductions (SORT). This is a laudable exercise, although in the United States reducing the number of weapons is primarily a legal activity achieved by transferring ownership of warheads from the Department of Defense to the Department of Energy.

Country	Warheads
United States	2,702
Russia	4,384
United Kingdom	160
France	300
China	186
India	60–70
Pakistan	60
Israel	80
Total	8,392

Information compiled by the Stockholm International Peace Research Institute.

The three nuclear-weapon states that are not part of the Non-Proliferation Treaty—India, Pakistan, and Israel—do not make public information on their nuclear weapon activities. Yet all three appear to be maintaining or increasing the size of their nuclear capabilities. Due to testing exercises in 2006, it is thought that North Korea is developing a weapons program, but it is not believed to have an operational weapon as yet.

Fast Fact

Nearly half of the United States' deployed nuclear warheads, almost 1,200, are carried aboard our fleet of twelve operational nuclear submarines. The shift of concern to China by U.S. war planners means that about sixty percent of submarine patrols take place in the Pacific Ocean, four times the level of the 1980s.

Anthropology

Anthropology is a social science that studies the origin, behavior, and cultural development of humans. Anthropologists are concerned with human biological and evolutionary history as well as social features that distinguish us from other animal species. Anthropology began to develop as a distinct field in the nineteenth century and, since the middle of the twentieth century, as a group of specialized disciplines. Fieldwork distinguishes anthropology from other social sciences.

Four Fields

Traditionally, anthropology is divided into four fields: cultural anthropology, archaeology, linguistic anthropology, and physical anthropology.

Cultural anthropology concentrates on the social and cultural constructions of human groups past and present. Cultural anthropologists may study contemporary communities in remote areas or specialized and distinct groups within local society.

Person of Importance
Franz Boas

Franz Boas (1858–1942) was a German-born American anthropologist who was associated with the American Museum of Natural History and who became the first professor of anthropology at Columbia. He is generally credited with establishing anthropology as an academic discipline in the United States, and was one of its most influential pioneers.

Boas employed rigorous methodology in his effort to understand the particular histories of societies. He founded a multidisciplinary approach, which later developed into the individual disciplines of modern anthropology. He also taught and mentored a generation of anthropologists including Margaret Mead and Ruth Benedict.

Archaeology investigates social and cultural evolution in prehistoric societies. Archaeologists study the remains of human activity to reconstruct life patterns and habits of societies.

Linguistic anthropology focuses on the development and relationships between languages and the relationships between culture and language. Linguistic anthropology may consider the biological

---

characteristics of a language, how a language evolves and spreads geographically, or how a language functions in society.

Physical or biological anthropology studies the biological evolution of humans, including anatomical development and the hereditary distribution of variations to diverse populations. Physical anthropologists focus on human paleontology and the study of race.

Cultural Anthropology

Cultural anthropology, one of the four main fields of anthropology, emerged as a distinct area of study as European explorers revealed the extent of global diversity. Sir Edward Burnett Tylor, one of the founders of anthropology, said culture is "that complex whole which includes knowledge, belief, art, morals, law, custom, and any other capabilities and habits acquired by man as a member of society." It is this emphasis on the whole that distinguishes cultural anthropology from other disciplines.

The Study of Cultures

Cultural anthropologists examine the systems at work in a culture. These systems include kinship, the customs of marriage, mate choice, family relationships; social systems, such as religion or spiritual beliefs and practices; and economic and political systems that shape relationships beyond the family and community. The cultural anthropologist focuses on the effects of these systems at the everyday, local level.

As a field-based science, cultural anthropology has developed methods of ethnography and direct observation. Because controlled experimentation is not possible, cultural anthropologists collect quantitative and qualitative data from repetitive, detailed observations over a period of time. Researchers employ surveys, interviews, and observations of behaviors and events and then compare the results of these methods to ensure accuracy and validity of the findings.

Person of Importance
Sir Edward Burnett Tylor

Sir Edward Burnett Tylor (1832–1917) was an English anthropologist and is considered the founder of cultural anthropology. In his most important work, *Primitive Culture* (1871), Tylor developed the theory that primitive cultures progressively evolved through cultural achievements to modern cultures. His work on the mental functioning of primitive people and on animism— the idea that all living things are produced by a spiritual force and have souls—was a great advance in the understanding of early religions.

Tylor's *Anthropology* (1881) is still regarded as a huge advancement in modern cultural concepts and theories. Due in part to the influence of Charles Darwin, Tylor's work promoted the idea of the unity of all humankind.

Archaeology

Archaeology, the scientific study of prehistoric and historic human societies on the basis of material remains, originally was concerned primarily with documenting and classifying the materials themselves. It evolved into a discipline that sought to explain the meanings of the findings in the context of the societies that produced them.

Fast Fact

Archaeological evidence from the site in Monte Verde in southern Chile shows that it is the earliest known settlement in the Americas. Seaweed from the site, which is fifty miles from the coast, is approximately 14,000 years old. This finding confirms the accepted theory that humans migrated to North America from Asia via the Bering Strait land bridge more than 16,000 years ago.

Archaeology in the United States

THOMAS JEFFERSON (1743–1826), third president of the United States, is credited as conducting the first systematic, organized archaeological investigation in the United States in 1784. He was interested in the source of an earthen mound on his Virginia property, and through careful techniques was able to demonstrate that it was built by the ancestors of Native Americans living in Virginia. Jefferson, as a result, is considered the "father of American archaeology."

Jefferson's research provoked the interest of Americans, and several organizations, including the Smithsonian Institution conducted their own investigations. In 1884, Congress appointed the first federally funded archaeologist at the Bureau of American Ethnology to study U.S. prehistory. Their work resulted in the *Handbook of North American Indians* in the late 1970s.

The need for cooperation between government agencies, academic institutions, and researchers was influential in the creation of archaeology as a discipline. The government, in a preservationist mood, passed the Antiquities Act in 1906 to protect archaeological sites, and began creating national parks and monuments.

The American Anthropological Association was founded in 1902, major universities created anthropological departments at about this time, and anthropological archaeology was formalized as a discipline with the founding of the Society for American Archaeology in 1934. The field became more scientifically based and multidisciplinary as chemists and astronomers contributed their expertise to the process of radiocarbon dating in the 1940s. New archaeologists with new thinking appeared in the 1960s and moved archaeology into the examination of processes and reasons behind cultural complexity and change.

- -

Person of Importance
Willard Libby

Willard Libby (1908–1980) was an American chemist who developed radiocarbon dating. Libby's work recognized that living plants and animals continually absorb carbon, some of which is radioactive carbon-14, which decays over time to a stable nitrogen-14 isotope. When an organism dies, its carbon-14 begins to decrease, decaying at a constant rate. By measuring the amount of radiocarbon remaining, it is possible to determine when the organism died.

Willard's technique is widely used by archeologists, as well as geologists and anthropologists, to date fossils and specimens between 500 and 50,000 years old. Willard received the 1960 Nobel Prize in Chemistry for his work.

Linguistic Anthropology

Linguistic anthropology is the study of language within the framework of anthropology. It recognizes that human cultural evolution was immeasurably facilitated by a means of effective communication, the most important component of which is language. Linguistic anthropologists study how speech was used during that evolution and how it shaped and was shaped by its cultural context.

Linguistic anthropology is a largely American discipline. It grew out of the government sponsored study of North American aboriginal cultures that was carried out under the auspices first of the Smithsonian Institution and then of the Bureau of Ethnology, later renamed the Bureau of American Ethnology (BAE). Documentation of native languages spoken in North America was a large part of the work of anthropologists at this time.

JOHN WESLEY POWELL (1834–1902) founded the BAE and was the primary motivator and organizer of the North American Indian language study. He believed that languages could be used to classify cultures and employed linguists to organize data gathered into language families. While supporting the importance of the role of language in culture, the hugely influential American anthropologist Franz Boas discredited the notion that language was correlated with race.

Boas also refused to view languages of less sophisticated cultures as primitive. **EDWARD SAPIR** (1884–1939), a distinguished American linguist and anthropologist and one of Boas' students, went on to point out that a well-ordered language is a characteristic of every known group of humans. Language is, therefore, the most sophisticated element of human culture and is essential to the study of anthropology.

Physical Anthropology

Physical anthropology, the scientific study of human evolution and biological diversity, traces its roots to the need to explain the variation in humans discovered by European explorers in the seventeenth century. The Bible provided guidance for early naturalists who sought to fit evidence to its teachings.

The first anthropology association, the Anthropological Society of Paris, was founded by French surgeon Paul Broca in 1859. Broca's work largely consisted of comparative studies of skulls, or racial craniometry. As a methodology, the use of anthropometric measurements spread to other institutions. In 1861, Broca discovered the brain's speech center, now referred to as Broca's area, the first anatomical proof that brain functions are localized.

Developments in the Field

In the United States, **ALES HRDLICKA** (1860–1943) became an active advocate in the field and established the *American Journal of*

Physical Anthropology in 1918. Hrdlicka argued that North America was populated by peoples crossing the Bering Straits in recent times, and he rejected the still popular ideas of racial superiority. He was influential in the founding the American Association of Physical Anthropologists.

Physical anthropology began to diversify at the beginning of the twentieth century. Many studies were conducted on nonhuman primates in the field and as a result of primate use in biomedical research. Field research was emphasized in the 1950s and 1960s and produced the well-known work of L.S.B. Leakey, Jane Goodall, and Dian Fossey. Genetics became a new tool for the physical anthropologist at this time.

Cheat Sheet for Social Sciences

The term *psychology* has its origins in the Greek words *psyche* (soul or self) and *logos* (logic and, in turn, science).

The publication of *Principles of Psychology* (1890) by William James (1842–1910) marks the beginning of modern psychology for most psychologists.

Cognitive psychology is a school of psychology that studies human internal mental processes such as problem solving, memory, and language, particularly as they affect learning and behavior.

At the University of Pennsylvania, Lightner Witmer, a student of Wilhelm Wundt, established the world's first psychological clinic in 1896 and originated the field of clinical psychology.

Economics is the study of how people and societies allocate resources to produce goods, how they decide what goods and services will be produced, how goods will be produced, and how they will be distributed for consumption among people in the society.

Economics is typically divided into microeconomics, the operation of markets on an individual level, and macroeconomics, the functioning of complete economic systems.

Physiocrats, the first economists, argued for free markets unencumbered by government intervention and regulation.

The Great Depression, the decade of the 1930s during which unemployment in the United States reached twenty-five percent, is often called a defining moment in U.S. history and in economic thinking.

Because people largely depend on social institutions to provide the norms that regulate human behavior, sociology attempts to determine the role of these institutions, how they are established and dissolve, how they interact with each other, and how they gain or lose influence.

Auguste Comte (1798–1857) was a French philosopher influential in sociology who founded the school of philosophy known as positivism, which maintains that the only knowledge is scientific knowledge.

Karl Marx (1818–1883), the German social philosopher and socialist, felt that the organization and development of society was economically motivated and class struggle the primary factor of social progress.

Political science is a social science concerned with the study of the state, government, and politics.

John Rawls (1921–2002) was an American political philosopher whose Theory of Justice (1971) is considered the major work in twentieth-century political philosophy.

Globalization can be broadly defined as the process of uniting—politically, economically, and culturally—nations and populations into a larger community.

As of January 2009, eight countries possessed nearly 8,400 active and operational nuclear warheads.

Anthropology is a social science that studies the origin, behavior, and cultural development of humans; it considers human biological and evolutionary history as well as social features that distinguish us from other animal species.

Traditionally, anthropology is divided into four fields: cultural anthropology, archaeology, linguistic anthropology, and physical anthropology.

Thomas Jefferson (1743–1826), third president of the United States, is credited as conducting in 1784 the first systematic, organized archaeological investigation in the United States.

Archaeological evidence from the Monte Verde site in southern Chile shows that it is the earliest known settlement in the Americas, some 14,000 years old.

Edward Sapir (1884–1939), a distinguished American linguist and anthropologist, stated that a well-ordered language is a characteristic of every known group of humans. Language is, therefore, the most sophisticated element of human culture and is essential to the study of anthropology.

Chapter Nine

Physical Sciences

The physical sciences encompass the natural sciences of physics, chemistry, astronomy, and the earth sciences. Some of these overlap to form such disciplines as astrophysics, chemical physics, physical chemistry, and geophysics. There is also an overlap between the physical and biological sciences—biophysics, for example—but, strictly speaking, the physical sciences consider only nonliving or inorganic matter.

Physics

Physics is the branch of science that studies matter and energy and the interactions between them. The term "physics" is derived from the Greek word meaning "to grow" and was known as natural philosophy until the late nineteenth century.

Physics is concerned with all natural phenomena from the macroscopic to the submicroscopic levels. The central components of physics are mechanics, which concerns the influence of forces on the motion of particles or bodies; and field theory, which examines and explains the properties of gravitation, electromagnetism, and nuclear force fields. Together, mechanics and field theory are science's attempt to provide an explanation of natural phenomena.

Physics can be divided into classical physics, which considers matter and energy on the normal scale of observation, and modern physics, which is concerned with activities at very large or very small scales.

Classical Physics

Classical physics includes traditional fields that had been fairly well developed prior to the twentieth century. These include mechanics, sound, light, heat, electricity, and magnetism. Mechanics, concerned with forces acting on objects, can be divided into statics, the study of an object at rest; kinematics, the study of motion regardless of its cause; and dynamics, the study of motion and its causes. Hydrostatics, hydrodynamics, aerodynamics, and pneumatics fall under the subcategory of fluid mechanics. Acoustics, the study of sound, and optics, the study of light, are also considered branches of mechanics because they can be explained by the laws of mechanics. Heat, a form of energy, is the province of thermodynamics. Finally, the field theory of electricity and magnetism has been a single discipline since their relationship was recognized during the early nineteenth century.

Modern Physics

Modern physics, which considers the behavior of matter and energy in untypical conditions or on abnormal scales, includes atomic and nuclear physics. Particle physics studies materials below the atomic level and, due to the extreme energy of particle accelerators needed to produce these particles, is also known as high-energy physics. Modern physics has given us the quantum theory and the theory of relativity to explain the nonintuitive nature of the unseen world.

Early Physics

The Greeks were concerned with discovering a universal theory of matter and suggested that such elements as earth, air, fire, or water constituted the smallest, indivisible foundations of the universe. **PYTHAGORAS** (ca. 580–500 B.C.) believed that numbers were the principle of the universe. The natural philosophies conceived by **PLATO** (ca. 428–348 B.C.) and **ARISTOTLE** (384–322 B.C.) in particular were influential in the development of physics and science in general. **ARCHIMEDES** (ca. 285–212 B.C.) studied a wide range of physical issues, and **ARISTARCHUS** (ca. 310–220 B.C.) proposed a

---

sun-centered universe. His theory, as well as earlier atomic theories, were not accepted.

Later, the Romans eagerly adopted Greek ideas and applied their engineering skills to practical concerns, such as the construction of aqueducts and bridges. Following the Empire's fall, few significant advances were seen for a millennium, although the Muslim world was able to preserve existing science and develop a useful numbering system.

The Scientific Revolution

The Renaissance brought renewed interest in ancient literature and scientific ideas, with mechanics and planetary motion receiving the most attention. In 1543, **COPERNICUS** (1473–1543) provided the great breakthrough in astronomy with his sun-centered model (again, not universally embraced) that was supported by the mechanical explanations of **GALILEO** (1564–1642). But the most significant work of this time, as well as one of the most significant scientific works of *any* time, was Sir Isaac Newton's *Principia* (1687). In it, Newton offered the three laws of motion and showed how the principle of universal gravitation could explain both earthly and celestial movements. Newton needed to invent calculus to explain his results, a new branch of mathematics essential to later developments in other areas of physics.

Developments in other fields included the work of **WILLIAM GILBERT** (1544–1603) who explained the earth's magnetism, and **ROBERT BOYLE** (1627–1691) who developed a law of gases. Newton also produced an important work on optics.

Mechanics Comes of Age

During the eighteenth and nineteenth centuries, physicists were refining our understanding of many of the concerns of mechanics. **DANIEL BERNOULLI** (1700–1782), a Swiss mathematician and physicist, established Bernoulli's principle. This states that a fluid produces less pressure as its velocity increases, and it is one of the foundations of aerodynamics.

Until the eighteenth century, heat was believed to be a kind of fluid, called caloric. Several scientists, **JOSEPH BLACK** (1728–1799) and **HENRY CAVENDISH** (1731–1810) among them, made significant contributions toward the development of a more modern theory. Count Rumford (who was born in America in 1753 as Benjamin Thompson, became a spy for the British, and fled the country) recognized that heat is directly related to mechanical energy. This relationship was clarified by the English physicist J.P. Joule in the 1840s and, as a result, had the mechanical unit of work named for him. Lord Kelvin formulated the second law of thermodynamics in the 1850s.

Wave Theory

Great advances in electromagnetism were also made in the eighteenth and nineteenth centuries. **ALESSANDRO VOLTA** (1745–1827) invented the electric battery. **H.C. OERSTED** (1777–1851) discovered that an electric current creates a magnetic field and, in 1831, **MICHAEL FARADAY** (1791–1867) discovered the opposite. These two principles form the foundation of electric motors and generators.

Scottish physicist **JAMES CLERK MAXWELL** (1831–1879) demonstrated that light is an electromagnetic wave and developed the concept of electromagnetic radiation, which was based on Faraday's concepts. The wave theory of light was widely accepted and the study of light, electricity, and magnetism were closely related thereafter.

So many accomplishments had been made by the end of the nineteenth century, so much of the physical world had been deciphered, that there were some who felt that the golden age of physics had passed and there was nothing left to discover. Modern physics was about to be born.

Person of Importance
Lord Kelvin

Lord Kelvin (1824–1907), born in Belfast as William Thomson, was a mathematics prodigy who entered the University of Glasgow at age ten and published papers by age seventeen. He was professor of natural philosophy at the university for fifty-three years. During his career he suggested the method that led to the invention of refrigeration, devised the absolute temperature scale named for him, invented the device that allowed telegraph signals to be sent across the Atlantic Ocean, and invented a marine compass.

Lord Kelvin published more that 600 scientific papers and won sixty-nine patents during his lifetime. He was unable to correctly estimate the earth's age, however; his last best guess pegged it at 24 million years.

Modern Physics

Modern physics, the study of the extremes, the very large and the very small, started out with big ideas about small things. Wilhelm Roentgen discovered X-rays in 1895. A.H. Becquerel, working with Marie and Pierre Curie, discovered radioactivity the following year, and J.J. Thomson identified the electron the next year. Meanwhile, in the United States physicist A.A. Michelson and chemist E.W. Morley were experimenting (with funds provided by Alexander Graham Bell) on the speed of light through the "ether." They discovered that the ether, a medium that supposedly was needed by light in order to travel through space, and was defended by Newton and accepted by all physicists, did not exist.

Quantum Mechanics

In 1900, German theoretical physicist **MAX PLANCK** (1858–1947) proposed the quantum theory. Planck stated that energy is not a continuous force but rather is emitted and absorbed in discrete packets he called "quanta." These packets had a definite size, what is now called Planck's constant. He received the Nobel Prize in physics in 1918 for his work. His theory overturned classical physics and opened the door to the quantum age.

Relativity

In 1905, a young Swiss patent office clerk named **ALBERT EINSTEIN** (1879–1955) published three papers, one of which was "On the Electrodynamics of Moving Bodies," in which he established his special theory of relativity. At its core, the theory states that matter and

---

energy are equivalent and that a body with mass could not travel faster than the speed of light, which was constant. It explained how uranium could throw off great amounts of energy without deteriorating, and how stars could burn for billions of years without using up their fuel.

In 1917 Einstein published his masterwork, the general theory of relativity. This theory, to oversimplify, says that space and time are not absolute but relative to the observer and the thing being observed. Time is variable; it has shape and is bound up with the three dimensions of space in the fabric of spacetime. What's more, the warping of spacetime produces gravity.

- - - - - - - -- - -- -- -- --

Person of Importance
Albert Einstein

Born in Ulm, Germany in 1879, Albert Einstein had a famously undistinguished childhood and education. He became a Swiss citizen in 1901 and took a job in the Swiss Patent Office in Berne, which allowed him time to think about physics. The 1905 publication of his paper showing that light has properties of both waves and particles won him a Nobel Prize in 1921. That same year he also proved the existence of molecules and gave the world the special theory of relativity. But it was the 1917 publication of his general theory of relativity that was called "the highest intellectual achievement of humanity."

Repeatable Quotable

Put your hand on a stove for a minute and it seems like an hour. Sit with that special girl for an hour and it seems like a minute. That's relativity.
—*Albert Einstein*

Person of Importance
John Bardeen

John Bardeen (1908–1991) was an American physicist and electrical engineer who won the 1956 Nobel Prize in physics for inventing the transistor with William Shockley and Walter Brattain. The transistor has made possible nearly every modern electronic device. In 1972, he again shared the Nobel Prize in physics for his work on a theory of superconductivity. He is the only person to have won the Nobel Prize in physics twice.

Chemistry

Chemistry is the branch of science that studies the properties, composition, and structure of elements and compounds, the changes they undergo, and the energy that is absorbed or released as they combine or react under certain conditions. Chemistry is concerned with material at the atomic level of all matter, and with all living things.

Divisions of Chemistry

Chemistry can be divided into organic and inorganic branches. Originally organic chemistry was concerned with compounds of biological origin, which had quite different properties from those of mineral origin. That distinction is no longer valid; today, organic chemistry is the study of carbon compounds and inorganic chemistry studies chemical elements and noncarbon compounds.

Chemistry can also be classified as physical or analytical. Physical chemistry involves the physical properties of materials—their magnetic and electrical behavior and how they interact with electromagnetic fields, for example. Subdivisions of physical chemistry include thermochemistry, the study of changes in energy and entropy during chemical reactions; electrochemistry, which concerns the relationship between electricity and chemical reactions; and chemical kinetics, which analyzes the details of chemical reactions. Analytical chemistry consists of a set of laboratory techniques that permit the exact determination of the composition of a given material.

Early Chemistry

The earliest examples of the practice of chemistry come from ancient metallurgy. A copper axe dating from 5500 B.C. was found in the area of Serbia, and other signs of metallurgy from the third millennium B.C. have been discovered in Portugal, Spain, and the United Kingdom. People in Egypt and Mesopotamia were making pottery and dyes as early as 3500 B.C., although we have no evidence that the practitioners of these crafts had an understanding of chemical processes.

The Greeks

Many Greek philosophers were concerned with the chemical concepts of element and compound during the period from 500 to 300 B.C. **DEMOCRITUS** (ca. 460–370 B.C.) posited that all matter was composed of atoms—tiny, indivisible, and indestructible particles that were in constant motion. **ARISTOTLE** (384–322 B.C.) believed that all matter was made of fire, air, earth, and water and had just four properties: hot, cold, dry, and wet.

Alchemy

The practice of alchemy arose about this time and was practiced widely, from China and India to Egypt and Greece, with Alexandria generally considered the early center of the practice. Alchemists believed that, under the right astrological or magical conditions, a base metal, usually lead, could be transformed to gold. The Arabs practiced alchemy for several centuries, and it reached Europe in the twelfth century. While many medieval alchemists earned a dishonorable reputation, they made some useful discoveries, such as alcohol and mineral acids, and their experimental methods presaged chemistry. **PARACELSUS** (1493–1541), a German-born Swiss physician and alchemist, straddled the fields of alchemy and modern chemistry and was influential in the development of pharmacology. It was not until the nineteenth century that the methods of alchemists were finally discredited.

Modern Chemistry

Chemistry as a science is usually considered to have formally begun with the publication of Robert Boyle's *The Sceptical Chymist* in 1661. **BOYLE** (1627–1691), an Anglo-Irish scientist with a wide range of interests, contributed to the laws of gases but is often called the founder of modern chemistry for his development of the modern concepts of element and compound, distinguishing between acids and bases, and incorporating the scientific method in his experiments.

Other "Oxford Chemists" include **ROBERT HOOKE** (1635–1703), another polymath, who provided the first rational explanation of combustion as involving air, and **JOHN MAYOW** (1641–1679) who experimented with animal respiration. During this period, and through the eighteenth century, scientists searched for and claimed to have found miraculous and nonexistent substances, including élan vital, the force that created life.

The eighteenth century did see many real advances in chemistry, however. **JOSEPH PRIESTLEY** (1733–1804), English theologian and physical scientist, discovered ten gases including nitrogen and oxygen. **HENRY CAVENDISH** (1731–1810), English physicist and chemist, discovered hydrogen and the fact that air and water are compositions. The French chemist **ANTOINE LAVOISIER** (1743–1794) and his wife engaged in extensive experiments, came up with the names for oxygen and hydrogen, discovered that a rusting object gains weight rather than losing it as everyone had supposed, and brought order and clarity to the field.

Nineteenth-Century Advances

The major advances in nineteenth-century chemistry were made by John Dalton and Humphry Davy. **JOHN DALTON** (1766–1844) was a British chemist and physicist best known for his atomic theory, published in his *New System of Chemical Philosophy* (1803), that revived the ancient Greek concept that all matter consists of tiny particles. Here he stated that each element is composed of atoms, and he went on to calculate their weights. The British chemist **HUMPHRY DAVY**

(1778–1829) used electrolysis to isolate new elements, including potassium, sodium, magnesium, calcium, and aluminum.

Fast Fact

The Swiss chemist Carl W. Scheele (1742–1786) discovered, using rather primitive equipment, eight elements, including chlorine, fluorine, and oxygen. His work was either overlooked or delayed, and so he did not receive credit for any of these discoveries. Scheele had the unfortunate habit of tasting the materials with which he worked and was found dead at his workbench at age forty-three, victim of one of his toxic chemicals.

The Chemical Society of London was founded in 1841 and began publishing a journal in 1848. Until this time, chemists used a number of different means to identify and represent elements. Common nomenclature was developed by the Swedish chemist **J.J. BERZELIUS** (1779–1848), and the Russian chemist **DMITRI MENDELEYEV** (1834–1907) invented the periodic table, both developments much appreciated by the chemist community.

As the nineteenth century was drawing to a close, Henri Becquerel, working with Pierre and Marie Curie, discovered radioactivity and the elements polonium and radium.

- - - - - - - - -- --- ----- ------------------------------ ----

Person of Importance
Marie Curie

Marie Curie (1867–1934) was a Polish-French chemist and physicist who pioneered work with radioactivity and discovered the elements polonium and radium. She directed the first studies into the treatment of cancers with radioactive isotopes.

Curie was the first woman professor at the Sorbonne. She was also the first woman to win a Nobel Prize (the 1903 prize in physics was shared with Becquerel and her husband) and with her 1911 Nobel Prize in chemistry, the only person to win in physics and chemistry.

Chemistry in the United States

The earliest known formal chemistry instruction was given at the medical school of the College of Philadelphia prior to 1769. The first American teacher of chemistry, and author of the first American chemistry textbook, was **BENJAMIN RUSH** (1745–1813), a physician who was also known for advocating the treatment of disease by bloodletting. The first American chemical journal, *Transactions*, was published in 1813 by the Chemical Society of Philadelphia.

J. WILLARD GIBBS (1839–1903) was one of the earliest great, although little known, American chemists. He taught at Yale from 1871 until his death and, in 1875–1878, produced a series of papers, *Equilibrium of Heterogeneous Substances*, that explained the thermodynamic principles of many substances. These papers showed that heat and energy was present at the atomic level of chemical reactions.

LINUS PAULING (1901–1994), an American chemist, was among the first to apply quantum mechanics to the study of molecular structures. His work provided most of what is known about chemical bonds and their properties.

GLENN T. SEABORG (1912–1999), an American nuclear chemist, was another pioneer in chemistry at the atomic level. Working at the University of California, Seaborg discovered plutonium in 1941 and eight more elements in 1944. He joined the Manhattan Project to develop the atomic bomb in 1942 and shared the 1951 Nobel Prize in chemistry.

Person of Importance
Linus Pauling

Linus Pauling (1901–1994) was an American chemist who studied quantum mechanics in Europe with pioneers Niels Bohr and Arnold Sommerfeld and then applied quantum theory to the analysis of chemical bonds. Using electron diffraction techniques, Pauling and his colleagues determined the molecular structure of more than 225 substances.

His book, *The Nature of the Chemical Bond* (1939), became one of the century's most influential chemistry texts, and remains the classic in the field. He won the 1954 Nobel Prize in chemistry, and for his work in disarmament won the Nobel Peace Prize in 1962.

Industrial Chemistry

With the growth of corporations in the early twentieth century and the supply of certain products made unstable by wars and political tensions, industrial chemical research grew rapidly. Industrial concerns recruited research chemists from academic labs to develop new and replacement products.

The U.S. chemical industry had significant native sources of important mineral deposits, including phosphate rock for fertilizers; salt; sulfur for insecticides, pharmaceuticals and the vulcanization of rubber; and soda ash for the manufacture of glass, ceramics, detergents, and soap. The United States also had major sources of oil, natural gas, and coal. By 1914, the U.S. chemical industry was 40 percent larger than was Germany's, with fertilizer comprising two-fifths of all chemical sales.

The availability of large quantities of power fueled the growth of the electrochemical industry, particularly the manufacture of aluminum. Innovations in chemical technology were used to produce other products such as carborundum.

Many industrial products produced from coal before World War II, like phenol, acetylene, methanol, and formaldehyde, were being made by U.S. industry less expensively and in larger quantities from petroleum and natural gas. This period between the world wars saw U.S. petroleum-based chemical production grow from 21 million pounds in 1921 to more than 3 billion pounds in 1939. Production of fuels was a primary area of concentration but, by the early 1930s, Union Carbide was manufacturing as many as fifty petrochemical derivatives.

World War II was a major catalyst for growth in the U.S. chemical industry. Synthetic rubber tires, nylon, and plastics were in great demand, and in the postwar period new uses were found for synthetic materials. Polyethylene, originally used as a cable shield, was developed for use in food and garbage bags, packaging films, and containers. Production grew from five million pounds in 1945 to 14.5 billion pounds in 2000. The production of polyvinyl chloride and polystyrene, also used in packaging, experienced similar gains.

In 2000, production of the top 100 chemicals in the United States totaled 502 million tons according to the American Chemical Council. Today, the U.S. chemical industry realizes sales of $450 billion annually.

Astronomy

Astronomy is the scientific study of the universe and the objects it contains. Astronomers consider the origin, evolution, composition, orientation, and motion of all celestial bodies and phenomena. It is the oldest of the sciences, having existed since the beginning of recorded civilization.

A Multidisciplinary Science

Because much of modern astronomy relies on the laws and methods of physics, astronomy and astrophysics are often used interchangeably. However, techniques from scientific disciplines such as chemistry, geology, and biology are also used in astronomy, giving rise to such concentrations as astrochemistry, planetary science, and astrobiology. Methods of analysis employed in geology have been used for the close-up observations of planets and their satellites as well as of asteroids and comets. The connection between geology and astronomy may grow closer due to our desire to understand the nature of planets discovered near distant stars.

Techniques taken from chemistry are used to analyze materials detected in interstellar clouds. And the astronomical search for life outside our solar system, as well as NASA's investigation of Mars for evidence of life, will require the cooperation of planetary science and astrochemistry.

Astronomy has always been a cutting-edge science, seeking and employing new technologies and using them to their utmost. Because they are 100 times more sensitive than photographic film, light-sensitive silicon chips known as charge-coupled devices now perform the work of astronomical imagery. Fiber optics permit the simultaneous capture of hundreds of images from a telescope's field of view. Spectrographs analyze electromagnetic radiation from distant objects. And active optics, rapidly changing a mirror's shape to compensate for blurring caused by atmospheric interference, promises to tame the twinkling of stars.

Ancient Astronomy

As the oldest of the physical sciences, astronomy has roots in the cultures of many early civilizations. The regularity of celestial motions was known during most of history for the purpose of forecasting seasons or events. Astronomy served the practical function of providing a basis for calendars, with units for day, month, and year defined by astronomical observations.

The earliest knowledge of celestial bodies is probably the Venus tables of the Babylonians from the seventeenth century B.C. Most of their surviving records, clay tablets that serve as astronomical calendars, were created between 650 and 50 B.C. The Babylonians divided the sky into zones and the Latin names for signs of the zodiac are translations from Babylonian.

The ancient Chinese had an active and productive interest in astronomy. They had a working calendar dating to the thirteenth century B.C. and, in 350 B.C., produced a star catalog with some 800 entries. They are also known for their observation and documentation of comets and supernovas.

Their limited understanding of geometry restricted the ancient Egyptians' knowledge of astronomy. A catalogue created by Amenhope ca. 1100 B.C. listed just five constellations, and the Egyptians also recognized thirty-six groups of stars, or decans, which were used on star clocks found on wooded coffin lids dating to the early Middle Kingdom (ca. 2055–1650 B.C.)

The Greeks

The Greeks, too, were concerned with using the regularity of celestial events as a guide for planting and harvesting. It is clear that the movement of constellations was observed and understood from about 700 B.C. Thales introduced the concepts of geometry into astronomy around 600 B.C. Around 500 B.C., Pythagoras recognized that the earth is a sphere and imagined all known celestial bodies as inhabiting their own moving spheres. But because much of Greek thought was aimed at finding a single, perfect theory, advances were somewhat delayed.

ARISTARCHUS (ca. 310–230 B.C.) used a more scientific approach to determine the sizes of the moon and sun and their distance from the earth. He advocated a sun-centered cosmos.

HIPPARCHUS (190–120 B.C.), one of the greatest of ancient astronomers, made important contributions to the understanding of celestial movements through his use of trigonometry and careful observations.

PTOLEMY (A.D. 85–165) summarized astronomical knowledge in his thirteen-volume work, the *Almagest*, that predicted motions of the planets with great accuracy. Although it posited an Earth-centered cosmology and claimed that planets move in perfect circles, it served as the authority for the next fourteen centuries.

Renaissance Astronomy

The Roman Empire contributed virtually nothing to the science of astronomy, and following its fall, the science, and indeed all sciences, lay dormant for a millennium. Fortunately, the Muslim world was actively translating Greek and Latin texts, and it was through Arabic translations that the Greek astronomical thinking reached Europe.

In 1543, the polish astronomer **NICOLAUS COPERNICUS** (1473–1543) published his *De revolutionibus orbium coelestium* (*On the Revolutions of the Celestial Spheres*). His system retained the Greek belief that the planets move in perfect circles, but showed the sun rather than the earth as the center of our solar system. By separating the movement of the planets from the stars, Copernicus also implied a much larger universe than before.

In 1576, Danish astronomer **TYCHO BRAHE** (1546–1601) established an observatory on the Danish island of Hveen. Without the aid of a telescope, he and his assistants made the most accurate and detailed astronomical observations possible over a period of twenty years, charting the position of 777 stars. When he died, his records passed to his pupil and assistant, **JOHANNES KEPLER** (1571–1630), who used Brahe's records to develop his principles of planetary motion. The following are referred to as Kepler's laws: the orbits of planets about the sun are ellipses, planets move faster as they near the sun, and a simple mathematical formula related the planets' orbital period to their distance from the sun.

A New Tool

GALILEO GALILEI (1564–1642), Italian scientist, was the first astronomer to make use of a telescope for observations, discovering the four largest moons of Jupiter and that the Milky Way was composed of stars. In *The Sidereal Messenger* (1610), he revealed that there were craters on the moon and blemishes on the sun, imperfections in the universe not accepted by the church. Tried and found guilty of heresy by the Inquisition, he was forced to recant.

ISAAC NEWTON (1642–1727) added his genius to astronomy, as he had to so many other scientific disciplines, by incorporating the laws of physics. His laws of motion and theory of gravitation provided a mathematical basis for Kepler's observations, and his work represented the pinnacle of astronomical thought until well into the nineteenth century.

In 1781, the German-born English astronomer **WILLIAM HER-SCHEL** (1738–1822), using telescopes of his own design and construction, discovered the planet Uranus by accident. By analyzing the orbit of Uranus, both the English astronomer John Couch

Adams and the French astronomer Urbain Leverrier independently predicted the existence of Neptune. In 1801, Giuseppe Piazzi discovered Ceres, the first asteroid (a small body orbiting the sun), and F.W. Bessel measured the distance to a star for the first time in 1838.

- - - - - - - - - --- ------ ---------------------------------- ----

Person of Importance
Edmond Halley

Edmond Halley (1656–1742), an English mathematician and astronomer, was a man of many talents and interests. During his lifetime, he was a sea captain, a cartographer, a professor of geometry at the University of Oxford, an astronomer royal, and the inventor of the deep-sea diving bell. In 1686, he produced the first meteorological charts, showing prevailing winds on the oceans. He described the parabolic orbits of twenty-four comets and noted, correctly, that the comets seen in 1456, 1531, 1607, and 1682 were one in the same and would return in 1758. His greatest contribution to science and human knowledge, however, was his involvement in Isaac Newton's *Principia*. Halley is said to have persuaded Newton to create it, edited the manuscript, and personally paid for its publication.

Modern Astronomy

The second half of the nineteenth century was a period of rapid development in astronomy. In the United States, the desire for better telescopes and the funds to pay for them prompted the development of observatories from the Naval Observatory in Washington, D.C., to the Lick Observatory of the University of California, to the forty-inch Yerkes instrument at the University of Chicago. The introduction of photographic and spectroscopic techniques during this period revolutionized astronomy and encouraged the development of new observatories with telescopes that permitted photography and the analysis of starlight.

As these new techniques were introduced, astronomers became more interested in the properties and structures of stars and objects than their location, giving rise to the field of astrophysics. **GEORGE ELLERY HALE** (1868–1938) founded the *Astrophysical Journal* in 1895 and the American Astronomical and Astrophysical Society in 1899. With funds from the Carnegie Institution of Washington, Hale built the Mount Wilson Observatory in Los Angeles in 1904. A 60-inch telescope was constructed there in 1908 and in 1919 a 100-inch telescope was built. These were the largest telescopes in the world and were used by Edwin Hubble for his observations that spiral nebulae are independent galaxies beyond our own and that the universe is expanding.

Fast Fact

American astronomer Edwin Hubble (1889–1953) is credited for discovering that the universe is expanding in 1927, although Vesto Slipher, an astronomer at the Lowell Observatory in Arizona actually made the observation first.

In 1948, the giant 200-inch Hale telescope, the largest in the world for the next forty-four years, was completed at Palomar

Observatory in San Diego County, California. But astronomy had taken a turn by this point: in 1931, American physicist **KARL JANSKY** (1905–1950) discovered that celestial bodies emitted radio signals, and radio astronomy was born. In the 1960s these instruments—at first, no one saw an application for them—would enable astronomers to date the universe from its birth in the big bang about 14 billion years ago.

With the launch of Sputnik in 1957, the world "discovered" space. The National Science Foundation built the Kitt Peak National Observatory, the largest collection of super telescopes in the Northern Hemisphere. The National Aeronautics and Space Administration (NASA) was created and began a program of manned space flight. NASA launched the Hubble Space Telescope in 1990 that, among other discoveries, was used to confirm that the universe is not only expanding but its expansion is accelerating due to a force called "dark energy."

Fast Fact

In 2006, the International Astronomical Union voted on a new definition of "planet," and in doing so, demoted Pluto to the status of dwarf planet. Pluto, which was discovered and classified as a planet in 1930, has a mean distance from the sun of 3.67 billion miles and a period of revolution of 248 years. It is classified as a dwarf planet because it does not clear its orbital path. The American Dialect Society selected "plutoed," meaning demoted or devalued, as its 2006 word of the year.

Astronomical Terms

Following are definitions of some selected astronomical terms:

Big bang
The rapid expansion of the universe from a state of high temperature and density some 14 billion years ago. The theory is based upon Einstein's general theory of relativity describing the gravitational relationship of all matter, and the cosmological principle that the universe is homogeneous.

Black hole
A cosmic object with a gravitational field so intense that nothing, not even light, can escape. It can be created by the death and collapse of a massive star. The term was coined by American theoretical physicist John Wheeler in 1967.

Cepheid variable
A type of star whose cycle time of variation matches its luminosity, making it useful in measuring interstellar distances. The relationship and its utility was discovered in 1912 by Henrietta Leavitt of Harvard Observatory.

Dark energy
A repulsive force opposing gravity that causes the expansion of the universe to accelerate. Its nature is not understood, but is theorized to constitute about 70 percent of the universe. Einstein originally introduced the force as part of his general

---

theory of relativity, and then retracted the concept believing he had made a mistake. It was confirmed in 1998.

Dark matter
Material that cannot be observed, except by its effect in bending light rays from distant stars, but is theorized to constitute nearly 30 percent of the universe. The existence of dark matter would explain the gravitational deviations observed in the distributions of galaxies.

Dwarf star
A star, like our sun, that fuses helium into hydrogen in a thermonuclear reaction. A dwarf star is in a certain stage of evolution.

Gamma-ray astronomy
The study of astronomical objects that emit gamma rays rather than visible light. Observations must be made from high-altitude balloons or spacecraft: military satellites designed to detect clandestine nuclear testing during the 1960s discovered the first space sources of gamma rays.

General theory of relativity
The theory that space and time are not absolute but relative to the observer and the thing being observed. Time and space are part of a single spacetime and matter and energy are equivalent, or $E = mc^2$.

Hubble constant
A value used in calculating the expansion rate of the universe and its age. The current value has an error factor of ±10 percent.

Infrared astronomy
The study of astronomical objects that emit infrared radiation. Infrared astronomy has permitted studies of the core of the Milky Way, whose dust obscures conventional telescopes.

Interstellar matter
The dust and gaseous material between stars. Interstellar matter is the source of new stars and is important to an understanding of the processes leading to the formation of the universe.

Pulsar
A class of cosmic object that emits short intense bursts of radio waves, X-rays, gamma radiation, or visible light. A pulsar is believed to be a rapidly spinning neutron star, the extremely dense, collapsed remains of a star. First discovered in 1967, more than 550 pulsars have since been detected.

Quantum theory
The theory that energy is emitted and absorbed in packets called quanta and can behave in certain situations as if they were particles. The theory was proposed by Max Planck in 1900 to explain the behavior of radiation.

Quasar
A class of cosmic object that is extremely distant, and whose light and radiation output is several thousand times that of our entire galaxy. They are typically observed at distances of 10 billion light years and their redshifts suggest they are moving away at speeds approaching the speed of light.

Radio astronomy
The study of celestial objects emitting electromagnetic radiation. Karl Jansky discovered radio emission from space in 1931.

Redshift
An observed shift in the light spectrum toward longer wavelengths emitted by distant galaxies. Redshift demonstrates that the universe is expanding.

Search for Extraterrestrial intelligence (SETI)
The ongoing effort to detect intelligent extraterrestrial life by analyzing radio signals. Currently the project is privately funded.

Special theory of relativity
The theory that the speed of light is the same in all reference frames, irrespective of the motion of the observer or the observed. Albert Einstein developed this theory in 1905.

Spectroscopy
The analysis of radiant energy emitted (in astronomy) by celestial objects to determine such qualities as chemical

composition, temperature, density, pressure, and the presence of magnetic or electric fields.

Stellar wobble

The variation in position of a star due to the gravitational effect of another body orbiting it. It can be detected in the visible spectrum or as redshift in the star's spectrum. Stellar wobble is an important tool in detecting distant planets and black holes.

Supernova

An exploding star with a temporary brightening and energy output many millions of times above its normal level. Supernovas are responsible for producing all elements heavier than iron. A supernova was described by Chinese astronomers in 1054.

Ultraviolet astronomy

The study of astronomical objects that emit ultraviolet (UV) radiation. Ultraviolet astronomy has been responsible for revealing much information about the chemical compositions and processes of interstellar matter. The Hubble carries a UV telescope.

X-ray astronomy

The study of astronomical objects that emit radiation at X-ray wavelengths. The observation of X-rays has produced information on the nature and quantity of black holes, the evolution of galaxies, and the composition of the remains of supernovas.

Earth Sciences

The earth sciences are physical sciences that study the nature, origin, evolution, and behavior of the earth and its parts. Earth sciences include geology, oceanography, and meteorology as well as their subdisciplines and variations involving techniques from other sciences.

The earth scientist attempts to observe, catalogue, and classify earth's features and develop theories or explanations for their development. The earth scientist is trained to understand natural processes of the earth and to apply that knowledge in ways that are environmentally sound. Today, scholars in the field recognize societal problems surrounding the sustainable use of energy and water resources, risks posed by natural hazards, and the consequences of human activity on the environment.

In addition to traditional courses of study in the earth sciences, academic programs are now offered in earth systems. This interdisciplinary program recognizes the complexity of environmental problems and combines fundamental knowledge in biology, calculus, chemistry, geology, physics, economics, statistics, and policy.

Geology

Geology, one of the earth sciences, is the scientific study of the composition, structure, physical properties, and history of the earth. It is commonly divided into the two major categories of physical and historical geology.

Physical geology includes the subdisciplines of:

Mineralogy
The study of minerals

Petrology
The study of rocks

Structural geology
The study of the forces that deform the earth's rocks

Geomorphology
The study of the origin and modification of landforms

Geochemistry
The study of the chemical composition and earth materials

Geophysics
The physics-based study of rock materials in response to stress

Sedimentology
The study of erosion and deposition of earth materials

Economic geology
The study of exploration and recovery of natural resources

Astrogeology
The study of celestial objects using geological techniques

Historical geology considers the earth's historical development. Its subdisciplines include:

Paleontology
The study of past life forms

Stratigraphy
The study of rock layers and their relationships

Paleogeography
The study of ancient land masses

Geologic mapping
The use of geologic information with existing topographic maps

History of Geology

The earliest knowledge of geology is exemplified by the mining of flint for tools in several areas of Europe between 5000 and 2500 B.C. In the Middle East, people started to mine minerals such as copper as early as 4000 B.C. and iron ore about 1300 B.C.

The ancient Greeks recognized natural processes at work; Aristotle, for example, noted erosion and deposition of material. ERATOSTHENES (ca. 276–194 B.C.), knowing the earth to be a sphere, made quite accurate measurements of its circumference. These were essentially the last advances made in the understanding of the earth for 1,500 years.

Not until the time of **LEONARDO DA VINCI** (1452–151᠌ did geologic ideas resurface. He recognized what fossils were and speculated on erosion of land by the action of rivers. The German **AGRICOLA** (1494–1556) made a systematic study of ore deposits, advancing significantly the knowledge of minerals. **NICHOLAS STENO** (1638–1686), a Dane, was one of the first to study rocks from a broad geological point of view and made important observations about sedimentation.

Person of Importance
Sir Charles Lyell

Sir Charles Lyell (1797–1875) was a Scottish geologist and principal advocate of uniformitarianism, the theory that all geologic events may be explained as the result of processes that have operated with uniformity over long periods of time. The theory gave rise to the phrase, "the present is key to the past" and is a foundational basis of the science of geology.

Lyell's three-volume *Principles of Geology* (1830) went through twelve editions during his lifetime and had a significant influence on Charles Darwin.

During the eighteenth century, many naturalists recorded their geological observations. One of these was James Hutton, a Scottish gentleman without any geological training, who published *Theory of the Earth* (1795) in which he theorized that volcanic activity was causing upheaval of the earth's crust over long periods of time. This theory was adopted and advanced by future geologists such as Sir

Charles Lyell. Another British geologist, **WILLIAM SMITH** (1769–1839), founded the science of stratigraphy and introduced the technique of using fossils for the dating of layers.

Modern Geology

The nineteenth century was a time of significant growth in geology. The Geological Society was established in London in 1807 with thirteen members and numbered 745 by 1830. And in the United States, Sir Charles Lyell would deliver geology lectures to sellout audiences of 3,000, a testament to the popularity of the science.

With the discovery of strata in rocks, there was a great deal of effort made by many geologists, and a great amount of heated controversy as a result, to name and organize the periods of earth's history. By the middle of the century, the basic geological time periods were established, although it was not understood yet what scale these periods represented.

During the twentieth century, the theory of plate tectonics was finally accepted, and advances in physics and chemistry would change the practice of geology. Atomic structure and the properties of radioactivity were discovered and put to use in geologic research.

Oceanography

Oceanography is an earth science that studies the physical and chemical properties, origin and geology, and biology of the world's oceans. Understanding and protecting the ocean is critical for life on earth; the oceans support nearly 50 percent of all species on earth and provide 20 percent of the animal protein and five percent of the total protein in the human diet.

The first organized investigation of the oceans was the *Challenger* expedition of 1872 which, after three and a half years covering 70,000 nautical miles of sea, netted more than 4,700 new species of marine life and created the term *oceanography* in the process. The International Council for the Exploration of the Sea, the first international organization dedicated to marine research, was created in 1901, but until the sinking of the *Titanic* (1912) and depredations on shipping during World War I, public interest in the oceans was limited to the fisheries industry.

Fast Fact

Submarine warfare during World War II provided a huge impetus to oceanographic research, as the U.S. government mapped the sea floors and set up hydrophone systems to monitor the movement of Soviet submarines. This led to the discovery of mid-ocean mountain ranges and canyons; undeniable evidence of seafloor spreading confirmed the theory of plate tectonics.

In the 1970s, oceanographers discovered deep-sea vents producing huge amounts of energy and hosting an astonishing variety of life never seen before. New appreciation for the ocean's role in the earth's weather, and the fact that 95 percent of the ocean remains unexplored, will continue to make oceanography a critical science for decades to come.

A seamount is "any geographically isolated topographic feature on the seafloor taller than 100 meters, including ones whose summit regions may temporarily emerge above sea level. . . ." (from *Oceanography* March 2010, The Oceanography Society). More than ninety-nine percent of all seamounts remain unexplored, but studies of a few—there may be as many as 100,000—show that they are literally at the core of the processes that build and alter the earth's surface. Volcanically active seamounts are the source of significant chemical change in seawater, can alter ocean currents, and are some of the richest biological hotspots in the ocean.

Meteorology

Meteorology is an earth science that studies the earth's atmosphere and its phenomena. Originally, meteorology and climatology developed from different roots, but are now considered a single atmospheric science.

Fast Fact

Approximately one-third of the gross domestic product of the United States comes from weather- and climate-sensitive industries.

The oldest known thorough discussion of meteorological subjects is Aristotle's *Meteorologica* (ca. 340 B.C.), which served as the authority for some 2,000 years. The first instruments to measure conditions were developed during the scientific revolution and include Leonardo da Vinci's wind vane (1500), Galileo's thermometer (c.1593), and Torricelli's mercury barometer (1643).

In the early twentieth century, theories of modern weather analysis were introduced and, by the late 1940s, high-speed electronic computers were used for weather forecasting. Weather satellites launched in the 1960s have improved the accuracy of forecasting and serve as early warning and detection systems for hurricanes and tropical cyclones.

Cheat Sheet for Physical Sciences

The Greek astronomer Aristarchus (ca. 270 B.C.) proposed the first theory of a sun-centered universe and attempted to measure the distances between the sun, moon, and earth.

Sir Isaac Newton's *Principia* (1687) presented the three laws of motion and showed how the principle of universal gravitation could explain both earthly and celestial movements.

In 1900, Max Planck proposed the quantum theory, stating that energy is not a continuous force but is emitted and absorbed in discrete packets called "quanta."

Einstein published his special theory of relativity in 1905, explaining that mass and energy are related by the equation $E = mc^2$.

Einstein published his masterwork, the general theory of relativity (1917), in which he describes the relationship between time and space.

A copper axe dating from 5500 B.C. was found in the area of Serbia.

Democritus (ca. 400 B.C.) developed the theory that all matter is composed of atoms, tiny, indivisible, and indestructible particles that are in constant motion.

Henri Becquerel, working with Pierre and Marie Curie, discovered radioactivity and the elements polonium and radium in 1901.

Marie Curie is the first woman to win a Nobel Prize and the only person to win in physics and chemistry.

In 2000, production of the top 100 chemicals in the United States totaled 502 million tons.

The earliest knowledge of celestial bodies is the Venus tables of the Babylonians from the seventeenth century B.C.

The Chinese had a working calendar dating to the thirteenth century B.C.

Galileo Galilei was the first astronomer to make use of a telescope and discovered that the Milky Way was composed of stars.

American astronomer Edwin Hubble is credited for discovering that the universe is expanding in 1927.

Dark energy makes up seventy percent of the universe and is responsible for its accelerating rate of expansion.

In the Middle East, people started to mine minerals such as copper as early as 4000 B.C. and iron ore about 1300 B.C.

The theory of plate tectonics was accepted by most geologists in the 1960s.

Sir Charles Lyell published *Principles of Geology* (1830), in which he stated that geologic phenomena were the result of natural forces occurring over long time periods.

In the 1970s, oceanographers discovered deep-sea vents producing huge amounts of energy and hosting an astonishing variety of life never seen before.

Aristotle's *Meteorologica* (ca. 340 B.C.) served as the authority on meteorology for some 2,000 years.

Chapter Ten

Mathematics

Mathematics is the science of structure, order, and relation, and concerns number, quantity, shape, and space. Mathematics involves quantitative calculation and logical reasoning. Its origins stem from the practical needs of commerce, agriculture, and industry, but since the seventeenth century it has been essential to the practice of physical sciences and technology. The entries in this chapter are arranged alphabetically by subject or name.

Algebra

Algebra is a branch of mathematics that uses symbols to represent quantities and involves methods for solving equations that contain unknowns. "Classical algebra," or the process of solving equations, has developed over a period of 4,000 years, and "abstract algebra," which is the study of groups, rings, and fields, appeared in the last 200 years.

Both the Babylonians and Egyptians were familiar with the concept of algebra, if not the rules and methods. They realized that mathematics, in addition to its practical uses in counting and measuring, could be used to solve problems and compute unknown values. The Egyptian *Ahmes Papyrus*, dating from 1650 B.C., contains nearly 100 mathematical problems demonstrating examples of rudimentary algebraic calculations.

Person of Importance
Al-Khwarizmi

Al-Khwarizmi (ca. 780–850) was an Islamic mathematician from Baghdad who wrote *The Compendious Book on Calculation by Completion and Balancing,* which was translated into Latin in the twelfth century. The work contains rules and demonstrates solutions for linear and quadratic equations. We get our word *algebra* from its title. Another of his works introduced Hindu-Arabic numerals, and was one of the first to use zero as a place holder in positional notation.

Greek Influence and Later

The practice of writing mathematical problems using words and diagrams was changed by the Greeks when Diophantus, working in the third century A.D., published his *Arithmetica*. This collection of mathematical problems contained symbols for unknown values. Islamic scholars got into the act in medieval times and al-Khwarizmi (al-Khowarizmi) gave the first book on algebra us in 825 A.D., as well as the word *algebra*. Still unsolved was how to deal with negative numbers.

In 1202, Fibonacci published his book and demonstrated the Hindu-Arabic numbering system to Europe. Then, in the seventeenth century, Descartes introduced an efficient system for representing real numbers using letters near the beginning of the alphabet (a, b, c), and unknown quantities or variables by letters near the end of the alphabet, particularly x, y, and z.

Person of Importance
Apollonius

Apollonius (ca. 240–190 B.C.) was a Greek mathematician, and possibly a student of Euclid, who produced the treatise *Conics*. This work was concerned primarily with the curves resulting from a flat plane intersecting a cone, namely, a circle, ellipse, parabola, and hyperbola. Most of his other works were lost, although later writers passed on their titles and a general indication of their contents. The work of Apollonius served to inspire much of the advancement of geometry in the medieval Islamic world, and Renaissance Europe's rediscovery of *Conics* formed a good part of the mathematical basis for the scientific revolution.

Person of Importance
Archimedes

Archimedes (ca. 285–212 B.C.) was one of the greatest ancient Greek mathematicians and scientists. He is the first person known to have used very large numbers. In his treatise *The Sand Reckoner*, he devised a numerical system based on the number 10,000, which he called the myriad. He then went on to calculate that it would require 1063 (1 followed by 63 zeros) grains of sand to fill the universe.

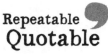
Archimedes is best known for his discovery of the relationship between the surface and volume of a sphere and a cylinder that will enclose it. He invented weapons of war effective enough to keep a Roman army at bay for three years, and a device for raising water, the Archimedes screw, that is still in use in developing countries. He also discovered a principle of hydraulics, known as Archimedes principle. Roman soldiers killed him in 211 B.C. while he was studying a geometrical diagram drawn in the sand.

Arithmetic

Arithmetic is a branch of mathematics; the term is usually applied to the basic skills involved with manipulation of numbers: addition, subtraction, multiplication, and division. It is considered a part of algebra.

Arithmetic was undoubtedly devised for counting—seeds, animals, tent poles, children, etc.—whenever people were able to acquire more than one of something. It arose independently in several cultures, and in a number of different formats. We have evidence that systems used a base of two, twenty, sixty, and ten, the system that we use today. The base-twenty system can be heard in the French term for eighty, *quatre-vingt*, literally "four-twenty," and in the now retired monetary system of the British, which divided a pound into twenty shillings. Remnants of the base-60 system show up in our time-keeping methods in which we use a sixty-second minute and a sixty-minute hour.

Many of these ancient systems were hampered by their cumbersome means of expressing and calculating numbers but, even so, were surprisingly precise in their ability to determine values when needed. The Babylonians, using their base-60 system, calculated the year as having 360 days. The Mayans computed the length of the year to be 365.242 days (the modern value is 365.242198 days).

Babylonian Contributions

Some of the earliest known examples of mathematic use are preserved in clay tablets created by the Babylonians (from the area of today's Turkey and Syria) between 2300 and 1600 B.C. The tablets were written in cuneiform, with one wedge-shaped symbol representing the number *1* and another, corner-shaped symbol for *10*.

These tablets are also notable for using positional notation, in which the position of a digit in a series of digits is significant, and a base-60 (as opposed to our base-10 decimal system) number system which, like cuneiform, was adopted from Sumerians before them. Although this system must have been cumbersome in use and apparently lacked a character for 0 until much later, the base-60, or sexagesimal, system survived to give us our current 60 seconds in a minute, 60 minutes in an hour, and 360 degrees in a circle.

Person of Importance
Geronimo Cardano

Geronimo Cardano (1501–1576) was an Italian mathematician and astronomer who received a medical degree in 1524. He published his chief work in 1545, the *Ars magna* (*The Great Skill*), the first important printed work on the subject of algebra. This book contained the first methods for solving cubics (algebraic equations whose highest exponent is three) as well as quartics (equations whose highest exponent is four).

A gambler who was notoriously short of money, Cardano wrote *Liber de ludo aleae* (*On Casting the Die*), which contains the first systematic treatment of probability, as well as a discussion of effective cheating methods.

Calculus

Calculus is a branch of mathematics concerned with the study of change. Calculus is based on and varies from other types of mathematics due to differentiation and integration, two operations that also define the subcategories of calculus for differential calculus and integral calculus. Differentiation refers to the computation of the rate at which one variable changes in relation to another at a given point in a process. Differentiation involves calculating smaller and smaller values to reach a limit, the value of the rate of change at any instant. Differential calculus studies how functions change when their inputs change. Integration is basically the opposite operation to differentiation; it takes an equation in terms of rate of change and converts it to an equation in terms of the variables that are changing. Integral calculus finds the limit of a sum of elements when the number of such elements increases without bound while the size of the elements decreases.

The Greeks, Archimedes in particular, had solved a number of specific problems concerning rates of change by treating a curve as an accumulation of infinitely short segments, or an area as a collection of infinitely fine slices. These "infinitesimals were used by mathematicians in the sixteenth and seventeenth centuries also; the German astronomer **JOHANNES KEPLER** (1571-1630) used a type of geometric calculus in his three laws of planetary motion. The French mathematician **PIERRE DE FERMAT** (1601-1665), working with Descartes, founded the modern theory of numbers and has been called the inventor of the differential calculus.

The work of these and other mathematicians paved the way for the major developments of English physicist Isaac Newton and the German mathematician G. W. Leibniz. Working independently, these two in created the fundamental theorem of calculus.

Person of Importance
René Descartes

René Descartes (1596–1650), French philosopher and scientist,
brought a fresh approach to the natural world by insisting that
it can be understood as obeying laws that can be determined
by observation and experimentation. By observing a fly buzzing around his room, Descartes realized that its position could
be defined by distances from nearby walls. This was the beginning of analytic geometry, which represents numbers as points
on a graph, geometric shapes as equations, and equations as
geometric shapes.

Chaos Theory

Chaos theory is a mathematical concept that describes random
results in a complex system. The fundamental principle in chaos
theory is the idea that small, seemingly insignificant, events can significantly affect long-term behavior of a system, the so-called "but-
terfly effect."

The French mathematician and theoretical physicist **JULES
HENRI POINCARE** (1854–1912) is credited as being the first to
discover chaotic behavior in a system and laid the foundations of
modern chaos theory. In the 1960s, American meteorologist Edward
Lorenz found chaotic behavior while working on computer models
of atmospheric processes.

Recognizing that normal linear analysis assumes a regularity that occurs infrequently in nature, theorists have employed chaos theory to explain behaviors in many practical applications including turbulent flow in fluids, biological systems, population dynamics, chemical reactions, meteorology.

Person of Importance
Diophantus

Diophantus was a Greek mathematician known as "Diophantus of Alexandria" who probably lived in the third century A.D. His fame rests on his *Arithmetica*, which is the first known work to contain algebra. Diophantus uses symbols for unknown values—the x of today's algebra—as well as positive and negative powers for some arithmetic operations. *Arithmetica* is a collection of 130 problems with emphasis on solving the problems rather than the development of algebraic theories. However, these examples of algebraic symbolism are the first and only occurrence prior to its introduction in Europe in the fifteenth century.

Chinese Contributions

The Chinese began to use paper during the first century B.C., but little has survived from the period before A.D. 700. There is evidence of a written numerical system from the Yin dynasty (ca. 1523–1027 B.C.), but the system may be substantially older.

There are three different styles of numerical symbols used in China: traditional national, official, and mercantile. Traditional national numerals are used most frequently, official numerals are used on banknotes and financial documents, and mercantile numerals (which were used by shopkeepers) are being used with less frequency. The traditional system is a decimal system using thirteen basic characters representing the numbers 1 through 9 plus 10, 100, 1,000, and 10,000.

Egyptian Contributions

Egyptian civilization existed prior to 4000 B.C. It was unified between 3500 and 3000 B.C. under the first dynasty, the pyramids were built about 2500 B.C., and was, until Alexander the Great's invasion of 332 B.C., relatively isolated from outside influences. Under these circumstances, the Egyptians developed a pictorial hieroglyphic system of writing words and numbers.

The Ahmes (or Rhind, for the Scottish Egyptologist who purchased the papyrus in 1858 in Thebes) Papyrus, now in the British Museum, is the primary source of our information on ancient Egyptian mathematics. It was created around 1650 B.C. but contained much older material, having been copied from a document dating back to the period 1849–1801 B.C. The mathematics contained in the papyrus probably represented the same system in use by the Egyptians as far back as 3500 B.C.

Egyptians used a decimal system, that is, a number system using ten as a base, and a set of seven hieroglyphic symbols to represent the numbers 1, 10, 100, 1,000, 10,000, 100,000, and 1,000,000. The papyrus also contained some of the earliest known symbols for mathematical operations including plus, minus, and equal symbols. Multiplication and division operations were calculated through addition, and the expression of fractions was complex.

Fast Fact

Egyptian hieroglyphics used symbols for numerals and, when used in combination could represent any number. The number 1 was represented by a vertical line, 10 by a heel-bone sign, 100 by a coiled rope, 1,000 by a lotus blossom, 10,000 by a bent finger, 100,000 by a tadpole, and 1,000,000 by a figure of a man with raised arms.

Egyptian mathematics was used for practical purposes: counting, measuring, determining volumes, calculating wages and taxes, and in constructing the largest buildings of their time. In conjunction with astronomical observations, Egyptian mathematics enabled the construction of a fairly accurate calendar, and temples situated to observe annual solar events. In the mathematics of ancient Egypt we find the beginnings of algebra as well as formulas, but no proofs, of geometry.

Person of Importance
Leonhard Euler

Leonhard Euler (1707–1783) was a prolific Swiss mathematician who authored more than 900 papers. A prodigy, Euler entered the University of Basel at the age of thirteen and studied under the noted mathematician Johann Bernoulli. Euler worked in the areas of both pure and applied mathematics, and his contributions span all fields.

Euler introduced many of the standard notation symbols to mathematics, was one of the first to develop calculus methods on a wide scale, and was a principal founder of complex analysis.

Person of Importance
Euclid

Euclid (born ca. 300 B.C.) was the greatest mathematician of antiquity and known as the father of geometry for his *Elements*. The *Elements* constituted thirteen books; the first six concern elementary plane geometry while the others deal with solid geometry, number theory, and the concept of infinity, now a part of calculus. The concepts in his book were not his own, but were collected, simplified, and organized from the works of others.

Fast Fact

Abraham Lincoln learned reasoning by studying Euclid. As a traveling lawyer, he kept a copy of Euclid's *Elements* in his saddlebags.

Euclid's accomplishments in geometry are echoed by his means of proving his ideas. First, he defined basic terms such as point and line, then made logical statements or axioms, and finally derived a number of theorems from the axioms by using deductive logic.

Elements became one of the most successful textbooks ever published and was in common use for more than two millennia. Euclid also was the author of several other works including Data, which includes ninety-four propositions, Phaenomena, about spherical astronomy, Caloptrics, about mirrors, Optics, which is a theory of perspective, and a work of music theory.

- -

Person of Importance
Fibonacci

In 1202, Liber Abaci, or Book of the Abacus, appeared in Italy. The book was written by Leonardo Pisano, Leonardo of Pisa, but more frequently known then as now as Fibonacci, and was the result of his discovery and mastery of the Hindu-Arabic numbering system. This system was much more useful and liberating than the Hebrew, Greek, or Roman systems of letter numerals used for counting and calculating. Fibonacci's book explained how to use Arabic numerals and contained calculations using fractions and whole numbers, square roots, solutions for quadratic equations It also demonstrated practical applications for bookkeeping and accounting. These applications ensured that Liber Abaci enjoyed wide circulation and his examination of the number of offspring rabbits that would be produced over time by a breeding pair led to the discovery of the "Fibonacci series." The Fibonacci series starts with the numerals: 1, 2, 3, 5, 8, 13, 21, 34, 55, 89, 144, 233 . . . . Each successive number is found by adding the two previous numbers. This series is special because if any number is divided by the preceding number, the result will be 1.6 (1.618 after 144). The Greeks called this proportion the "golden ratio" and may have used it to establish the proportions of the Parthenon.

Person of Importance
Carl Friedrich Gauss

Carl Friedrich Gauss (1777–1855) was a German mathematician, astronomer, and physicist. He was an astounding prodigy; at the age of nineteen, he constructed a seventeen-sided regular polygon, the first major new construction since the Greek period. His contributions include the fundamental theorem of algebra, the least squares method, a method for solving matrix equations, non-Euclidian geometry, and the bell curve. His greatest work, however, was done in the area of higher arithmetic and number theory.

Fast Fact

Gauss published more than 150 works; his *Disquisitiones Arithmeticae* (1801) is one of the masterpieces of mathematical literature. He is considered the greatest mathematician of his time and the equal of Archimedes and Newton.

Geometry

Geometry is a branch of mathematics dealing with the shapes of objects, spatial relationships, and the properties of surrounding space. Its name is derived from two Greek words for *ge*, meaning earth, and *metron*, meaning measurement. The Egyptians used geometry to build the pyramids and survey fields; they were able to measure lines and angles and calculate areas and volumes.

> **Repeatable**
> # Quotable
>
> Mathematics is the language in which God has written the universe.
> —*Galileo Galilei*

The Greeks, who provided us with the name for the science, were better practitioners and developed geometry beyond mere practical applications. **THALES OF MILETUS** (ca. 600 B.C.) used deductive reasoning to develop geometric concepts and founded the geometry of lines.

PYTHAGORAS (ca. 580–500 B.C.), a student of Thales, applied scientific reasoning to proofs. **EUCLID** (ca. 300 B.C.) put together all the extant teachings of geometry and mathematics in his masterpiece *Elements*. In the next century, Apollonius released his treatise on conic sections, which made important contributions to astronomy and ballistics.

Later Work

In the late eighteenth century, the French mathematician **GASPARD MONGE** (1746–1818) invented descriptive geometry as a means of representing three-dimensional objects on a two-dimensional surface. He then went on to develop, with Carl Friedrich Gauss (German, 1777–1855), differential geometry, in which concepts from

---

calculus are applied in the analysis of curves and surfaces. The modern period in geometry is marked by Jean-Victor Poncelet's (French, 1788–1867) work in projective geometry, and the development of non-Euclidean geometry.

Branches of Geometry

EUCLIDEAN GEOMETRY describes the relationships between lengths, areas, and volumes of physical objects. This geometry was codified in Euclid's *Elements* through ten postulates, from which several hundred theorems were proved by deductive logic. The *Elements* epitomized the deductive method for many centuries. Until the second half of the nineteenth century, geometry was synonymous with Euclidean geometry.

ANALYTIC GEOMETRY was developed by the French mathematician René Descartes, who demonstrated how rectangular coordinates could locate points, and how lines and curves could be represented with algebraic equations. Algebraic geometry is a modern extension of analytic geometry in multidimensional spaces.

PROJECTIVE GEOMETRY concerns the relationships between geometric figures and the images that result from projecting them onto another surface. Shadows cast by objects are examples of projections.

Greek Contributions

Around 450 B.C. the Greeks, whose civilization dates to 2800 B.C., developed an alphabetic numbering system. Unfortunately, the

---

Mathematics

original works of the great Greek mathematicians have not survived; our sources are critical copies, with unknown changes, made 500 to 1,500 years after the originals. Despite gaps in our knowledge, and some unavoidable assumptions, we have works in one form or another from Euclid, Apollonius, Archimedes, Ptolemy, and Diophantus.

There were two major systems: Attic numeration was used in Athens and the surrounding province of Attica, and the Ionic system, named for Ionia, the Greek colony established around 1000 B.C. in what is now Turkey. The Attic system was not suitable for calculations and went out of use, while the Ionic system appears to have been established by the eighth century B.C.

The Ionic system used twenty-seven letters of the Greek alphabet, three of which fell out of use. Numbers 1 through 9 each were represented by its own letter, and the multiples of 10 and 100 each had a letter. Numbers were written by combining letters as needed, the additive principle. Often a horizontal bar was placed above the letters representing numbers to distinguish them from text. However, lack of any standards among the Greek city-states meant there were considerable variations in the expression of large numbers. While this system was handy enough for recording the results of calculations, performing the calculations was quite difficult.

While their mathematical system was competent enough to permit the design and construction of magnificent buildings, the Greeks encountered the limitations of an awkward numbering system and were unable to progress beyond geometry. Calculus was unknown to them and they failed to discover even simple algebra.

Mathematics Through History

The timeline below shows the first known occurrence of some mathematics fundamentals as well as the dates for several mathematic pioneers.

3000 B.C.	Hieroglyphic numerals
1850 B.C.	Arithmetic
518 B.C.	Pythagoras
300 B.C.	Euclid
180 B.C.	360 degree circle
140 B.C.	Trigonometry
150	Ptolemy
250	Diophantus
775	Arabic translations
830	Al-Khwarizmi
1202	Fibonacci
1489	Use of + and −
1609	Johannes Kepler
1637	René Descartes
1687	Newton's Principia
1748	Leonhard Euler
1801	Carl Friedrich Gauss
1915	Einstein's relativity

Incas

At the time of the Spanish conquest in 1532, the Inca empire, centered in Cuzco, Peru, consisted of about 12 million people and stretched some 2,000 miles along the Pacific coast from the northern border of today's Ecuador to central Chile.

The Incas had a well-developed social system and strong bureaucracy to govern the lands and people they conquered. They were proficient in building terraced fields for agriculture and precisely constructed fortresses and temples. Yet, the Incas lacked a system of writing and instead used quipos (quipus) to record and convey information. The quipo was a cord of cotton with additional knotted cords attached. The number of knots, their position, size, and color all were significant to what could be a complicated message; the largest quipo found contained 1,800 cords.

Only about 400 quipos have been recovered, all from graves in desert regions. The Spanish considered quipos and many other artifacts as ungodly and destroyed them; more were lost due to humid conditions in other areas.

Person of Importance
Gottfried Leibniz

Gottfreid Leibniz (1646–1716) was a German mathematician and philosopher. His wide-ranging interests led him to acquire knowledge in fields from engineering and mechanics to political theory and theology, and he was one of the most influential thinkers of eighteenth-century Europe.

He is considered to have invented infinitesimal calculus in the 1670s, before Sir Isaac Newton published his work, but Newton is given the credit for his earlier conceptions. It is Leibniz's notations, however, that are used today. He did early work in symbolic logic and binary systems.

Mayans

The Mayans have inhabited the Yucatan Peninsula and what is now southern Mexico since approximately 2000 B.C. The classical period of Mayan civilization, A.D. 290 to 925, saw significant achievements in art, astronomy, and mathematics. They had the only fully developed language in the pre–Columbian Americas as well as an efficient mathematical system, for which they developed the concept of zero.

Mayan mathematics used a base 20, or vigesimal system, and expressed numerals with symbols: a dot, a bar, and a shell (representing zero). There is no indication that the system was used for multiplication or division, and it did not seem to allow for fractions It was efficient, however, for counting and was used to calculate very large numbers. The Mayans also were able to calculate the values for the length of the year and lunar month with remarkable accuracy.

--- ------- --- ------ -------------- --- -------------------- ----

Person of Importance
Menelaus

Menelaus of Alexandria was a Greek mathematician and astronomer active in the first century A.D. He was the first to conceive and define a spherical triangle, a triangle formed from three arcs of great circles on the surface of a sphere, thereby founding spherical trigonometry.

Menelaus's most important work is *Sphaerica*, a treatise on the geometry of the sphere, which has been preserved only in an Arabic translation. Book I established the basis for a mathematical treatment of spherical triangles similar to Euclid's treatment of triangles in two dimensions. He originates the use of arcs of great circles instead of arcs of parallel circles on the sphere, a major turning point in the development of spherical trigonometry. Book II established theorems that apply to problems in spherical astronomy. Finally, Book III concentrates on spherical trigonometry and presents Menelaus's theorem, which became of fundamental importance in spherical trigonometry and astronomy.

Person of Importance
Isaac Newton

Isaac Newton (1643–1727) was an English mathematician, physicist, astronomer, alchemist, philosopher, and theologian. He was considered by many of his contemporaries and modern current scholars as one of the greatest scientists and thinkers who ever lived. His *Philosophiæ Naturalis Principia Mathematica* (the *Principia*), published in 1687, is considered to be among the most influential books in the history of science.

Newton was an obsessive who would forget to eat or sleep while conducting experiments, and was extremely secretive about his accomplishments. Albert Einstein, a capable thinker in his own right, said of Isaac Newton: "Nature to him was an open book, whose letters he could read without effort."

In addition to explaining the behavior of celestial bodies, providing the law of gravitation, and explaining the motions of fluid, the *Principia* gives a sound, albeit dense, mathematical grounding for Newton's theories.

Numbering System

In A.D. 500, the Hindus developed the numbering system we use today. This system was encountered and adopted by the Arabs after 622 when followers of Mohammed entered India.

The Hindu-Arabic system includes a zero, which the Hindus called *sunya* and the Arabs named *cifir*. It forms the basis of our word "cipher." The zero enabled all numbers to be written, and all calculations made with just the digits 0 through 9. Using the zero as a placeholder in larger numbers clarified the numbering system, and sequences in particular became obvious.

This numbering system spread to Europe, carried by Moors from northern Africa in the eighth century, and was taught in Spain and in use in Italy by the year 1000 A.D. The first known use of the system is found on a Sicilian coin dated "1134 Annoy Domini," but the numbering system was resisted until the early 1500s. Part of the reluctance to employ the new system was simply natural opposition to change—the previous system had been in place for centuries. Also, the new system presented a greater danger of fraud; one number could be changed for another quite easily. This is why Europeans still add a horizontal line to the numeral 7. And despite the wide circulation of Fibonacci's 1202 *Liber Abaci*, in which he explains and demonstrates the advantages of the Hindu-Arabic system, in 1229 an edict was issued in Florence prohibiting bankers from using the numerals. People wanting to learn the new system had to disguise themselves as Moslems.

Not until the invention of printing from movable type did Arabic numerals overcome their opposition. It was no longer possible to fraudulently alter numerals. When it became obvious that they represented great advantages over the complicated Roman system, the system enjoyed welcome commercial adoption. The zero proved to be a difficult and foreign concept, but it enabled mathematics to move from the realm of purely practical to the abstract.

Person of Importance
Blaise Pascal

Blaise Pascal (1623–1662) was a French mathematician, scientist, and religious philosopher. He was a child prodigy; he attended meetings of a mathematical society when he was twelve, published a paper on the geometry of conical sections when he was sixteen, and invented a calculating machine that used gears at the age of nineteen.

He is credited with founding the theory of probability and statistics and contributed to the advance of differential calculus. He experimented with pressure and developed the theory of hydraulics known as Pascal's law.

Pythagoras

Pythagoras (ca. 580–500 B.C.), a student of Thales, founded his own school in Croton, a Greek city in southern Italy. This religiously oriented Pythagorean brotherhood, which influenced the thinking of Plato and Aristotle, contributed to the development of mathematics and Western philosophy.

None of his writings have survived, and because his students typically noted the authority of their master, it is difficult to attribute his teachings with any certainty. He is credited with the theory that numbers constitute the true nature of things and that music could be expressed in numerical ratios; he is also the first to use the term "philosophy." The Pythagorean theorem, demonstrating the relationship between the sides of a right triangle, had been used by the Babylonians and Egyptians for 1,000 years, but was finally proven by his school if not by Pythagoras himself.

Roman Influence

The oldest example of Latin is an inscription in Greek characters from the sixth century B.C.

The Roman Empire split in two in A.D. 395; the Western Empire fell in 476, the Eastern Empire not until 1453.

Latin ceased to be spoken in the period between the seventh and tenth centuries, although it remained the official language of the

Church. It was also the language of scientists, and served the diplomatic service until the eighteenth century when that role was taken over by French.

Roman numbers were derived from the Greek system and used letter symbols: 1, 5, and powers of 10. Like the Greeks, the Romans used the additive principle and symbols were simply strung together in order of descending value to create the desired number. To prevent a symbol from being repeated four times, the subtractive principle was introduced. By putting a symbol of lower value before one of higher value, the lower value was subtracted from the higher number.

Romans expressed fractions using dots and the letter *S* for *semis* (one-half). Although the Roman system was decimal, base 10, fractions were based on the number twelve. So, one dot equaled 1/12, two dots equaled 2/12 or 1/6, *S* equaled 1/2 (6/12), *S* with one dot equaled 7/12, and so on.

Despite the fact that expressing numbers, particularly large numbers, with Roman characters was cumbersome and multiplication and division were quite difficult, Roman numerals could be readily added and subtracted. Bookkeepers used the Roman system well into the eighteenth century.

Person of Importance
Bertrand Russell

Bertrand Russell (1872–1970) was an English mathematician, philosopher, and political activist. He studied mathematics and philosophy at Cambridge University, where he later taught. In both his *The Principles of Mathematics* (1903) and *Principia Mathematica* (3 vol., 1910–1913), which he wrote with Alfred North Whitehead (1861–1947), Russell sought to demonstrate that the whole of mathematics was an extension of logic. His ideas would have a profound influence on twentieth-century work in both logics and mathematics.

In 1925 Russell published *The ABC of Relativity* in which he attempted to explain Einstein's theory of relativity for nonscientists. He received the 1950 Nobel Prize for Literature.

Set Theory

Set theory is a branch of mathematics concerned with the study of sets or collections of objects. Modern set theory was developed by **GEORG CANTOR** (1845–1918), a German mathematician, who proved that the set of real numbers could not be put into a one-to-one correspondence with the set of natural numbers.

The three principle operations of set theory are union, intersection, and complement. Given a set of teachers and a set of women, for example, a union of the two sets would yield a set of all teachers and women. An intersection of the two sets would yield a set of women teachers. A complement would create a set of teachers who are not women, or a set of women who are not teachers.

Trigonometry

Trigonometry is a branch of geometry concerned with the properties and relations of parts of a triangle developed from the study of right triangles. Plane trigonometry concerns triangles in two dimensions, and spherical trigonometry studies triangles on the surface of spheres. Its applications, however, extend well beyond geometry into surveying, navigation, cartography, and astronomy.

The word "trigonometry," constructed from Greek units of speech and meaning "measurement of triangles," seems to have been invented by Bartholomaeus Pitiscus, a German mathematician and astronomer who used the word in a publication in 1595. However, the understanding of triangular measurement, which serves as the basis of trigonometry, goes back at least to the Babylonians, whose interest in astronomical events was recorded in a table of trigonometric functions on a clay tablet dating to around 1900-1600 B.C. This knowledge was passed on to and developed by the Greeks, including Menelaus and Eratosthenes. **THALES OF MILETUS** (ca. 600 B.C.) is said to have calculated the height of the pyramid at Cheops and the distance from shore of ships at sea using these principles. The Greeks also expressed sides of triangles as parts of circles and, using their base-60 numbering system, divided the circle into 360 parts, our 360° convention.

Functions

Trigonometric functions, which describe the ratios between sides of right triangles and form the basis of trigonometric study familiar to generations of high school students, include: sine (sin), cosine (cos), tangent (tan), cotangent (cot), secant (sec), and cosecant (csc). The Hindu mathematician and astronomer Aryabhata in the fifth century A.D. originated the term "sine" and first defined it in its modern form in the *Surya Siddhanta*. Islamic scholars such as Al-Khwarizmi adopted Indian mathematics and numerals and had calculated their value and were using all six functions by the tenth century.

Person of Importance
Alan Turing

Alan Turing (1912–1954) was an English mathematician and logician who contributed to logic, mathematics, biology, philosophy, cryptanalysis as well as to the areas that would become known as computer science, cognitive science, and artificial intelligence.

In 1936 Turing published a paper, "On Computable Numbers," describing the abstract digital computing machine—the Turing machine—and suggested that computers would eventually be capable of human-like thought. During World War II, Turing was instrumental in breaking the German Enigma code, work that was considered to have shortened the war by two years. After the war, his efforts in designing and programming an electronic digital computer formed the foundation for the field of artificial intelligence.

Europe was exposed to trigonometry by Latin translations in the fifteenth century. Regiomontanus, a German astronomer and mathematician, compiled *De triangulis omnimodis* around 1464, a compendium of contemporary trigonometric knowledge. Trigonometry was modernized largely through the efforts of the Swiss mathematician Leonhard Euler, who published his *Introductio in analysis infinitorum* in 1748.

As measuring devices made technical advances, from knotted ropes, wooden rods, and carpenter's squares, trigonometry also became more precise.

Cheat Sheet for Mathematics

"Classical algebra" or the process of solving equations, has developed over a period of 4,000 years. "Abstract algebra," which is the study of groups, rings, and fields, appeared in the last 200 years.

Conics, by the Greek mathematician Apollonius (ca. 240–190 B.C.), formed a good part of the mathematical basis for the scientific revolution.

Arithmetic is considered a part of algebra and is usually applied to the basic skills involved with manipulation of numbers: addition, subtraction, multiplication, and division.

Some of the earliest known examples of mathematic use are preserved in clay tablets created by the Babylonians between 2300 and 1600 B.C.

The German astronomer Johannes Kepler (1571–1630) used a type of geometric calculus in his three laws of planetary motion.

There is evidence of a written numerical system from the Chinese Yin dynasty (ca. 1523–1027 B.C.).

Analytic geometry was founded by René Descartes (1596–1650) who observed a fly buzzing around his room and realized that its position could be defined by distances from nearby walls.

Egyptian hieroglyphics used symbols for numerals (as opposed to words) and could represent any number when used in combination.

Euclid (born ca. 300 B.C.) was the greatest mathematician of antiquity and known as the father of geometry for his *Elements*.

In 1202, Fibonacci discovered and mastered the Hindu-Arabic numbering system, which was much more useful for counting and calculating than the Hebrew, Greek, or Roman systems of letter numerals.

Geometry is a branch of mathematics dealing with the shape of objects, spatial relationships, and the properties of surrounding space.

Around 450 B.C. the Greeks, whose civilization dates to 2800 B.C., developed an alphabetic numbering system.

The Incas lacked a system of writing, and instead used cords of cotton with additional knotted cords attached to convey mathematical information.

The Mayans used a base-20, or vigesimal, system of mathematics, and expressed numerals with symbols: a dot, a bar, and a shell (representing zero).

Menelaus of Alexandria was a Greek mathematician active in the first century A.D. who founded spherical trigonometry.

In A.D. 500, the Hindus developed the numbering system we use today.

Blaise Pascal (1623–1662) was a French mathematician who, at age nineteen, invented a calculating machine that operated with gears.

The Pythagorean theorem, demonstrating the relationship between the sides of a right triangle, had been used for 1,000 years before it was proven.

Although the Roman numbering system was decimal, base 10, fractions were based on the number twelve.

Thales of Miletus (ca. 600 B.C.) is said to have calculated the height of the pyramid at Cheops and the distance from shore of ships at sea using trigonometric principles.

Bibliography

Angel, Allen R. and Stuart R. Porter. *A Survey of Mathematics with Applications*. (Reading, MA: Addison-Wesley, 1981).

Baker, Timothy B., Richard M. McFall, and Varda Shoham. "Toward a Scientifically Principled Approach to Mental and Behavioral Health Care." *Psychological Science in the Public Interest* Volume 9 Number 2, November 2008

Bernstein, Peter L. *Against the Gods: The Remarkable Story of Risk*. (New York, NY: John Wiley, 1998).

Cajori, Florian. *A History of Mathematics*. (New York, NY: Macmillan, 1919).

Clarfield, Gerard H. and William M. Wiecek. *Nuclear America: Military and Civilian Nuclear Power in the United States, 1940–1980*. (New York, NY: Harper & Row, 1984).

Drabble, Margaret ed. *The Oxford Companion to English Literature*, Fifth Edition. (Oxford, UK: Oxford University Press, 1985).

Gullberg, Jan. *Mathematics: From the Birth of Numbers*. (New York, NY: W.W. Norton, 1997).

Hart, James D. ed. *The Oxford Companion to American Literature*, Fifth Edition. (Oxford, UK: Oxford University Press, 1983).

Hazen, Kirk. Teaching About Dialects. (Center for Applied Linguistics, 2001).

Internet Encyclopedia of Philosophy, *www.iep.utm.edu*.

Jacobs, David. *Architecture*. (New York, NY: Newsweek Books, 1974).

Kennedy, X.J., Dana Gioia, and Mark Bauerlein. *The Longman Dictionary of Literary Terms*. (New York, NY: Pearson Education, 2006).

King, Kendall and Lyn Fogle. Raising Bilingual Children: Common Parental Concerns and Current Research. (Center for Applied Linguistics, 2006). *www.cal.org*.

Kline, Morris. *Mathematical Thought from Ancient to Modern Times*. (Oxford, UK: Oxford University Press, 1990).

Lewis, M. Paul (ed.). *Ethnologue: Languages of the World*, Sixteenth edition. (Dallas, TX: SIL International, 2009). *www.ethnologue.com*.

Malone, Margaret E. and Benjamin Rikkin. *Attaining High Levels of Proficiency: Challenges for Foreign Language Education in the United States*. (Center for Applied Linguistics, 2005).

Maynard, Senko K. *Japanese Communication: Language and Thought in Context*. (Honolulu, HI: University of Hawaii Press, 1997).

McDermott, John D. *A Guide to the Indian Wars of the West.* (Lincoln, NB: University of Nebraska Press, 1998).

Mencken, H.L. *The American Language: An Inquiry into the Development of English in the United States,* 2nd ed. (New York, NY: Alfred A. Knopf, 1921).

National Institute on Deafness and Other Communication Disorders (NIDCD), National Institutes of Health, *www.nidcd.nih.gov.*

Norman, Jerry. *Chinese.* (Cambridge, UK: Cambridge University Press, 1988).

Norwich, John Julius, ed. *Great Architecture of the World.* (New York, NY: Bonanza Books, 1978).

Salzmann, Zdenek. *Language, Culture, and Society: An Introduction to Linguistic Anthropology,* 2nd ed. (Boulder, CO: Westview Press, 1998).

School of Mathematics and Statistics, University of St Andrews, Scotland, *www-history.mcs.st-andrews.ac.uk.*

Stockholm International Peace Research Institute, *SIPRI Yearbook 2009*

Staudigel, Hubert et al. "Defining the Word "Seamount," *Oceanography*, March 2010.

Struik, Dirk J. *A Concise History of Mathematics*. (Mineola, NY: Dover, 1987).

Index

Marlowe, Christopher, 218
Márquez, Gabriel García, 210
Martial, 89
Marx, Karl, 20, 28–29, 211, 271, 276, 280, 298
Maslow, Abraham, 265
Materialism, 22–23, 28–29, 36–37
Mathematics, 3, 22–25, 341–71
Maupassant, Guy de, 212
Maxwell, James Clerk, 305
Mayall, John, 71
Mayans, 345, 360, 371
Mayow, John, 312
McKinley, William, 162
Mead, George Herbert, 280
Mead, Margaret, 289
Mechanics, 305–8
Medieval thought, 12–14, 16, 20
Medieval times, 88–89, 133, 140, 215–16, 311, 343
Meditations on First Philosophy, 21
Meiji, Emperor, 250
Mein Kampf, 127
Mendeleyev, Dmitri, 313
Menelaus, 360–61, 367, 371
Merriam, Charles E., 282
Merton, Robert, 280
The Metamorphosis, 215
Metaphysics, 32, 35, 37
Meteorologica, 336, 339
Meteorology, 336–37, 339
Michelson, A. A., 307
Middle Ages, 42–47, 151–53, 181
Middle English, 124, 193
Middletown, 278
Military expenditures, 286
Milky Way, 321, 339
Mind-body relationship, 21, 35
Minh, Ho Chi, 178
Miró, Joan, 214, 215
The Mirror and the Lamp, 196, 198
Mitchell, Mitch, 72
Modern English, 124, 193
Modern geology, 334

Modernism, 207–8
Modernist literature, 207–8
Modern languages, 115–48
Modern physics, 303, 307–9
Molière, 216
Monads, 23
Monet, Claude, 207
Monge, Gaspard, 355
Monk, Thelonious, 65
Montgolfier brothers, 166
Morley, E. W., 307
Morton, Ferdinand "Jelly Roll," 62
Moses, 239, 244
Mozart, Wolfgang Amadeus, 50, 52–54, 76
Mrs. Dalloway, 208
Muhammad, 239–40, 361
Murakami, Haruki, 215
Murray, Sir James, 202–3
Music, 39–77
Muslims, 239–40, 259
Mussolini, Benito, 135

Naked Lunch, 210
Nanak, Guru, 251–52
NASA, 324
Native Americans, 158–59, 255–59, 292–93
Natural History, 90, 112, 113
Natural History of Religion, 25
Naturalism, 15, 211
The Nature of the Chemical Bond, 315
Nero, 89, 96
New Deal, 171, 273–74
Newell, Allen, 264
New Organon, 18–19
New System of Chemical Philosophy, 312
Newton, Sir Isaac, 23–25, 304, 321–22, 338, 347, 354, 360–62
Nicolas II, Tsar, 168
Nihilism, 37
Nixon, Richard, 180
Nobile, Umberto, 164

North Atlantic Treaty Organization (NATO), 178

Norton Anthology of English Literature, 196, 198

Novels, 195-96, 221-22

Novoselic, Krist, 74

Nuclear Age, 172-73

Nuclear politics, 287-88, 298

Nuclear weapons, 172-73, 182, 315

Number set theory, 366

Numerical symbols, 119, 147, 350-51, 357-63, 370-71

Oceanography, 334-36, 339

The Odyssey, 85, 88, 113

Oersted, H. C., 305

Ogden, C. K., 134

Old English, 124-25, 193

Oliver, Joseph "King," 61, 62

Olympians, 99-100

On Casting the Die, 346

"On Computable Numbers," 368

On the Revolutions of the Celestial Spheres, 320

One Hundred Years of Solitude, 210

Orbits, 320-22

Organon, 7, 95

Othello, 217

Ovid, 88

The Oxford English Dictionary, 202-3, 221

Paleography, 194, 220

Panaetius, 96, 114

Panama Canal, 165-66, 182

Pantheon, 108, 114

Papyrus, 194, 342, 350-51

Paracelsus, 311

Parker, Charlie "Bird," 64-65, 67, 76

Parmenides, 3

Parsons, Talcott, 279, 280

Pascal, Blaise, 30, 363, 371

Passions of the Soul, 21

Patton, Charley, 57

Pauling, Linus, 314

Pavlov, Ivan, 264

Peary, Robert, 163

Peirce, Charles, 31-32

Peloponnesian War, 80-81, 151

Pentecostalism, 246, 259

Peret, Benjamin, 215

Pericles, 80, 108

Periodic table, 313

Petronius, 89

Pheidias, 82, 108

Philosophy, 1-37, 92-96, 101

Physical sciences, 301-39

Physics, 302-4, 307-9

Physiocrats, 270, 297

Piaget, Jean, 264

Piazzi, Giuseppe, 322

Pindar, 85

Pisano, Leonardo, 353

Pissarro, Camille, 207

Pitiscus, Bartholomaeus, 367

Plague, 42, 181

Planck, Max, 307, 327, 338

Plate tectonics, 334-35, 339

Plato, 4-6, 14, 19, 82, 86, 95, 114, 197, 269, 303

Plautus, 87

Pliny the Elder, 90, 109, 112, 113

Pliny the Younger, 90

Poe, Edgar Allan, 195, 205, 207, 213, 220

Poetics, 196, 217, 221

Poincare, Jules Henri, 348

Political science, 281-88, 298

Polo, Marco, 156

Polyclitus, 82, 109

Polyglot, 145

Poncelet, Jean-Victor, 356

Portuguese language, 137-39, 148

Positivism, 33, 36

Postmodernism, 210

Pound, Ezra, 205, 207, 208

Powell, John Wesley, 294-95

Prabhupada, Srila, 245

Pragmatism, 31–32, 197
Praxiteles, 109
The Predestined Prince, 195
Preface to Shakespeare, 216
Presley, Elvis, 68, 69
Prez, Josquin des, 46
Pride and Prejudice, 212
Priestley, Joseph, 312
Primitive Culture, 291
The Prince, 17
Principia, 23, 304, 322, 338, 361–62
Principia Mathematica, 366
Principles of Geology, 333, 339
Principles of Mathematics, 366
Principles of Psychology, 262–63, 297
Principles of Sociology, 275
Probability, 346, 363
Protestant Ethic and the Spirit of Capitalism, 276
Protestantism, 17–18, 247–48, 259
Psychic Factors of Civilization, 278
The Psychological Clinic, 266
Psychology, 262–68
Ptolemy, 320, 357
Punic Wars, 83–84
Punk rock, 74
Pure Sociology, 278
Pushkin, Alexander Sergeyevich, 141
Pynchon, Thomas, 210
Pyramids, 237, 258, 349–50, 355, 367, 371
Pythagoras, 2–3, 94, 114, 303, 319, 355, 364
Pythagorean theorem, 364, 371

Quantum mechanics, 307, 327
Quintillian, 89
Qur'an, 118, 240–41

Radioactivity, 307, 313–14, 329, 338
Radio signals, 324, 328
Rainey, Ma, 56
Rastafarianism, 246

Rational choice theory, 284
Rationalism, 12, 19, 22, 27, 37
Rawls, John, 283, 298
Ray, Man, 214
Realism, 212, 221
Redding, Noel, 72
Reformation, 17–18, 247–48, 259
Regiomontanus, 369
Reincarnation, 3, 94, 227, 238–39
The Reivers, 209
Relativism, 36, 210
Relativity, 307–8
Religion, 223–59
Remus, 83
Renaissance period, 16–18, 44–47, 50, 76, 320–22
Renoir, Pierre Auguste, 207
Republic, 6, 95, 114, 269
The Return of the Native, 211
Revolutionary War, 156–57, 181
Ricardo, David, 271
Richards, Keith, 58
Rimbaud, Arthur, 214
Robinson Crusoe, 196
Rock music, 67–75, 77
Rogers, Carl, 265
Roman architecture, 105–8, 114
Roman art, 110–12
Romance languages, 139–40, 148
Roman Empire, 79, 82–85, 97, 110, 113, 151–52, 181, 364–65
Roman gods, 100–102, 114
Roman mythology, 100–102, 114
Roman numerals, 364–65
Roman philosophy, 96
Romanticism, 213, 221
Rome, fall of, 85, 151–52, 181
Romulus, 83
Roosevelt, Franklin D., 171, 273
Roosevelt, Theodore, 162
Rumford, Count, 305
Rush, Benjamin, 314
Russell, Bertrand, 34, 365–66
Russian language, 141–42, 148

Russian Revolution, 167–68
Ryle, Gilbert, 35

St. Anselm, 12, 13
St. Augustine, 10–11
St. Jerome, 92
The Sand Reckoner, 344
Sapir, Edward, 295, 299
Sappho, 86
Sartre, Jean-Paul, 34–35
The Sceptical Chymist, 311
Scheele, Carl W., 313
Schleyer, Johann Martin, 133
Schlick, Moritz, 33
Scholasticism, 12–14, 20, 37
Science of Society, 277
Scientific revolution, 16–17, 304, 336–
    37, 343, 370
Scientology, 247
Scripture, 235, 246, 248, 250. *See also*
    Religion
Seaborg, Glenn T., 315
Seneca, 89, 96
Shakespeare, William, 87, 216–19, 222
Shelley, Mary, 213
Shelley, Percy Bysshe, 213
Sherman, William Tecumseh, 159
Shinto, 249–50, 259
Shockley, William, 309
The Sidereal Messenger, 321
Sikhism, 251–52, 259
Simon, Herbert, 264
Simon, Paul, 184
Simon, Theodore, 267
Sinatra, Frank, 63
Sinclair, Upton, 212
Sinube, 195
Sister Carrie, 211
Slaughterhouse Five, 210
Slipher, Vesto, 323
Small, Albion Woodbury, 278
Smith, Adam, 270–71
Smith, Bessie, 56–57, 76
Smith, William, 334

Socialism, 28–29, 271
Social sciences, 261–99
The Social System, 279
Social Theory and Social Structure, 280
Sociology, 274–81, 298
Socrates, 4–5, 82, 94–95
Sommerfeld, Arnold, 315
Sophocles, 82, 86
The Sound and the Fury, 208
Spanish-American War, 161–63, 181
Spanish language, 142–44
Speech, learning, 191–92, 220
Spencer, Herbert, 275
Sphaerica, 361
Spinoza, Baruch, 22
Spirituality, 21, 255–57, 290. *See also*
    Religion
Stalin, Joseph, 168
Stanford-Binet IQ tests, 267
Stendhal, 212
Steno, Nicholas, 333
Stoicism, 8–9, 37, 96, 114
Stokoe, William, 117
Strindberg, August, 206
Structure and Process in Modern Societies,
    279
The Structure of Social Action, 279
Sumner, Graham, 276–77
The Sun Also Rises, 208
Surrealism, 214
Surrealist Manifesto, 214
Syllogism, 7, 37

Tacitus, 90
The Tale of Genji, 196
Talmud, 244–45
Taoism, 253–55, 259
Ten Commandments, 229, 231, 244
Terence, 87
Terman, Lewis M., 267
Thales, 2, 93, 355, 364, 367, 371
Theogony, 85, 97
Theory of Justice, 283, 298
Theory of relativity, 307–8, 326, 328, 338

Sources

The Lazy Intellectual contains material adapted and abridged from: *The Everything® American Government Book*, by Nick Ragone, copyright © 2004 by F+W Media, Inc., ISBN 13: 978-1-59337-055-8; *The Everything® American History Book, 2nd Edition*, by John McGeehan, copyright © 2007 by F+W Media, Inc., ISBN 13: 978-1-59869-261-7; *The Everything® American Presidents Book*, by Martin Kelly and Melissa Kelly, copyright © 2007 by F+W Media, Inc., ISBN 13: 978-1-59869-258-7; *The Everything® American Revolution Book*, by Daniel P. Murphy, copyright © 2008 by F+W Media, Inc., ISBN 13: 978-1-59869-538-0; *The Everything® Bible Study Book with CD*, by James Stuart Bell and Tracy Macon Sumner, copyright © 2007 by F+W Media, Inc., ISBN 13: 978-1-59869-398-0; *The Everything® Buddhism Book*, by Jacky Sach, copyright © 2003 by F+W Media, Inc., ISBN 13: 978-58062-884-6; *The Everything® Christianity Book*, by Amy Wall, copyright © 2004 by F+W Media, Inc., ISBN 13: 978-1-59337-029-9; *The Everything® Civil War Book, 2nd Edition*, by Brooke C. Stoddard and Daniel P. Murphy, PhD, copyright © 2009 by F+W Media, Inc., ISBN 13: 978-1-59869-922-7; *The Everything® Classical Mythology Book, 2nd Edition*, by Nancy Conner, PhD, copyright © 2010 by F+W Media, Inc., ISBN 13: 978-1-4405-0240-8; *The Everything® Creative Writing Book, 2nd Edition*, by Wendy Burt-Thomas, copyright © 2010 by F+W Media, Inc., ISBN 13: 978-1-44050-152-4; *The Everything® C. S. Lewis and Narnia Book*, by Jon

978-1-59337-652-9; *The Everything® Psychology Book*, by Linda L. Warwick and Lesley Bolton, copyright © 2004 by F+W Media, Inc., ISBN 13: 978-1-59337-056-5; *The Everything® Saints Book, 2nd Edition*, by Jenny Schroedel, copyright © 2007 by F+W Media, Inc., ISBN 13: 978-1-59869-265-5; *The Everything® Shakespeare Book, 2nd Edition*, by Cork Millner, copyright © 2008 by F+W Media, Inc., ISBN 13: 978-1-59869-453-7; *The Everything® Understanding Islam Book*, by Jenny Schroedel, copyright © 2009 by F+W Media, Inc., ISBN 13: 978-1-59869-867-1; *The Everything® World's Religions Book, 2nd Edition*, by Kenneth Shouler, PhD, copyright © 2010 by F+W Media, Inc., ISBN 13: 978-1-4405-0036-7; *The Everything® World War II Book, 2nd Edition*, by David White and Daniel P. Murphy, PhD, copyright © 2007 by F+W Media, Inc., ISBN 13: 978-1-59869-641-7.

DAILY BENDER

Want Some More?

Hit up our humor blog, The Daily Bender, to get your fill of all things funny—be it subversive, odd, offbeat, or just plain mean. The Bender editors are there to get you through the day and on your way to happy hour. Whether we're linking to the latest video that made us laugh or calling out (or bullshit on) whatever's happening, we've got what you need for a good laugh.

If you like our book, you'll love our blog. (And if you hated it, man up and tell us why.) Visit The Daily Bender for a shot of humor that'll serve you until the bartender can.

VISIT THE DAILY BENDER BLOG TODAY AT
www.adamsmedia.com/blog/humor